Do I Kneel or Do I Bow?

Published in Great Britain by
Kuperard, an imprint of Bravo Ltd
59 Hutton Grove, London N12 8DS
www.kuperard.co.uk
Enquiries: office@kuperard.co.uk

Distributed in the United States and Canada
by Random House Distribution Services
1745 Broadway, New York, NY 10019
Tel: +1 (212) 572-2844   Fax: +1 (212) 572-4961
Inquiries: csorders@randomhouse.com

Series Editor Geoffrey Chesler
Design Bobby Birchall

ISBN 978 1 85733 524 8

British Library Cataloguing in Publication Data
A CIP catalogue entry for this book
is available from the British Library.

Printed in Thailand

This book is available for special discounts for bulk purchases
for sales promotions or premiums. Special editions, including
personalized covers, excerpts of existing books, and corporate
imprints, can be created in large quantities for special needs.

For more information in the USA write to Special
Markets/Premium Sales, 1745 Broadway, MD 6–2, New York,
NY 10019, or e-mail specialmarkets@randomhouse.com.

In the United Kingdom contact Kuperard publishers at the
address at the top of this page.

Do I Kneel or Do I Bow?

WHAT YOU NEED TO KNOW WHEN ATTENDING RELIGIOUS OCCASIONS

ROMAN CATHOLIC | PROTESTANT | ORTHODOX CHRISTIAN
JEWISH | MUSLIM | HINDU | SIKH | BUDDHIST

Akasha Lonsdale

·K·U·P·E·R·A·R·D·

Chapter 2
ORTHODOX CHRISTIAN CEREMONIES 82

Chapter 3
JEWISH CEREMONIES 122

Chapter 6
SIKH CEREMONIES

Chapter 7
BUDDHIST CEREMONIES 298

INTRODUCTION

As an Interfaith Minister working in modern multicultural Britain, I have enjoyed the privilege and pleasure of being welcomed into the lives and homes of people across the social and religious spectrum. My experiences have deepened my respect for all sacred traditions and their wisdoms. What has impressed me, time and again, is the truth of the core Interfaith Foundation tenet, 'Many Ways: One Truth', and how rich and imaginative are the different ways of expressing basic human wants and spiritual needs. I hope that this introductory guide to unfamiliar religious occasions will convey not only the excitement of discovery, but also a warming recognition of our common humanity. We really are all the same under the skin.

In our rapidly changing society, I believe that there is real need for a book of this kind. We live in an age of unprecedented mobility and today Western Europeans and North Americans are many times more likely than their parents to find themselves meeting people from a variety of religious backgrounds. We may well find ourselves invited to an unfamiliar ceremony, and when this happens there can be few of us who know exactly what to expect, or are confident about how to behave.

This guide introduces eight major religious traditions. It describes and explains the ceremonies in each that you may be invited to attend, and offers advice on how to behave, so that you do not inadvertently give offence or cause embarrassment to yourself or others. Because of the variety of traditions, customs and cultural influences even within each religion, you may experience some differences from what is described – but the basic forms and features of the ceremonies will be the same.

While many people have friends of different faiths, other groups continue to struggle to understand each other. If this book helps to raise awareness, stimulate interest and offer useful guidance, my intention will have been met.

So many wonderful and gracious people have helped me on this journey, some to a huge extent and others in a passing conversation. Every contribution has been invaluable. I am deeply grateful to everyone, and humbled by the extreme generosity shown by several of the contributors. Thank you again to Liz and Jon Papier; Suresh Namdhari, Bristol Hindu Temple; Mother Sarah, St John of Kronstadt Orthodox Church, Bath; Father J. Blacker, St Thomas More Catholic Church, Marlborough; Swindon Gurdwara; The Reverend Dr R. Sharma, Hindu Council UK; Lynda Ford-Horne; Farzana Saker, West Wiltshire Interfaith Group; Anstice Fisher; Ruwan Uduwerage-Perera; Panditji, Bristol Hindu Temple; Helen Renton; Morris Banks, St Andrew's Church, Chippenham; Anne Cooper; and Alison Paginton. And thank you to my commissioning editor, Geoffrey Chesler, who remained steady through sometimes choppy seas.

Last, but no means least, a huge thank you to my wonderful husband, John Gloster-Smith, who with his extensive knowledge of history was able to suddenly give a totally clear perspective on otherwise complex issues. As always, a rock and a loving support.

EXPERT ADVISORS

I am indebted to the following expert advisors, who ensured that their respective religions were fairly portrayed, and who have given their blessing to my attempts to explain their complex and nuanced traditions in simple terms:

The Reverend Malcolm Warren, Industrial Chaplain for Severn Side; Father Robert King, University of Bristol; Father Luke Holden, Holy Orthodox Church, Wales; Rabbi Rodney Mariner, Belsize Square Synagogue, London; Imam R. Azami, Bath Islamic Centre; Swami Ambikananda Saraswati, Reading Hindu Temple; Mr Jaspal Sagoo; and the Buddhist Society, London.

Chapter 1

WESTERN
CHRISTIAN
CEREMONIES

WHAT CHRISTIANS BELIEVE

The Christian concept of God is 'triune'. The one, righteous, compassionate Creator is revealed in Three Persons, as God the Father, God the Son (Jesus Christ) and God the Holy Spirit – known as the Holy Trinity. This fundamental doctrine, agreed at the Council of Nicea in AD 325,* is known as the Nicene Creed, and also as the Apostles' Creed.

As a living statement of Christian faith, the Creed declares that Jesus Christ, the Son of God, was born human, and that his suffering and death by crucifixion (nailing to a wooden cross) redeemed (saved) us from our sins. His

ABOVE The Crucifixion. Detail from an altarpiece by Andrea Mantegna, 1459.
PREVIOUS PAGE Mass in the Church of Our Lady of Lourdes, Philadelphia.

resurrection, when he rose from the dead on the third day, instilled hope and gave the promise of eternal life after death. We are able to enter into a relationship with God the Father through the gift of the human incarnation and sacrifice of Jesus Christ, His son, and through the Holy Spirit working within us personally.

The historical Jesus was a Hebrew preacher born into the tribe of Judah and the House of David, the second king of Israel. The word 'Christ' comes from the Greek *Christos*, a translation of the Hebrew *Messiah*, meaning 'anointed one', and Christians believe that he was the Messiah prophesied in the Old Testament who would usher in the final redemption at the end of days. Jesus was born and died a Jew, and it was not until some time after his death that his disciples travelled widely to spread his teachings.

After waves of persecution and martyrdom, and through the support of the Emperor Constantine, who converted to Christianity in 312, the new Christian religion became respectable, and finally, in 380, the state religion of the Roman Empire. It was then that the apostle Peter, who had taken Jesus' message to Rome some two hundred years earlier, was posthumously recognised as a saint, the first Bishop of Rome and so the first Pope. For a thousand years all Christians belonged to a united worldwide 'Catholic' Church. (Catholic, from the Greek *katholikos*, means general or universal.)

SACRED WRITINGS

The Holy Bible, the Christian holy book, is a complete instruction book for life and for salvation. It consists of two parts: the Jewish Old Testament, which contains the Ten Commandments, the code of moral conduct given to Moses on Mount Sinai, and the New Testament, containing post-crucifixion accounts of the life and teachings of Jesus by those who either knew him or were under the guidance of those who did. Of several New Testament Gospels (Old English *godspel*, good news) current at the time, only those of the disciples Matthew, Mark, Luke and John were accepted as being canonical, or authoritative religious texts.

The New Testament was written in Greek in the course of the first century AD;

---

* AD, for *Anno Domini*, 'in the year of our Lord', signifies 'years after the birth of Christ.' Today, in non-Christian contexts, this is often replaced with CE, for 'common era.' The actual date of Christ's birth is now, however, thought to be about 4 BC.

the Old Testament texts were a third-century BC Greek translation from the Hebrew scrolls. Both Testaments were translated into Latin, the language of scholarship in Western Europe, and in the Western Church all prayer was conducted in Latin until the Protestant Reformation in the sixteenth century.

Differences between Roman Catholic and Protestant Christianity revolve around the question of spiritual authority and matters of doctrine. The Catholic Church has a single worldwide hierarchical structure of ordained bishops and priests, whose authority is guaranteed by their direct descent through a line of succession from Christ's apostles. At their head is the Pope, the Bishop of Rome, who is considered Christ's Vicar (representative) on earth and the successor to St Peter. The many different Protestant Churches, broadly speaking, accept only the Bible as the source of revealed truth, believe in the doctrine of 'justification' (salvation) by faith alone, rather than through sacraments or personal merit, and in the priesthood of all believers (discarding the need for a priest to represent them before God). Today the Christian ecumenical movement is attempting to bridge this theological gap.

BRANCHES OF CHRISTIANITY
Division
The early Church was universal. However, the seeds of disunity were sown in AD 330, when Constantine moved his capital from Rome to the Greek city of Byzantium, which he renamed Constantinople (modern-day Istanbul, in Turkey). This became the capital of the Eastern Roman Empire, later known as the Byzantine Empire, and latterly the home of the Orthodox Church (see chapter on Orthodoxy).

As security within the Empire deteriorated,

ABOVE Bronze statue of St Peter Enthroned in St Peter's Basilica in the Vatican, Rome. One foot is largely worn away by pilgrims kissing it over centuries.

communication between the Eastern and Western Church Councils became difficult; despite differences in theology and language – Greek in the East and Latin in the West – the two remained in communion until the great doctrinal schism of 1054. The rift was made final in 1204, when Western Crusaders, on their way to war in the Holy Land, sacked Constantinople, committing acts of savagery and sacrilege.

The Reformation

In Europe, Roman Catholicism continued undivided until the sixteenth century saw the rise of the Protestant Reformation, launched by the German monk Martin Luther. The chief branches of Protestantism were Lutheranism, Calvinism and Zwinglianism. As religion became enmeshed with power politics, the continent was devastated by wars of religion until the middle of the seventeenth century.

In England, after the Act of Supremacy of 1534, King Henry VIII dissolved the monasteries, which finalised his break from Rome and established him as head of a new Church of England, the

Anglican Church, whose doctrine was finally established in the Thirty-Nine Articles of Faith. Apart from a brief five-year break under the Catholic Queen Mary Tudor, persecution of Catholics continued in England until the Catholic Relief Act of 1829 – although religious antagonism between Catholicism and Protestantism has never been one-sided.

Since the Reformation, all non-Catholic denominations have been referred to as Protestants. In the United Kingdom, however, the official State Church is the Church of England, whose supreme

ABOVE Bronze statue of the theologian and reformer Martin Luther, outside the Frauenkirche (Church of Our Lady) in Dresden, Germany.

governor since the time of Henry VIII has been the reigning monarch. The Archbishop of Canterbury, also known as the Primate of All England, is the spiritual leader of the worldwide Anglican community and head of the South of England Province, while the Archbishop of York heads the Northern Province. The established Church of Scotland is Presbyterian (Calvinist) and, until recent times, the established Church in Northern Germany and Scandinavia was Lutheran.

Differences

The Roman Catholic Church has a global hierarchy with ultimate authority vested in the Supreme Pontiff, the Pope, who resides in the Vatican, an independent state within the city of Rome.

Fundamental to Catholic belief and practice are the seven sacraments, solemn religious acts that convey God's grace to the recipient. These rituals are baptism, the Eucharist, confirmation, penance and reconciliation, sacrament of the sick, marriage, and holy orders (ordination). The origin of the word 'sacrament' is the Latin *sacramentum* (sacred pledge or oath), a translation of the Greek *mysterion* (mysteries). In Anglican theology a sacrament is defined as 'an outward and visible sign of an inward and spiritual Grace'.

Protestants differ from Roman Catholics in key respects. They do not recognize the supremacy of the Bishop of Rome, or that only celibate men may be ordained as priests. They reject Catholic devotion to the Virgin Mary, mother of Christ, belief in the power of holy intercessors, and the Church's total opposition to contraception and abortion (although some Anglicans and evangelical Churches also oppose these); they also reject the Catholic belief in transubstantiation (that the bread and wine become the body and blood of Christ during the celebration of the Eucharist), and the granting of

ABOVE Pope Bendict XVI performing a blessing during a canonization Mass in St Peter's Square in Rome.

WHAT CHRISTIANS BELIEVE

indulgences (remission by the Church of a penalty for sin in consideration of prayers or other good works). Generally, Protestants accept just the two biblical sacraments of baptism and Holy Communion. Quakers and the Salvation Army have done away with these altogether.

The Anglican Church, however, tends to be divided between the 'High Church' – often called Anglo-Catholic because it closely resembles Catholicism in its forms of worship – and the more liberal tendency that tolerates greater diversity, including the ordination of women, although some evangelical churches also oppose this. Core to Anglican worship are the sacraments of baptism and Holy Communion/Eucharist. Other important rites in common are confirmation, reconciliation (confessions of sins), matrimony, holy orders and anointing the sick.

In Britain, other Protestant Churches are referred to as Non-Conformist. The worldwide Protestant tradition is very diverse and includes the Lutheran Churches, the Reformed Churches (Presbyterians and Congregationalists),

Methodists, Baptists, Amish, the Society of Friends (Quakers), the Salvation Army, Unitarians, Pentecostalists, Evangelicals, the Church of Jesus Christ of Latter-day Saints (Mormons), Christian Brethren, Seventh Day Adventists, Jehovah's Witnesses, Pentecostalists and the African Independent Churches.

Despite the great variety of Protestant ministries there are shared practices, and this chapter will look at Anglicanism (known in the USA as Episcopalianism) as a representative Protestant Church and at Catholicism.

ABOVE The Anglican parish church of St Andrew in the village of Wraysbury, Berkshire, England.

PLACE OF WORSHIP

The main places of worship for Christians are cathedrals (the seats of bishops, city based), abbeys, originally used by a religious order of monks or nuns, and churches, located

in towns and villages. Historically built in the shape of a cross, they vary in decoration from plain and simple to ornate and elaborate. A key aspect of the early Reformation was the simplification of places of worship by the removal of the 'idolatrous' images – icons, paintings, statues, carvings and stained-glass windows – that characterised opulent Catholic churches.

Traditionally, the congregation sat on rows of wooden pews, or benches, designed with upright backrests and a shelf at the back to hold the hymn and prayer books of the people behind. On the floor were hassocks, or firm cushions, on which to kneel in prayer. Now, many churches have replaced pews with chairs that still have book holders, and there are often no hassocks, as most people just bow their heads to pray. The traditional pulpit, a raised enclosed platform used by the preacher, and reached by several integral curved steps, can still be seen in older churches, but most clergy now preach from the front of the church using a lectern (stand) and microphone.

ABOVE Western front of the magnificent Gothic cathedral of York Minster, seat of the Anglican Archbishop of York.

INSIDE AN ANGLICAN CHURCH

As you approach a typical traditional Anglican church with its spire, you may hear the bells that are rung for an hour beforehand to let the community know of the forthcoming service.

Inside there will probably be a central aisle and two outer aisles dividing the pews or seats and leading, from west to east, to the front of the church and the altar – a rectangular table draped with a white cloth and colours appropriate to the liturgical season. On the altar will be a large cross in the centre and candles at each end, and behind it might be a wall-mounted crucifix – a statue of Christ on the cross. There may be flowers, beautifully arranged, at the side.

Many churches have stained-glass windows, which often depict saints or scenes from Jesus' life. In older churches, these were often paid for by the landed gentry who lived in the local manor house and whose tombs may form part of the church floor, or who are otherwise remembered with memorial inscriptions around the walls. The stained glass in modern churches is likely to be more contemporary, and the overall look and feel lighter and brighter. At the back or side of the church will be the font, the stone or metal container for blessed water, usually mounted on a pedestal, used in

A B O V E Interior of the small church of St Martin in Coney Street, York.

welcoming babies formally into the Christian faith in the ceremony of baptism, or christening.

Some churches may have a small play area for very young children to use during the service, and many progressive churches have a separate room for children to receive age-appropriate teaching.

Other places of worship in the Protestant tradition might be a chapel (Methodist, Baptist, Free Church), a 'meeting house' (Quaker), a village hall, someone's home or a purpose-built venue, as it is recorded (Matthew 18) that Jesus said 'When two or more are gathered in my name, there also shall I be'. In larger congregations, usually outside Britain, services might be held at venues that accommodate hundreds, if not thousands, of worshippers.

INSIDE A CATHOLIC CHURCH

The layout of a Catholic church will be similar to that described above. However, there are differences. Just inside the main entrance is a wall-mounted, or sometimes free-standing, container of holy water, and you will notice an area (or areas) of candles on circular stands. These candles are votive offerings, which people may light to ask for a prayer to be answered, or to give thanks. In return a small monetary or flower offering is usually given. The Holy Rosary (prayer beads) is still used by many Catholics as a focus of devotion to the Virgin Mary; it consists of a crucifix and five sections of 'decades' (ten beads) separated by single beads. Special prayers, starting with the Lord's Prayer and ending with 'Hail Holy Queen', are said at each bead.

Behind and above the altar will be a wall-mounted statue of Jesus or his mother, the Virgin Mary. Also behind the altar, and slightly elevated, is the Tabernacle,

which contains the reserve sacraments (consecrated bread and wine kept for emergency use, such as sudden illness). An altar-lamp burns continuously in front of it. Around the walls you will notice fourteen Stations of the Cross. These are either pictures or carvings in wood or stone that depict the Passion of Christ – his journey from condemnation to death by Pontius Pilate to the placing of his body in the tomb. They are a visual pilgrimage and a focus for both individual and group devotion, especially during Holy Week.

Confession, the sacrament of Reconciliation, is a once-yearly obligation for Catholics, although many will go more frequently. You may notice the confessionals (special divided booths) in which the priest, who can only hear what is said, sits on one side with the person making the confession on the other.

ABOVE The nave of Westminster Cathedral in London, headquarters of the Roman Catholic Church in Britain.

SERVICES

Although the range of daily services offered has diminished because of busy lives and smaller numbers of attendees, morning Communion and Evensong (an early evening prayer service) may be available on at least a couple of weekdays. Details of services and times are usually posted on a notice board outside the church. Devout Christians not attending a daily service may say prayers at home in the morning and at night, before they go to bed. (The Lord's Prayer, said to have been taught to his disciples by Jesus, is popular.)

The Clergy

The key person in an Anglican church is a vicar, who can be male or female and is free to marry if he or she chooses. A rector is a vicar who looks after more than one church in a geographical area. Both have the title of 'Reverend'. Additional help will come from a curate or deacon (ordained ministers awaiting parish appointments) and 'lay members' (not ordained) of the congregation who have been specially trained to assist during services and ceremonies.

The Catholic Church ordains only male priests, who must remain celibate (no marriage or sexual relations) and who are addressed as 'Father'. Assistance with services comes from altar servers and 'ministers', who are members of the congregation specially trained to help with the Holy Eucharist (Thanksgiving).

The colours of clergy vestments (ceremonial clothing) worn for services and the altar dressings will vary depending on the focus of worship in the Christian year but will include purple, green, white, gold and red. Usual clerical daywear includes the stiff white circular collar. In strong Catholic communities, you might still see a Catholic priest wearing a traditional button-fronted cassock (floor-length robe) and biretta (a square hat). Some 'High Church' Anglicans also wear a cassock.

Sunday Service

Every Sunday, known as the Lord's Day, is a celebration of the resurrection and therefore the most popular day to attend a service, which probably starts between 10:00 and 11:00 a.m. and lasts from one and a half to two hours, depending on the individual church. For Catholics, this is a Holy Day of Obligation, and everyone must attend Holy Mass unless they have a good reason for not doing so. A 'High Church', or Anglo-Catholic, service is very similar in structure to that of the Roman Catholic Mass.

Central to both Catholic and Anglican worship is the Holy Eucharist, also called Holy Communion or the

ABOVE Cardinal Joseph Ratzinger (now Pope Benedict XVI) celebrating Mass in Poland in 2003.

Lord's Supper. This sacrament relates to the last supper that Jesus shared with his disciples before his arrest and crucifixion. During this meal he instructed them to remember him when breaking bread and drinking wine, representing the sacrifice he made of his body and blood for the salvation of those who follow him.

Not all Protestant denominations include this sacrament in the main family service, but they may offer it as a separate early-morning service. Therefore the two Sunday services outlined here are an informal Anglican family service without Holy Communion, and the Catholic Mass, where the Holy Eucharist is always the nucleus. English Protestant services use *The Book of Common Prayer* or *Common Worship*, while Catholics use two versions of *The Missal*, and *A Simple Prayer Book*.

WHAT HAPPENS IN AN ANGLICAN FAMILY SERVICE?

◆ In formal churches, the service starts with everyone standing for the processional entry led by a church member carrying the cross, followed by the choir (if there is one), church servers or other attendants, and finally the vicar. All are appropriately robed. At an informal service there might be musicians playing at the side of the church, and the service begins when the vicar, or appointed lay person, walks to the lectern. Usually, after a few words of welcome, the congregation is reminded of why they have gathered. Prayers of confession and absolution are often said, to put right the relationship with God at the opening dialogue with Him. Prayers end with all joining in the final 'Amen' ('So be it'). There may now be a hymn, which all stand to sing.

◆ Once the congregation is seated again there might be comment on a topical issue, or an announcement of interest to the community, such as a fund-raising endeavour, with a prayer for success and wellbeing. The children may then leave for their own service. Everyone stands to sing again, and remains standing while a sectional prayer is offered, to which the responses by the congregation might be 'Lord, have mercy' (the response for the day will be on the screens or in the Order of Service).

◆ The congregation sits again. A reading from the Bible is given, and ends 'This is the word of the Lord,' to which all respond, 'Thanks to the Lord'. If there is to be a baptism or vow renewal in the service, this will take place now. All then stand for the 'Song of Faith'.

◆ Once seated, Prayers of Intercession, such as prayers for the Church, for the community, for individuals who might be sick, or for world communities struck by tragedy, are offered. Each section of prayer might end with 'Lord in your mercy', and the response 'Hear our prayer'.

◆ A further reading from the Bible may be given, and ends as before, and at this point the children return to join their parents. This will be followed by a sermon, story, or address, usually given by the vicar and linked to the reading. After this all speak the Creed, declaring faith in God and Jesus Christ.

◆ Church notices are then given, and other announcements made. This is the time when Banns, the formal announcement of a couple's intention to marry, will be read. Banns must be read on three Sundays, over three months, in the church where the marriage is to take place, and in the couple's local parish church, or churches. This gives an opportunity for anyone knowing of a lawful objection (such as one of the couple being already married) to raise it in good time. (This is only done in the Anglican Church, which has the status of registrar.)

◆ Everyone stands for a last hymn, or song, and the closing Lord's Prayer. The service finishes with a blessing, after which people greet friends and enjoy the refreshments provided.

WHAT DO I DO?

❖ At a family service in an Anglican church you will be greeted by helpers at the door and given an Order of Service for the day. You may also be handed a prayer book and a hymnbook, or these might be at your seat. A church with a modern approach may have the words to the hymns (songs of praise) displayed on large power point screens on either side of the church; if this is not the case the hymn numbers (not the page numbers) will be displayed on a board and probably be listed in the Order of Service, and you will then need the hymnbook.

* Older churches can be quite cold, so go prepared, and remember to turn your cell phone off.

* Generally you can sit where you like, and it is customary, once seated, to bow your head for a moment's silent prayer.

* If there has not been a chance to give a voluntary offertory (donation of money) during the service (sometimes a cloth bag on a stick is handed along for you to put money in before passing it on) there is usually a collection box at the back of the church. Should you wish to contribute, £1 is an acceptable amount, and it generally goes towards the upkeep of the church.

* As you leave, the vicar, together with those helping him, will be at the door to thank you for coming and possibly shake hands. If you have enjoyed the service, it is customary to say something like, 'That was a very good service (or sermon), thank you.'

WHAT HAPPENS IN A CATHOLIC MASS?

Opening Rites

◆ You will be greeted at the door to the church and probably given an Order of Mass, which will help you to understand what is happening. On entering, Catholics touch their fingers into the holy water, and make the sign of the cross on their bodies (forehead to heart, left shoulder to right). Their intention for the service is to leave the outside world behind and turn their attention to God and spiritual matters. As they approach their seat, they genuflect (with hands held in front of the chest they bend the right knee) in reverence to the altar and the cross. As a guest there is no need for you to do this. From their seats, they will then either kneel or bow their heads for a few moments' silent prayer.

◆ As the priest enters, either alone or in procession with attendants, worshippers stand and might say or sing the brief Entry Antiphon or a hymn. After kissing the altar, the symbol of Christ, he turns to the congregation, makes the sign of the cross and says 'In the name of the Father, and of the Son, and of the Holy Spirit'. Everyone crosses themselves and responds with 'Amen'.

◆ All are then greeted in God's name, to which the response is 'And also with you'. After outlining the theme for the Mass, the priest leads the congregation in the Penitential Rite, a confessional prayer. (In one of the prayers that might be said, people strike their chest after the third line.) The prayer ends with 'Lord, have mercy' (Greek, *Kyrie eleison*).

◆ Except in Advent or Lent, when it is omitted, the hymn known as the Gloria is either said or sung. It is introduced by the priest with the words 'Glory to God in the Highest', to which the response, spoken by both priest and congregation, starts 'and peace to his people on earth'. It ends with 'Amen'. There is a short pause for silent prayer before the priest says or sings the prayer known as the Collect.

Liturgy of the Word

◆ The opening rites have prepared the congregation to receive the word of God, and everyone sits as the first reading (possibly from the Old Testament and linked with the reading from the previous week) is given. It ends with 'This is the Word of the Lord' and the response 'Thanks be to God'. Then follows a reflection on what has been heard in the form of a sung responsorial psalm.

◆ After a second reading (probably from the New Testament), ending as before, everyone stands to say or sing the Gospel Acclamation 'Alleluia' (different during Lent). This heralds the Gospel reading, which will be preceded by a responsorial prayer as the congregation touch their foreheads, lips and heart with a cross, to signify opening their minds, hearing the word of God and letting the Spirit of His Gospel into their hearts. 'This is the gospel of the Lord' ends the reading, with the response 'Praise to you, Lord Jesus Christ'.

◆ Everyone sits to hear the homily (sermon), which signifies the 'breaking open of the Word' for reflection.

◆ Then all stand and speak the Creed, the Profession of Faith (you will notice that for three particular lines people will bow), followed by Prayers of Intercession, sometimes called Bidding Prayers or Prayers of the Faithful. These are sectional prayers, some of which will have been requested in advance by church members and will include prayers for those who are sick, bereaved, at war, and so on. Each section ends 'Lord, hear us' with the response 'Lord, graciously hear us,' and are completed with an invocation prayer to Mary, Mother of Jesus.

Liturgy of the Eucharist

◆ The Eucharist, also known as Holy Communion, is the taking of bread and wine to represent the body and blood of Christ, as instructed by him at the Last Supper. If a hymn is sung while the gifts of bread and wine are brought to the altar and prepared, then everyone stands, and this is also the time of the monetary collection, or offertory, which is how worshippers show their thanks for the Grace received from God and contribute to the upkeep of their church. The offertory is then taken to the altar. For a guest, £1 is an acceptable amount.

◆ However, it is possible that the priest will quietly say prayers as he prepares the bread and wine (into which he will place a drop of water to symbolise that as Christ shared his humanity with us, so we may share his divinity), in which case the congregational response is 'Blessed be God for ever'. The priest may now wave a brass incense container over the gifts of the altar and towards the congregation to acknowledge the presence of Christ. He will then rinse his hands to symbolise freedom from sin.

◆ Everyone then stands as a call and response prayer is spoken, before the priest speaks the Prayer over the Gifts, to which all reply 'Amen'. The Eucharistic Prayer, or Prayer of Thanksgiving, commences with the Preface and leads to the Prayer of Acclamation that starts 'Holy, Holy, Holy' (Latin, *Sanctus*) and is said or sung by all. The congregation then kneels as the triumphant prayer continues and a bell is rung as the priest spreads his hands over the bread and wine. (This gesture is seen as calling the Holy Spirit to change the bread and wine into Christ's body and blood. Known as 'transubstantiation', this change is not accepted within the Protestant tradition.) The priest continues his invocation and as the bell is rung again, the consecrated bread (which is special unleavened bread or a circular rice-paper substitute) is held up before the congregation and then placed on a special plate. The process is repeated for the wine, before the priest leads a brief acclamation and prayers that end with the great 'Amen', said firmly and clearly. Non-Catholics are not required to join in with this, although you are welcome to do so if you wish.

Liturgy of the Communion

◆ The Communion Rite is the final part of the service, starting with all standing to recite the Lord's Prayer. This is followed by the invitation to greet one another with the sign of peace, which is done by shaking hands with those around you while saying 'peace be with you' or responding 'and with you'.

◆ The priest then breaks the Host (bread) and the congregation either say or sing the 'Lamb of God' (*Agnus Dei*) three times, after which the priest says a prayer quietly before holding up the Host and leading a short pre-communion responsorial prayer.

◆ Once the priest has received Holy Communion (the eating of the bread and the drinking of the wine – the body and blood of Christ) everyone moves towards the altar rail and kneels. If the congregation is large, the priest will be helped by appointed lay members. Each person accepts Communion with the words 'The body of Christ' (and/or 'The blood of Christ'), to which the response is 'Amen'.

WHAT DO I DO?

❖ Only Catholics can receive this sacrament, but as a guest you are most welcome to receive a blessing. To do this you join the others in kneeling at the altar rail and place your arms upwards across your chest (right fingertips touch the left shoulder, left fingertips touch the right shoulder). This also applies at Protestant services.

❖ After Communion there might be a short period of silence before thanksgiving and post-Communion prayers are led.

❖ The Concluding Rite consists of general church notices, followed by a final responsorial blessing where the priest makes the sign of the cross, and everyone crosses themselves again. The service ends with the Dismissal words 'Go in the peace of Christ', response: 'Thanks be to God' (the words may vary). Everyone again genuflects as they leave their seats. If refreshments are offered, you will be welcome to stay.

FESTIVALS AND HOLY DAYS

THE CHRISTIAN CALENDAR

The liturgical year consists of a cycle of seasons: Advent (the lead-up to Christmas), Christmas (the birth of Christ), Lent (Christ's ministry and time in the wilderness) and Easter (the death and resurrection of Christ). The date of Easter varies between 21 March and 25 April. It is determined by the Paschal full moon, a Church calculation, which changes connected dates accordingly. The prayers of each season, as well as the colours adorning the altar and the vestments worn by the priests, are laid down in the Lectionary, a scriptural readings guide. The periods outside the seasons are known as 'Ordinary Time', and number thirty-three or thirty-four Sundays in the year. There are also additional Feast days and Saints' days in both traditions. Key patron saints of the British Isles are St George (England, April), St Patrick (Ireland, March), St David (Wales, March) and St Andrew (Scotland, November). This calendar follows the liturgical year.

THE FEAST OF THE IMMACULATE CONCEPTION (8 December)

This feast, occurring within Advent, is a Catholic honouring of the belief that Mary, Mother of Jesus, was conceived immaculately (without sin), meaning that her conception was God-given.

ADVENT
(December)

Christmas is one of the most important festivals in the Christian calendar, and is steeped in rituals. (When abbreviated to 'Xmas', the 'X' stands in for the Greek letter *chi* of Christ's name and 'mas' is 'mass', Christ's Mass.) Advent, meaning 'arrival', is the twenty-four-day period preceding the eagerly awaited birth of the Christian saviour. Until 17 December it is a time for reflection that then changes to anticipation; a popular hymn sung during Advent is 'O Come, O Come, Emmanuel'.

Churches will have an Advent candle with twenty-five markings, a portion being burnt each day until Christmas Day on 25 December.

You might also see an Advent wreath. Circular and made of flat evergreen branches to symbolise eternal life, it contains four candles, traditionally red or purple, sometimes with a central white candle (white for purity). The four candles represent Hope, Peace, Love and Joy, with one being lit each Sunday leading to Christmas Day. Christians might also hang an Advent wreath on their front doors – but without the candles!

Children are often given an Advent calendar, traditionally in the form of a picture with twenty-four small windows. Daily from 1 December, the child opens a numbered window to reveal a miniature picture on the theme of the nativity (the story around Christ's birth) such as a candle, a shepherd, a star, an angel, and so on, with the last one showing the baby Jesus in the manger. More recently some Advent calendars open to reveal celebrity pictures and chocolates!

In homes over the Christmas holiday period it is usual to decorate at least the main living room. The central feature will be a festive Christmas tree, adorned with coloured baubles and lights, and the upper part of the walls might be strung with decorative tinsel that shimmers in the light. Many people also hang their Christmas cards around the walls, and windowsills often have a candleholder in a shape similar to the Jewish *menorah*.

Christmas trees were first introduced to Britain and America in Victorian times. The colour scheme was traditionally red and green, and the lights were candles. Pride of place is still the top of the tree, which is crowned with either an angel (who first brought the news of Jesus' birth to Mary), or a star (as followed by the three wise men). The tree is normally put in place around mid-December, which is also the time that many people start to send their Christmas greeting cards, a custom that has been adopted into mainstream life. Town centres and shops will be brightly decorated and many people string coloured lights outside their homes. The overall feeling is one of celebration.

CHRISTMAS EVE
(24 December)

Christmas Eve is the twenty-fourth day of Advent, when children look forward to receiving presents, as the infant Jesus received presents from the three wise men. In a night-time visit, Santa Claus (Father Christmas – based on Saint Nicholas, fourth-century Bishop of Myra) traditionally climbed down the chimney and left presents in a stocking for each child; now that fewer houses have chimneys, the presents may miraculously appear under the Christmas tree in time for Christmas morning.

More importantly, though, for Christians this marks the period of Christmastide, which continues until the start of Epiphany on 6 January. It is a time of anticipation, with important church services and re-enactments by children of the nativity. Both the Catholic and Protestant traditions will include an early evening family Carol Service to herald his birth with joy, and a Midnight Mass to welcome him.

The singing of Christmas carols is an ancient tradition that had its roots with beggars who would sing for money, and was introduced into formal church services by St Francis of Assisi in the early thirteenth century. Some of the most popular carols are 'O Come all ye Faithful'; 'Once in Royal David's City'; 'O Little Town of Bethlehem'; 'Silent Night' (originally Austrian) and 'Away in a Manger'.

DO I SING?
❖ Everyone stands to sing the hymns and carols, but as a guest you are not expected to sing unless you want to!

During the service, candles might gradually be lit from the west of the church to the east, to symbolise the move away from the darkness of sin to the light of Christ. Church colours will be gold.

CHRISTMAS DAY
(25 December)

The actual date of Christ's birth is not known, but in AD 440 it was fixed at 25 December, and in many countries around the world with large Christian communities it is a public holiday (Holy Day). In the morning, Christian families attend church for a special service, and on these two days, Christmas Eve and Christmas Day, the church is likely to be full.

WHAT DO I DO?

❖ After church, families gather to exchange gifts. It is becoming quite popular now for adults to give each other 'alternative gifts' by making financial donations to charitable foundations working in poorer countries. If you are unsure what to give, this is a good option. Another acceptable gift would be wine, or a decorative *Poinsettia* plant.

❖ Apart from church and presents, another tradition is the Christmas meal, and you might find that a short Grace (prayer) is said before eating. As a guest, it is polite just to lower your head while the prayer is being offered. It ends with 'Amen'.

❖ On the table next to you may be a paper cracker, which you will pull with the person beside you. Alternatively everyone crosses arms around the table, with a cracker end in each hand, and pulls at the same time. A chemically impregnated strip creates the 'cracking' sound and, depending on the cost of the crackers, the gift inside will vary, but there will always be a joke or motto to read out and a paper hat or 'crown' to wear.

❖ Traditionally the meat was goose but is now often turkey, served with 'all the trimmings' – meat, herb and vegetable stuffings, a variety of vegetables, cranberry sauce and gravy. If you don't eat pork for any reason, be aware that bacon has usually been draped across the breast of the bird to keep it moist during cooking, and may be served with the meal, as may a pork stuffing. Obviously, if you are vegetarian, tell your hosts in advance!

❖ Dessert is usually a rich fruit Christmas pudding, originally plum, over which brandy is poured and the top briefly set alight (to ward off evil spirits). The traditional accompaniment is brandy butter. The pudding used to be made on 'Stir-Up Sunday', at the beginning of Advent. It was always stirred from east to west in honour of the three wise men, and contained thirteen items representing Christ and his disciples. Some cooks still put a coin in the pudding for good luck, but will usually tell you first so that you don't accidentally bite on it.

❖ If you are asked to 'pull the wishbone' (the forked 'collarbone' of the turkey or chicken), you hook your little finger around one side while someone else does the same with the other side, and you both pull. Whoever gets the bigger piece as it breaks makes a secret wish.

❖ Many years ago, this meal would have been followed by Christian study, but these days people generally just relax together. In Britain, the tradition is to listen to the Queen's speech at 3:00 p.m.

EPIPHANY
(January)

The start of Epiphany (Greek, manifestation) on 6 January ends the 'twelve days of Christmas' that started on 25 December, and celebrates the manifestation of Christ to the three gentile (non-Jewish) Magi (wise men, or kings) who came with gifts of gold, frankincense and myrrh for the baby Jesus. It is also the day that Christmas decorations are traditionally removed. The first Sunday after this date is a popular family choice for a baptism ceremony, as it celebrates Jesus' baptism by John the Baptist in the River Jordan. Overall, the Feast of Epiphany celebrates the many miracles, signs and preachings of Jesus that revealed him to be the Son of God, and representations of these stories might be included in church services. At this time the altar dressings and vestments are white and gold, for purity and holiness.

CANDLEMAS
(2 February)

This day ends Epiphany and is traditionally when all the Church candles to be used throughout the coming year are blessed. Symbolically, candles bring light to the dark, in the way that Christians say Jesus is the 'light of the world'. This date also commemorates the day that, in accordance with the law of the time, Mary presented Jesus in the Temple at Jerusalem, and is also known as 'Presentation of Christ in the Temple' and in the Roman Catholic tradition 'Purification of the Blessed Virgin Mary'. In the United States this coincides with Groundhog Day, which has its roots in ancient European weather lore.

SHROVETIDE
(February/March)

Shrove Sunday marks the start of the three days leading to Lent, and is also known as Quinquagesima Sunday (Latin, fifty days), starting a fifty-day period to Easter Day and the Resurrection. In early Christian times, this is when fasting would have begun. The word 'shrove' derives from the medieval word 'shriven', which means confessed and absolved, but in its more frequent use it denoted the time to eat before the fast began.

In England, Shrove Monday, with the eating of collops (pieces of bacon) and eggs, preceded Shrove Tuesday, or 'Pancake Day', when the fat from 'Collop Monday' was used for making the pancakes. This used to be a half-day holiday that started with the ringing of the Shriven bell, still rung in some English villages. Though no longer a holiday, the tradition of pancake tossing survives – with many dropped in the process! This is the last day to use up and enjoy foods forbidden during Lent – fat, butter and eggs, although only very strict Christians would observe this. In the USA, Roman Catholics call Shrove Tuesday by its French name, Mardi Gras ('Fat Tuesday').

LENT
(February/March)

Quadragesima (Latin, forty days) is the period leading to Easter and in part commemorates the time that Jesus spent in the wilderness, fasting and being tested by the Devil. As a 'fast', Christians will usually 'give something up for Lent' – such as chocolate or alcohol, or watching TV. It only includes weekdays because Sundays are always kept as a celebration of the resurrection.

ASH WEDNESDAY
(February/March)

This is the first day of Lent, a solemn day for Catholics and Protestants alike. For Catholics it is a compulsory day of fasting and abstinence. In many cultures, fire represents purification, and in the Christian tradition the ashes created by burning the palm leaves from last year's Palm Sunday symbolise the freedom from sin that came through Christ's crucifixion and resurrection. Mixed with holy water, the ashes form a paste, which the priest then uses to make the sign of the cross on worshippers' foreheads during the Ash Wednesday service. This signifies that they repent their wrongdoings of the past year and are seeking God's forgiveness.

MOTHERING SUNDAY
(February/March)

Commercially, this is known as Mother's Day, and is a day for special attention for their mothers from sons and daughters; in former times, domestic servants were given a rare half-day holiday to visit their mothers. It has now become popular to send Mother's Day cards, and perhaps give presents or flowers, as a sign of appreciation.

Falling on the fourth Sunday in Lent, it is also when Christians give special thanks for their 'mother church'.

PASSION SUNDAY
(March/April)

This, the fifth Sunday in Lent, marks the start of a two-week period known as Passiontide that culminates in the death of Jesus.

PALM SUNDAY
(March/April)

The sixth Sunday in Lent celebrates the entry of Jesus into Jerusalem. The modern way of greeting honoured guests is to wave a flag, but then the tradition was to wave palm leaves, which were also laid on the ground before him. The celebration was short-lived, as Jesus' death by crucifixion came a week later. The ash used on Ash Wednesday symbolically reminds worshippers that defeat quickly follows triumph. For both Protestants and Catholics this is the beginning of Holy Week, and congregations might carry palm leaves or palm crosses to or from their church. Catholics in particular pray and reflect at the Stations of the Cross, which follow Christ's journey to crucifixion.

ABOVE Palm procession in San Cristóbal de las Casas, Mexico.

MAUNDY THURSDAY
(March/April)

Also known as Holy Thursday, this is the day of the Last Supper that Jesus shared with his disciples, during which he broke bread and drank wine, asking that he be remembered in this way. Knowing that he would be betrayed, he also gave a new commandment to 'love one another' and, as an act of humility, he washed the feet of his disciples. Congregations might also choose to follow this example during a special evening Eucharist service. This marks the start of the Easter Triduum (Good Friday, Holy Saturday and Easter Sunday) and might be followed by an all-night vigil. Alternatively,

some Christians might have a 'Last Supper' meal together at home.

In Britain there is an ancient tradition in which the monarch used to wash the feet of the poor in Westminster Abbey before giving them 'Maundy money'. Today the monarch just gives the specially minted coins to a group of pensioners, the amount of money and number of pensioners being determined by the age of the monarch.

ABOVE The Anglican Bishop of St Asaph, in Wales, washing feet on Maundy Thursday.

GOOD FRIDAY
(March/April)

Good Friday, or Holy Friday, is a key focus for Christians because on this day Jesus was tried, found guilty and crucified. It is considered 'good' because Jesus died so that humanity might be freed from its sins. In many countries, Good Friday is a public holiday, which means that shops and businesses are closed, and in many parts of the world there will be a 'procession of witness', in which a cross will be carried through the streets to the church. In extreme cases, individuals will also either be nailed to a cross or draw blood through self-flagellation, as a reminder of the suffering of Jesus. For Catholics, this is an obligatory day of fasting and abstinence.

WHAT HAPPENS?

◆ Both Anglican and Catholic churches will hold special services. Some might start at midday or 3:00 p.m., said to be the time that Jesus died, and are likely to last for three hours, during which time there may be passion plays and special readings. As it is considered a day of mourning, the altar will be empty and pictures and statues might be covered. Clergy vestments are likely to be red, to represent the blood of Christ's wounds.

◆ Traditionally, as a penance, Catholics would only ever eat fish on a Friday, not meat, but this is now only observed during Lent. 'Hot cross buns' (sweet and spicy fruit buns with a white cross baked into the top) are often eaten on this day, with the cross being the reminder of the crucifixion.

◆ Among more observant Christians it is also popular to send Easter cards, which became fashionable during Victorian times.

HOLY SATURDAY
(March/April)

This is a day of reflection on Christ's death, burial in the tomb and forthcoming resurrection, which leads Christians into the service known as the Great Vigil or Paschal Vigil. This takes place sometime between sunset on Holy Saturday (which marks the end of Lent) and sunrise on Easter Day (Sunday), hence it is also called the Sunrise or Dawn Service. It is more likely to be the latter. Some congregations gather at outdoor crosses placed at high spots in the landscape, while others meet at their church.

EASTER SUNDAY
(March/April)

Easter Sunday marks the start of Eastertide, the period of joyous celebration of Christ's Resurrection that ends fifty days later at Pentecost. It includes his Ascension into heaven after forty days.

Also known as the Feast of the Resurrection, Easter Sunday itself is the most powerful of the Christian holy days, when Christ's rising from the dead is celebrated with a four-part Easter Eucharist.

WHAT HAPPENS?

◆ Commencing with the Service of Light, the congregation is led into the darkened church with a Paschal candle, a special candle representing the wounds of Christ, which is used to light their own candles to acknowledge Christ as the 'Light of the World'.

◆ Once the candle is ceremoniously placed in its holder, the congregation is greeted with the words 'Alleluia, Christ is Risen', to which they respond 'Thanks be to God'.

◆ There follow the Liturgy of the Word, the Liturgy of Baptism and the Liturgy of the Eucharist (Holy Communion).

◆ As this is a time of celebrating joyous new life, baptisms/christenings or congregational Renewals of Baptisms (re-affirming Christian commitment) are often held during the service. Clerical vestments are white and gold. If this service has taken place at sunrise, it will be followed by a hearty community breakfast.

As in the original Passover in Egypt, where a lamb was ritually killed and the blood smeared on the Israelites' doorposts to ensure that the Angel of Death 'passed over', for Christians, the Paschal Lamb is Christ, ' the Lamb of God', whose sacrifice is said to have freed us from sin. Therefore lamb is the usual meat for the Easter Sunday lunch. Afternoon tea will often include

Easter biscuits and simnel cake, made with fruit and topped with eleven small balls of marzipan – one for each of the Apostles (excluding Judas Iscariot, who betrayed Christ).

It has long been the tradition to give Easter eggs, which are now usually chocolate but were originally decorated birds' eggs, and although these eggs remind Christians of the empty tomb, there are also strong links with Eostre, the Anglo Saxon Goddess of Fertility, and the new beginnings of Spring. An afternoon activity that children love is the Easter egg hunt!

Easter Monday is another public holiday in many countries, and one of the traditional pursuits was 'egg rolling', again a merging of Christianity with ancient traditions, with the egg as a pagan fertility symbol and the rolling symbolising rolling away the rock from Jesus' tomb to reveal his resurrection. In the USA, the Easter Egg Roll is a race held on the lawn of the White House.

ASCENSION
(May/June)
Marking the day when Jesus last appeared to his disciples, telling them to wait for the Holy Spirit, this day is always a Thursday, but is honoured on the Sunday.

PENTECOST
(May/June)
Pentecost (Greek, fiftieth day) falls on the seventh Sunday after Easter Sunday and is the day when the Holy Spirit touched the disciples, causing them to speak in tongues, and inspiring them in their mission to spread the teachings of Jesus throughout the world.

It was, in effect, the start of what is now the Christian Church. It is also another popular occasion for baptisms and christenings, where churches and Christian homes might be decorated with symbols of the white dove said to represent the Holy Spirit, present at the baptism of Jesus.

Also known as Whitsun (Old English, 'White Sunday') in England, Pentecost is often celebrated in local towns and villages with a fair to include the old customs of Morris dancing and cheese rolling. The link with cheese might be because Pentecost took place on Shavuot, the Jewish Festival of Weeks, when it is traditional to eat cheese.

TRINITY SUNDAY
(May/June)

This is the first Sunday after Pentecost and is the only day in the liturgical year that particularly Catholics (for whom it known as 'Solemnity of the Most Holy Trinity') and Anglo-Catholics recite the Athanasian Creed, which focuses on Trinitarian doctrine, confirming God's triune nature in the Father, the Son and the Holy Spirit. Historically, among non-Christians this led to the mistaken belief that Christianity is polytheistic. Different symbols from nature have been used to illustrate the three aspects of God, the best-known being the three-leaved shamrock made famous by St Patrick, the patron saint of Ireland. This Creed may or may not be recited in other Protestant services.

THE FEAST OF CORPUS CHRISTI
(May/June)

This feast, also known as 'the Body and Blood of the Lord' occurs on the Thursday after Trinity Sunday. It celebrates the institution and gift of the Holy Eucharist of the Lord's Supper, and is the Catholic equivalent of Maundy Thursday. In some countries it is celebrated not only with a special mass, but also with a procession through the streets. In Britain, it is now held on Sunday.

THE SOLEMNITY OF SAINT PETER AND SAINT PAUL
(29 June)

This is a Catholic Holy Day of Obligation, and commemorates the martyrdom of these two saints.

THE FEAST OF THE ASSUMPTION
(August)

A Catholic feast day, this commemorates the belief that Mary, Mother of Jesus, also ascended into heaven when she died. This belief remains controversial in the Protestant tradition. The Anglican Church commemorates this as 'the Blessed Virgin Mary'.

HARVEST FESTIVAL
(September/October/November)

Celebrating a successful harvest of crops, and with roots in many cultures, this unofficial festival is usually held at the end of September, but occasionally at the beginning of October, depending on the time of the full moon. Churches are creatively decorated with produce, plants and special displays of food donated by the congregation and local schools. After a service of thanks with prayers and singing, the food is usually packed up and distributed to those in the community who are less fortunate. In some cases, money will be donated, too, which will be used to help other countries in need.

In the USA, on the fourth Thursday in November, and in Canada, on the second Monday in October, this day takes the form of Thanksgiving, and is a national holiday with families gathering to celebrate.

THE FEAST OF THE DEDICATION OF SAINT MICHAEL, THE ARCHANGEL (29 September)

THE FEAST OF THE GUARDIAN ANGELS (2 October)

On these two feast days, Catholics affirm their belief in Angels and Archangels with special readings and prayers at Mass.

ALL HALLOWS' EVE (31 October)

This is more commonly known as Hallowe'en – the eve of All Hallows' (Old English, sanctified or holy), or All Saints', Day. There are strong links between Hallowe'en and the early pagan festival of Samhain, and children dress up as witches and play 'trick or treat' – words they still say when they knock on your door.

BE PREPARED!
❖ Have some sweets handy for the treat, or you may be the victim of the trick!

Many people have 'pumpkin parties' where, having scooped out the flesh of the pumpkin, they cut a scary face in the shell and put a lighted candle inside. This is called a jack o'-lantern in the USA. In ancient folklore it is said that if you are single and look in the mirror at midnight on 31 October you will see the face of the person you are going to marry.

ALL SAINTS' DAY
(1 November)
Usually commemorated on 1 November, this day venerates all saints, known and unknown, for whom prayers are said.

ALL SOULS' DAY
(November)
This day, usually on 2 November, is the Commemoration of the Faithful Departed, sometimes called the 'Day of the Dead', and linked with pre-Christian traditions. As a day of remembrance for friends and family who have died, candles are lit and special prayers said for the souls of the departed to be free of sin and received into heaven. This may not happen in some Protestant Churches. In some countries, families may visit the graves of their loved ones.

REMEMBRANCE SUNDAY
(November)
Also known as Poppy Day or Veterans' Day, this commemorates the signing of the Armistice ending the First World War on 11 November, 1918. It is held on the second Sunday of November in Britain, and observed by Commonwealth countries, to honour and remember all those who have given their lives in war.

Although this is a secular ceremony, churches hold special services, during which the National Anthem is sung. The service is followed by a town parade, usually organised by the Royal British Legion, an ex-veterans' association, and includes various youth groups such as scouts, guides and cadet forces. Standard-bearers from each group lead marches to the local war memorial, and at 11:00 a.m. a two-minute silence is observed and the standards are lowered. At the Cenotaph in London's Whitehall, the largest commemoration in Britain, this is preceded by cannon fire and followed by buglers of the Royal Marines playing the 'Last Post'. The Monarch then leads the laying of poppy wreaths.

Church services may also be held on 11 November, when this does not fall on a Sunday. Other countries, of course, have equivalent services for their fallen.

WHAT DO I DO?

❖ In the weeks before Remembrance Sunday, red paper poppies – which are worn on the lapel area and signify the flowers that grew in some of the worst battlefields of the First World War – are given to the public in exchange for donations to the British Legion. If you are invited to attend a service, it is polite to wear a poppy.

THE FEAST OF CHRIST THE KING (November/December)

This feast day occurs on the last Sunday before Advent and triumphantly ends the liturgical year. This day was also known as Stir-Up Sunday (see Christmas Day), from the opening words of the Collect for the day, and is when Catholics and many Anglicans affirm their belief in Jesus Christ as Lord over all creation.

RITUALS AND CEREMONIES

BIRTH

When a baby is a few months old – often around six months – Christian parents will have him or her 'baptised', or 'christened'. In this ceremony family and friends gather together to celebrate the Sacrament of Initiation that makes the child 'one with Christ' and formally welcome him or her into the Christian community. The ritual use of water is to wash away the 'original sin' created by Adam and Eve's eating of the forbidden fruit. The parents may be required to undertake a period of instruction with the minister or priest to ensure they fully understand the commitment that is being made on behalf of their child. As Catholics

ABOVE Infant baptism in the Stora Sköndals church in Sweden.

forbid the use of contraception, it is hoped that a healthy couple will have a child early in their marriage.

Parents will ask trusted friends or family members to be godparents (spiritual guardians), who will not only take some responsibility for the child should anything happen to them, but who will also ensure that Christian values are adhered to, until such time as the child can affirm his or her own commitment during the next sacrament of Confirmation. It is usual for a boy to have two godfathers and one godmother, and a girl to have two godmothers and one godfather. Godparents must have been christened, and preferably confirmed as well.

Catholic and Anglo-Catholic baptisms are similar, entailing a threefold pouring of water over the head, but other Protestant denominations differ depending on their particular approach. For example, Baptists usually wait until children are old enough to understand what they are committing themselves to, and their baptism is likely to be a full body immersion. Consequently, they do not also have a service of Confirmation.

WHAT DO I DO?

❖ It is customary to send a congratulatory letter or card to new parents.

❖ If you are invited to a christening, you will probably receive a formal invitation giving the date, time and venue, to which you will be expected to reply.

❖ A christening is usually on a Sunday, as part of the main church service for that day, so that the congregation is witness to the event and can welcome the new member, but it can also be a private church service.

❖ Take your lead from others as to when to stand or sit. There is usually an offertory (giving of money) at some point in the service, so have some change easily available, although it is not compulsory to contribute. £1 is an appropriate amount.

❖ Family, godparents and friends usually bring christening presents, which will probably include a Bible, for the child. As a guest, you may wish to bring a small gift, such as a child's cup or spoon or other keepsake or toy.

After the christening, friends and family usually gather at a separate venue to celebrate the event. Dress code is smart, and the baby as star guest may be wearing an embroidered white or cream christening gown, which may have been handed down through generations, and be wrapped in a special white shawl.

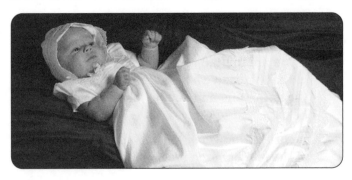

WHAT HAPPENS AT AN ANGLICAN/EPISCOPALIAN CHRISTENING?

◆ At the appointed time during the service the parents, baby and godparents will join the minister at the font.

◆ After confirming that the child has not already been baptised, there will be an opening prayer by the minister, followed by a prayer by all and words from the Gospel.

◆ Attention will then be turned to the parents and godparents, who will be asked a series of questions, and after giving the required answers will pass the baby to the minister, who confirms his or her name.

◆ The minister will then hold the child with the head above the font, and gently pour some water over the forehead three times, using the words, 'I baptise you in the name of the Father, Son and Holy Ghost. Amen'. The sign of the cross is then made on the child's forehead.

◆ Further prayers will be offered before the minister seeks the assurance of the godparents that they will present the child for confirmation (re-affirmation of the baptismal vows) at the appointed age.

◆ The service then continues as usual, or will end at this point with a final prayer.

WHAT HAPPENS AT A CATHOLIC BAPTISM?

◆ Where the Rite of Baptism is during Sunday Mass, the Reception of the Children (Child) will be part of the Introductory Rites, which on this occasion exclude the Penitential Rites. Once the priest has confirmed the name of the child and that the parents and godparents are clear what their Catholic responsibilities are, he will make the sign of the cross on the child's forehead and invite the family to do the same.

◆ The Gloria and the Collect are followed by the Liturgy of the Word, and the celebration of baptism continues after the Prayers of Intercession with a Prayer of Exorcism, so that the child may be free from Original Sin.

◆ The ceremonial shawl will be put aside and the mother holds her child while its chest area is anointed with holy oil of catechumens in preparation for the baptism. With family positioned at the font, the priest leads a responsorial blessing over the holy water followed by a Renunciation of Sin and Profession of Faith by the parents and godparents.

◆ After confirming that it is their desire for the child to be baptised, the mother places the head of the child towards the holy water, which the priest gently pours over the forehead three times, saying the same words as in the Anglican service. A further blessing is offered before the priest anoints the child with sacred chrism in the sign of the cross on the forehead.

◆ The white ceremonial shawl is then wrapped around the child as a symbol of purity and Christian dignity, before a special candle 'to receive the light of Christ' is lit and a joyful baptismal hymn might be sung before everyone recites the Lord's Prayer on behalf of the child. The service then continues in the usual way, ending with a final blessing for the parents as well as the congregation.

If the baptism is outside Mass, with only family and friends, there will be variations to the structure of the service, which will exclude the Liturgy of the Eucharist but include the Invocation of Saints to pray for those present.

FIRST COMMUNION

The First Communion is a major event in the life of a Catholic child, and is when he or she receives the Eucharist for the first time. It takes place when the child has reached the age of understanding and discretion: seven or eight years is typical, but some communities wait until the child is older. Before the date the children are prepared at Sunday School by a member of the community or their priest, and make their first confession. At the next Mass, after the consecration of the Host and Wine, they are called up to the altar to receive the Eucharist ahead of the rest of the congregation.

In Irish and Hispanic communities especially, and in much of Continental Europe, this occasion calls for a costly celebration. Little girls wear special white dresses, perhaps with tiaras or flowers in their hair, little boys are dressed up in page-boy outfits or smart white uniforms, and all receive cards and presents. There is a lavish party for family, godparents and friends after the ceremony. Elsewhere the celebration may be more modest, but it is nevertheless an important occasion for the family.

Gifts from the family and godparents might include religious items such as missals and rosaries, but it is quite suitable for friends to give an ordinary present such as a watch, necklace, book or toy.

CONFIRMATION

In both the Catholic and Anglican/Episcopalian traditions, Confirmation is the coming of age sacrament during which the Holy Spirit is conferred upon a child who is now considered mature enough to understand what is required within the Christian faith and to confirm the vows taken on their behalf at baptism. It usually takes place when the child is around fourteen years of age. In preparation, children will have attended confirmation classes and prepared a Statement of Faith to demonstrate their understanding of the commitment

ABOVE First Communion in Asturias, Spain, in the 1960s.

they are making. Only after their confirmation do Anglicans take Holy Communion.

The service of Confirmation will vary according to the tradition, but essentially it is conducted by a bishop, who confirms a number of individuals at the same time. The ceremony, which may last several hours, might therefore be held in a cathedral rather than the local church. In some services there may be people who are being baptised and confirmed at the same time.

WHAT DO I DO?

❖ Smart dress is required, and there may be a celebratory gathering afterwards.

❖ As with any service there will be times to stand or sit, when hymns are sung and prayers recited, so take your cue from your neighbours. Be sure your cell phone is turned off.

WHAT HAPPENS?

◆ The Catholic and Anglican services are very similar. Those to be confirmed answer a series of questions: they confirm their previous baptism, that they are ready to be confirmed, and that they intend to follow the teachings of their faith.

◆ After the Laying on of Hands, where the bishop and those assisting him extend their hands over the confirmands' heads and a special invocation prayer is spoken, a large candle is lit.

♦ The godparents then present the confirmands individually to the Bishop, who confirms their names and may also anoint their foreheads with chrism in the sign of the cross.

♦ A number of special prayers are offered and the service will continue as usual with the Liturgy of the Eucharist/Holy Communion. After the final Dismissal, each confirmand might light a candle from the central flame and be led from the church by the bishop.

♦ In some Protestant denominations, confirmation may just involve a person making a public declaration of faith to an assembled congregation, while in others they might share their Statement of Faith with family during a special dinner. Where time permits this may also happen during the service of confirmation, which would also be the case in the Catholic tradition.

MARRIAGE

For Catholics marriage is a sacrament. For all Christians, it is a holy commitment and celebrated in various ways both before and after the ceremony itself. Catholics must be baptised, confirmed, and marry in their local church of worship, while in the Church of England it is not necessary for those marrying to have been baptised or confirmed or to attend church regularly, although they do need to affirm their desire to live as followers of Christ. Couples can also now elect to marry in a church outside their normal parish, providing they meet certain criteria.

In both traditions, once the date is fixed for the ceremony, it is likely that the couple will have spent some time with the minister not only agreeing hymns and readings, but also discussing the importance of marriage and their future relationship. They may even have attended a pre-marriage event arranged by the church.

Catholics marrying non-Catholics must undertake to baptise any children into the Catholic faith, and

those who are divorced are not permitted to marry in church again unless they can obtain a decree of nullity – a long and sometimes costly procedure. A divorced Catholic marrying again without this dispensation is no longer permitted to receive Holy Communion, although he or she may attend Mass and receive a blessing. In the

Anglican Church, divorced people who remarry can apply to have a Service of Prayer and Dedication after a civil ceremony.

Pre-Wedding Celebrations

The night before the wedding, but more usually a few days or even weeks before, bride and groom may have separate celebrations with their respective friends for their 'last night of freedom'. Different countries have their own rituals and in the USA there will be a 'bridal shower', where female friends host a meal and give gifts, and a 'bachelor party', where the groom will give thank-you gifts to those supporting him. The bride might also host a 'bridal brunch' for close family as thanks for their support, and as a way of spending some time with people she might not see again for a while. The evening before the wedding there may be a 'rehearsal dinner', which is the equivalent of the 'wedding breakfast' mentioned below.

In the United Kingdom the groom's celebration is known as a 'stag night', and the bride's a 'hen party'.

How they are celebrated is very individual, but the occasions may involve alcohol and, depending on the company, can become very raucous!

An Anglican Wedding

A wedding usually takes place on a Saturday rather than a Sunday, so that the church can be reserved for private use. Everyone dresses smartly, the bride and groom's families particularly so, with the men possibly wearing formal 'morning suits' (waistcoats, cravats and long-tailed jackets) and a 'buttonhole' flower. Traditionally, the bride wears white as a sign of purity and carries or wears 'something old [perhaps the family bible], something new [her dress], something borrowed [such as a family necklace] and something blue [maybe a blue garter concealed under her dress]'. She will carry a bouquet of flowers and may wear a veil over her face, although this is now less fashionable.

As you arrive the church bells may be ringing to announce that a marriage is about to take place. Inside, the church is likely to be decorated with floral displays and ribbons and, if booked for the occasion, the organist will be playing appropriate music.

WHAT DO I DO?

❖ Smart dress is required. Male guests wear suits, and although this is not required in church, women often wear hats.

❖ It's a good idea to arrive at the church about half an hour before the service is due to begin, and also to take your invitation with you in case you are asked to show it.

❖ At the door you will probably be greeted by an usher, who may ask to see the invitation, and who will give you an Order of Service, which explains the format for the ceremony. At a traditional wedding you will be asked whether you are a friend of the bride (in which case you will sit on the left side) or of the groom (seats to the right).

❖ You may be shown to a seat but, if not, bear in mind that the first few rows at the front of the church will be reserved for the immediate families of the bride and groom.

❖ During the service, guests are not required to sing, even if the words are printed in the Order of Service, but you are of course welcome to do so.

WHAT HAPPENS?

◆ The groom will traditionally enter the church first with his 'best man' (brother or close friend and ring holder). They wait for the bride at the front of the church, on the right-hand side, facing the altar and the minister. It is said to be the bride's prerogative to be late, which can often cause some tense moments for the groom.

◆ When the minister asks everyone to stand, processional music plays to welcome her walk down the aisle, usually accompanied by her father, possibly preceded by a young 'flower girl' and followed by a chief bridesmaid, or maid of honour (matron of honour if a married woman), other bridesmaids and pages – or all!

◆ The overall service consists of two parts – the Introduction and the Marriage – and lasts approximately forty-five minutes. The Introduction starts once the couple is standing together facing the minister, who offers a short welcoming prayer, which might be followed by a communal prayer.

◆ In the preface, the minister reminds everyone why they are gathered and explains the purpose of Christian marriage. The Declarations of Intent allow the minister to make a final check as to whether anyone knows of a legal reason why the couple should not marry, before asking both the groom and the bride individually if they will love, honour, protect and be faithful to each other, to which they both respond positively. The minister is also likely to ask family and friends, who are not just considered as visitors but as witnesses to a sacred event, for a 'pledge of support' for the couple, to which the response is 'we will'.

◆ A brief period of silence for private prayer is followed by the Collect (a short invocation for blessings on the marriage) and ends with everyone saying 'Amen', after which the first hymn is sung.

◆ Once seated, a reading from the Bible is followed by a prayer and a sermon from the minister on the sanctity of marriage. Another hymn marks the start of the marriage, when the bride and groom turn to each other to speak their vows (sacred commitment), which are repeated after the minister.

◆ The best man presents the wedding ring (or rings) for the minister's blessing before the bride and groom exchange them 'as a sign of their marriage'. The Proclamation announces them to be 'man and wife', as they kneel to receive the nuptial blessing, at the end of which everyone says 'Amen.' The couple are then invited to kiss and in the USA at this point, the couple might also light a 'unity' candle to seal their bond of togetherness.

◆ While music plays, the couple go with two witnesses to a separate area to sign the register and receive their marriage certificate. Upon their return, another hymn might be sung before a series of special short responsorial prayers is offered (which could include one for the gift of children, when previously agreed with the couple), before all recite the Lord's Prayer. The service concludes with the Dismissal, a final blessing, ending with 'Amen'.

◆ Joyous recessional music will then be played as the bride and groom leave together, and once again the church bells might be rung. Outside, confetti (tiny pieces of coloured paper in the shape of horseshoes or bells) would traditionally have been thrown over the couple for good luck, but many churches no longer allow this. Official photographs are often taken now, before the bride and groom leave first in their chosen vehicle (which might be a vintage car, or horse and carriage) and make their way to the hall, hotel or other venue to welcome their guests to the reception and 'wedding breakfast' (celebratory meal).

A Catholic Wedding

Catholics are required to marry in one or the other's regular place of worship, and prior to the wedding they will have attended a marriage preparation class. However, the ceremony is not very different in format from that described above. One difference, of course, is that as Catholics enter the church they lightly dip their fingers into holy water, cross themselves, and genuflect towards the altar before sitting down.

WHAT HAPPENS?

◆ The priest, groom and best man enter through a side door and wait at the altar for the bride and those accompanying her.

◆ Where the marriage is part of the regular Mass, the ceremony follows the service order with the Rite of Marriage, which includes the vows, exchange of rings and signing of the civil register, taking place after the Liturgy of the Word and before the Liturgy of the Eucharist, where the bride and groom may bring the bread and wine to the altar. A nuptial blessing will be given after the Lord's Prayer as part of the Communion Rite.

◆ If the marriage takes place outside Mass, the Penitential Rite, the Gloria, and the Liturgy of the Eucharist are omitted, but Holy Communion is given during the conclusion of the celebration and the couple sign the civil register after the Dismissal. They will then leave for photographs and their reception.

The Wedding Reception

Traditionally, it is the bride's parents who host the reception, but today costs are often shared. It may be a modest or lavish occasion, and held at a private home, hall, hotel, restaurant or other venue.

The bride and groom may have a 'wedding list' with a store, so when you receive your invitation you can ask if there is one, which makes it easy to buy a gift of their choice from the store, which will deliver it for you. Otherwise, something for the house is usually appropriate, and you can take this with you to the reception and ask where you can leave it before you join the party; there will be an allocated area.

WHAT HAPPENS?

◆ Where there is a large number of guests and a formal seating arrangement, there will probably be a table plan in the main reception area, so you can check the number of the table where you will be sitting.

◆ You may be offered a welcome drink as you enter the main reception room, and you can expect to join a line of guests waiting to be greeted by the bride and groom and their respective parents in a 'receiving line'. It is usual to congratulate the couple and wish them a happy future, and to shake hands with their parents. Then the guests mingle until it is time to find their places at the tables. There may be a toastmaster to make announcements. Later in the proceedings there may be a 'paying bar', so take enough money in case you want to buy drinks after the meal.

◆ Traditionally, the bride, groom, their families, best man and bridesmaids will sit at a 'top table' and everyone stands until they are seated. Later in the meal, there will be speeches by a variety of people including the bride's father, the best man, the groom, and the maid/matron of honour. Increasingly these days, the bride might speak too, but this is not traditional. At varying times, there will be toasts to the 'happy couple', who then lead the first dance.

- ◆ At some point everyone gathers around the elaborately iced wedding cake, which the couple formally cut, to much applause. Of the three or four tiers of cake, traditionally the smallest, top tier was kept for the christening of the first child. Everyone receives a slice, and pieces are often mailed to those who were unable to attend.

- ◆ Towards the end of the evening, the couple will leave the room to change into smart but less formal 'going-away clothes', before everyone gathers outside to wave them off for their honeymoon – often in a car to which well-meaning friends have attached tin cans and a 'Just Married' sign. Once the couple have left, the celebration either begins to wind down or continues into the night!

DEATH AND MOURNING
The Anglican/Episcopalian Tradition

For the sick or dying, it is likely that the minister and congregation at the person's regular church will pray for healing, or strength in their dying. The minister might visit them at home or in hospital to offer spiritual support and administer holy unction (anointing the sick) with special oil.

Once death has been officially declared, local funeral directors remove the deceased to a funeral parlour. In the case of sudden death an autopsy may be required to determine the cause, and the funeral directors take responsibility for transportation and the later preparation of the body for family and friends to view in their chapel of rest, if they wish to do so.

For a cremation, the service may be led by the minister in the crematorium's chapel or at the local church, after which the body is taken for cremation. For a burial, the majority of the service will be inside the church, with the Final Committal at the graveside.

WHAT DO I DO?

❖ It is customary in both traditions to send a letter or card of sympathy. When meeting members of the bereaved family, it is usual to express your sorrow for their loss.

❖ If you are attending the service, you can send flowers in advance to the funeral directors, and these will be placed with the coffin. However, many families now request donations to charities instead, and a box may be provided on the day of the service.

WHAT HAPPENS?

◆ On the day of the funeral, the coffin is taken to the church or crematorium in a hearse – this can be a horse-drawn carriage or a limousine provided by the funeral directors. Either way, there are large glass windows on three sides so that the coffin, usually adorned with special flower wreaths, can be seen. Following the hearse in funeral cars are the close family, usually dressed in black – although these days lighter colours are sometimes worn and occasionally the deceased has previously stipulated that no dark colours are to be worn.

◆ At the church or chapel, mourners are usually asked to take a seat inside to await the arrival of the coffin, and appropriate music will be playing. The first few rows of seats are reserved for family members, and there will often be an Order of Service provided so that you know what will be happening. This will also state where donations can be sent.

◆ Once the hearse arrives, the coffin is removed and placed on the shoulders of six pallbearers, several of whom might be family members. On some occasions the coffin might be placed on a wheeled stretcher. Music signals the entrance, and everyone will stand and bow their heads as the coffin passes to the front. In a church it will be laid close to the altar, and in a crematorium, in an area fronted by open curtains.

◆ The minister welcomes everyone, introduces the service and says an opening prayer. Several hymns might be sung and, as well as readings from the Bible and/or a psalm, such as 'The Lord is my Shepherd', family members might give a special reading or eulogy (a formal expression of praise). In more modern funerals, the music might include a favourite song of the deceased.

◆ After prayers of thanks and prayers of comfort for the family, a period of silence leads to the prayers of commendation and farewell, which entrust the deceased to the mercy and love of God. All prayers end with everyone saying 'Amen'. At this point in a crematorium chapel, unless asked not to by the family, the minister will press a button and the curtains close to conceal the coffin. This is often a moment of much grief and part of the final act of closure.

◆ After the service for a burial, the coffin, followed by family and mourners, is carried to the graveside, where it is suspended over the grave on leather straps held by the pallbearers. With everyone gathered, it is gently lowered as the minister speaks the final words of committal. Mourners are then often offered a box containing some earth. It is your choice whether you take a small amount and throw it into the grave. Close family members might also throw in a single flower.

◆ The total service, including committal, is likely to take about an hour (or half an hour at a crematorium), but allow extra time for additional travel and attendance at the wake (the post-funeral gathering) for refreshments and the exchange of further memories of the deceased. This can be quite an enjoyable time, with laughter and tears as people share their recollections of the deceased. There may even be a photographic montage, slides or a video of the person's life.

The Catholic Tradition

As in the Anglican Church, for those who are ill, a priest will perform the Sacrament of the Sick, which includes prayers for recovery or strength in preparing for the afterlife, and anointing with oil in the sign of the cross on the forehead and palms of the hands.

If the person is dying, the priest will first determine where possible that the sacraments of baptism, communion and confirmation have been undertaken, before administering the Last Rites, consisting of confession (where the person is able), absolution and anointing with oil. Finally, and again if the person is able, Viaticum (a special Eucharist) is given as 'food for the journey'. After death and before the deceased is moved, 'Prayers after Death' will be said, either by the priest or by a layperson.

The two purposes of a Catholic funeral are to honour the dead and care for the bereaved, and the funeral itself consists of three parts: the Reception of the Body and Vigil, the Funeral Mass (no longer called a Requiem) and the Rite of Committal. In the case of a funeral falling on a day when the Eucharist is not celebrated, no priest is available, or the family, not having attended regularly, deem it inappropriate, it is called the Funeral Liturgy outside Mass.

Generally, Catholics are buried rather than cremated. Catholics believe that the body of the deceased must be treated with the utmost dignity because, on the Day of Judgement, when Christ returns, it will be reunited with its soul, and it is not therefore a 'shell'. However, since 1963, when Pope John XXII proclaimed it legal to seek cremation, and 1966, when the ban on Catholic priests conducting services in crematoria was lifted, cremation has become a family decision, but it is preferred that the body be present for the Funeral Liturgy/Mass and cremated later. The ashes should not be scattered, but buried in consecrated ground in a biodegradable container.

The 'Reception of the Body' and 'Vigil'

This is a pre-funeral service and the first moment of public prayer. It takes place in the candlelit church on the evening before the Funeral Mass.

If there is no Holy Mass this lasts about fifteen to twenty minutes and may be led by a deacon or appointed layperson, often referred to as 'the minister'. Otherwise it will be up to an hour long and led by the priest. It will be attended by family, friends and those who might not be able to attend the next day.

As well as Holy Communion the service will probably include a hymn, a poem or a reading; a brief tribute to the deceased; prayers of intercession, together with a final prayer and blessing that excludes the Rite of Committal (which will take place at the graveside or, in the case of cremation, the end of the Mass). In some Catholic countries or strong Catholic communities, the coffin may be open and a rosary placed in the crossed hands of the deceased.

WHAT DO I DO?

❖ Should you wish to attend, black is the traditional colour of mourning, but other dark colours are acceptable.

❖ If a visitors' book is provided, make sure you sign it so that the family of the bereaved knows who has been to 'pay their respects'.

❖ **Appropriate words for the bereaved are 'I'm sorry for your loss', and as you sit you might want to offer silent prayers from your own tradition.**

The Funeral Mass

The Funeral Mass in church on the day of Committal lasts approximately fifty minutes, although extra time will usually be needed to move to the graveside or the crematorium. As an act of the Church, it is usual for regular members of the congregation to be present to join in the prayers for the deceased. Essentially, the format follows that of the regular Mass.

WHAT HAPPENS?

◆ Mourners will be greeted at the door to the church and probably given an Order of Service before taking their seats. Music plays, and all stand to receive the coffin, which is draped with a plain white pall (cloth) with a crucifix or cross and/or a Bible placed on top. Flowers will have been removed and placed nearby, together with sympathy cards brought on the day.

◆ After an opening hymn, the priest welcomes the congregation and leads a prayer, after which a family member might say some brief words of remembrance, although this may have already taken place during the Vigil.

◆ The core of the service is then as for Mass: the Liturgy of the Word, and the Liturgy of the Eucharist, if held.

◆ The service concludes with the Prayers of Farewell, and mourners may be invited to sprinkle the coffin with holy water before it is either carried to the graveside or driven to the crematorium, for the Rite of Committal.

◆ The Rite of Committal is the final act of the community in caring for the body of the deceased and ends with mourners being offered a box containing earth, from which a small handful is taken and thrown into the grave.

For a cremation, where the Funeral Mass has already been held in church, the service at the crematorium chapel will just consist of the Rite of Committal prayer and, unless the family has chosen to leave it revealed, the closing of the curtains to conceal the coffin. If, however, the whole service is held at the crematorium, which is time-limited, it will be considerably shorter and will usually consist of a gathering prayer, an introduction, a short scripture reading and a prayer before Committal; and only the family will sprinkle the coffin with holy water before it is concealed.

As Catholics believe that we are only stewards of our bodies, and that it is God who determines when we depart this life, those who commit suicide have committed a sin and therefore cannot receive the Funeral Mass or liturgy, or be buried in consecrated ground. The Church, however, prays for them.

Chapter 2

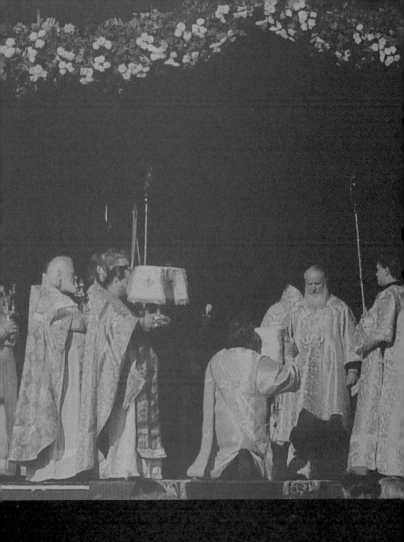

ORTHODOX
CHRISTIAN
CEREMONIES

WHAT ORTHODOX CHRISTIANS BELIEVE

Essentially, all Christian belief is the same: that God is 'triune': the one righteous, compassionate creator revealed in Three Persons – God the Father, God the Son (Jesus Christ) and God the Holy Spirit – known as the Holy Trinity. This fundamental doctrine, agreed at the First Council of Nicea in AD 325, is stated in the

ABOVE The angels visiting Abraham at the oak of Mamre. Holy Trinity Icon, c. 1400.
PREVIOUS PAGE Patriarch Kiril I in Arkhangelsk, Russia.

Nicene Creed and is the 'Symbol of Faith' of Orthodox Christians.

The word Orthodox is derived from two Greek words: *orthos* (right), and *doxa* (teaching, or worship). Orthodox Christians believe they faithfully adhere to the teachings of Jesus Christ as passed on through the unbroken line of his Apostles. While the Holy Mysteries of Baptism, Chrismation (Confirmation), Holy Eucharist (Communion), Confession, Matrimony, Ordination (reception into the priesthood) and Holy Unction (the sacrament of healing and forgiveness of sins and the anointing of the sick) are central to worship, in the Orthodox view all life is sacramental, or part of the Sacred Mystery, and cannot be easily compartmentalised. However, these seven Holy Mysteries have particular importance, with the Liturgy of the Eucharist having precedence.

Orthodox Christians have preserved the faith, as defined by the Seven Ecumenical Councils from the fourth to the eighth centuries, unchanged. The great schism that separated the Greek Orthodox and Roman Catholic Churches in 1054 was essentially a dispute over authority to rule on spiritual matters, not about fundamental differences in belief or doctrine. Orthodox believers take personal responsibility for their faith and, believing that God's voice speaks through the Church as a whole, they are willing to challenge authority when considered appropriate.

THE ORTHODOX CHURCH STRUCTURE

The early administrative structure of the Orthodox Church was created in Constantinople (modern-day Istanbul), but today it has a collegial system of government. There are fifteen autocephalous (self-governing) and four autonomous (self-ruling) Orthodox Churches worldwide in communion with each other. There is no single focus of authority, such as the Pope in the Roman Catholic Church, and supreme authority rests with an international Council or Synod, with representatives from the Orthodox Churches around the world meeting to decide questions relevant to Orthodox belief.

The hierarchy of clergy within the Church consists of

just three main orders: bishops, priests and deacons. However, bishops of large cities may be called archbishops, and bishops of cities with historical importance to the Orthodox Church, such as Constantinople, Alexandria, Antioch and Jerusalem, have the honorary rank of Patriarch, with the Ecumenical Patriarch of Constantinople being the most revered. Patriarchs, archbishops and bishops are drawn from the ranks of monks and are therefore celibate. Women are not ordained. Those entering the priesthood may already be married, but are not permitted to marry once ordained. Monastic communities of both men and women play an important part in the life of the Church.

The largest concentrations of Orthodox Christians outside Greece are found in Eastern Europe, the Balkans, the United States, Canada and Australia.

SACRED WRITINGS

The key texts of Orthodox Christianity are the Holy Bible, and a selection of seasonal service books among which is the Lenten Triodion, containing special hymns and prayers for use during Lent and Passion Week. The Trebnik (Book of Needs) is used for special services such as marriage, burial, baptism and various blessings. A calendar similar to that of the Lectionary in Western Christianity is used to determine the yearly liturgical (church service) structure.

BRANCHES OF ORTHODOXY

The Coptic, Ethiopian, Eritrean, Armenian, Syrian and (Indian) Malankara Orthodox Churches are known as Oriental Orthodox, and have not been in communion with the Eastern Orthodox Churches since the fifth century. They rejected the doctrine about the nature of Jesus – as one person with

ABOVE Greek Orthodox Archbishop Christodoulos visiting the Monastery of the Panagia Soumela in the village of Kastania, northern Greece.

two natures, both human and divine – agreed at the Fourth Ecumenical Council held at Chalcedon in 451 and re-affirmed by subsequent Synods. This is a controversial area and, while still highly regarded, these Churches are generally referred to as Monophysite (holding the belief that Christ has only one nature: human and divine totally entwined) or Non-Chalcedonian. Today they are in dialogue with the Eastern Orthodox Church, exploring the possibility of a return to unity.

ABOVE The Mother of God the Most Holy Theotokos and Ever-Virgin Mary. A contemporary Greek icon.

PLACE OF WORSHIP

The main places of worship for Orthodox Christians are cathedrals, the seat of the bishop and the centre of a diocese; churches, which are usually the centre of a parish (although in Greece there can be several in close proximity); and monasteries. In a parish with a relatively small Orthodox community, services may be held in converted houses. Orthodox churches tend to be square with a domed roof, giving a sense of God coming down to us (in contrast with Western churches, which are long buildings with a tall spire pointing heavenwards, suggesting power striving to reach upwards to God.) A particular feature of Russian

ABOVE Newly built church in Vladikavkaz in southern Russia.

Orthodox churches is the onion-shaped dome, often said to symbolise a candle flame burning upwards to heaven. All purpose-built churches are crowned by a cross.

The greatest Byzantine cathedral in Constantinople was the Hagia Sophia, or Church of the Holy Wisdom, which was commissioned by the son of Constantine the Great. Nine hundred years later, during Muslim rule, it became a mosque and minarets were added. It is now the Ayasofya Museum in modern-day Istanbul, and is considered an architectural wonder.

THE ORTHODOX CROSS

The Orthodox cross differs in design from that of Western Christianity, and is known as the tri-bar cross. The small top bar represents the words of Pontius Pilate nailed above the cross, declaring that this was 'Jesus of Nazareth, King of the Jews', and often bears the letters INBI or INRI, acronyms of the Greek and Latin translations. Crucified alongside Jesus were two thieves, and the upward angle of the lowest bar (to which the feet of Jesus were nailed) represents the thief who acknowledged Christ for who he was, while the downward angle signifies the thief who didn't.

HOLY ICONS

Icons – sacred images of key people and stories from the Scriptures and important saints – are a main focus of devotion for Orthodox Christians. Varying in size, they are usually simple, colourful, two-dimensional paintings that traditionally were created by monks after prayer and fasting. Historically, when many people couldn't read, icons were essential reminders of their faith, and most followers will have one or more in a

special place within the home. A permanently lighted lamp either hangs above or burns below each icon. Icons may be adorned with flowers or basil, the herb said to have grown above the site of Christ's crucifixion.

INSIDE AN ORTHODOX CHURCH

Generally, Orthodox churches have three distinct sections. At the western end, the entrance vestibule is the narthex, where votive candles may be taken in return for a small monetary donation. (How much you give is generally your decision, though some churches may state a specific sum.)

This area leads into the cross, or basilica-shaped nave, which tends to be a large open area without seating where the faithful stand to worship. At the eastern end of the church, behind the iconostatis (see below) is the area called the altar, where the Divine services are performed by the priest, who enters through the central portal known as the Royal Door or Holy Gate.

ABOVE Wall paintings and the Orthodox tri-bar cross in an Orthodox church in Trebic, Czech Republic.

The iconostasis is a long, ornate, wooden screen spanning the church. The screen is broken by three doors. In the centre is the Royal Door, which consists of a full-length, two-leafed door, or, in smaller churches, part curtain, part door. The left door leads to an area containing the Prothesis, or Proskomide, sometimes known as the Table of Oblation, where the holy gifts of bread and wine are prepared for the Holy Eucharist. The right door, sometimes called the Deacon's Door, gives further access to the altar area.

Within the altar the central feature is the Holy Table (known in Western Christianity as the altar). This is covered with white linen and overlaid with rich fabric that may be changed for different church seasons. Among the sacred items on the table will be a cross, the book of the Gospels and the Tabernacle, which may be an ornate coffer or a carved wooden box. This contains the Holy Gifts (consecrated bread and wine) kept in reserve for emergency use, such as sudden illness.

ABOVE Iconostasis of the Cathedral of Saints Vera, Nadezha, Lyubov and Sophia in Samara, Russia.

The icons of the Royal Door could show the story of the Annunciation, in which case the left-hand leaf shows the Archangel Gabriel, and the right the Virgin Mary, or could contain images of the four Evangelists, Matthew, Mark, Luke and John. The icon to the right of the Royal Door will be of Jesus Christ, and to the left, his mother, the Virgin Mary. These are replicated directly in front on sloping, cloth-covered icon stands, and these are the icons that worshippers revere and kiss on arrival. Worshippers never go behind the iconostasis screen.

Some Orthodox churches can seem quite dim on entry, but when your eyes have adjusted you will notice colourful frescoes and icons around the church, and in many instances completely covering all the walls and the ceiling. Candles or lamps will be burning and there will be a strong smell of the incense that is used during services. Items of gold and silver will shine in the light, which is also reflected by the gold paint of icons. Generally the only seating will be bench-style, along the sides of walls. In larger churches there will also be smaller prayer corners with icons and votive candle stands.

WHAT HAPPENS?

◆ On entering the church, worshippers take one or two votive candles. Offering silent prayers, they light them from existing candles and place them in the candle stands, which may be deep trays of sand. You may also do this if you wish.

◆ They will then move between various icons, starting with those at the iconostasis. At each icon they make the sign of the cross on their bodies, and touch the floor. The sign of the cross is an act of body worship made by putting together the thumb, index and middle finger of the right hand (the other two fingers are folded towards the palm) and touching the  forehead, the heart and across the body from the right to the left shoulder.

♦ They might also kiss the icons, which are accredited with healing powers and regularly cleaned. Throughout a service, worshippers cross themselves at different times. Outside service times, worshippers might visit just in order to perform these 'wordless prayers'.

The key people in a local parish are the bishop, presbyter (priest) and deacon. Liturgical vestments are rich, brightly coloured and elaborate, to remind the faithful that they are worshipping in the Kingdom of Heaven, and different colours may be worn for each liturgical (church) season. Most Orthodox priests have beards. In the monastic tradition, everyday clerical clothing tends to be black, and the most recognisable item is the distinctive *klobu*k, stiffened raised headwear covered with a draped veil extending down the back and over the shoulders. For ranks above Bishop, and depending on the tradition, the *klobu*k might be white and decorated, probably with a central cross.

SERVICES

Orthodox services are held in the language of the country, or of the congregation. This can vary, depending on the community, and may be Biblical Greek, Romanian, Church Slavonic or English.

There are four different types of prayer: the Liturgical Prayer following a prescribed format set out

in the service books, with the Divine Liturgy being the most important of these services; the monastic prayers, a twenty-four-hour cycle of prayer (the evening service, or Vespers, Compline, Matins and the Hours); specific home-based prayers including a special 'Jesus' prayer usually recited using prayer beads (a woollen rope of knotted beads) to count repetitions; and personal self-composed prayers.

Note that the liturgical day starts at sunset, which means that the first service of the day is evening Vespers. Feast days actually start on the eve of the appointed day, for the same reason.

In a parish setting, the priority is the Divine Liturgy. Where there are a number of priests, this will take place more than once a week. However, it is generally celebrated on a Sunday morning. If the morning service, Matins, is celebrated before the Liturgy, as in Greek Orthodoxy, the devout will also attend this. However, because these combined services are approximately three hours long, and therefore not really suitable for families with young children, most people will attend

ABOVE Russian Orthodox priests entering the Royal Door during Vespers.

what suits their personal circumstances. Where possible, worshippers will also attend the forty-five-minute weekday evening Vespers service, or the Great Vespers, the Saturday evening vigil, which in the Russian Orthodox tradition combines Vespers and Matins. This joyful service lasts between two and four hours, during which there are hymns and special prayers.

Sunday Service

The Divine Liturgy is the weekly celebration of the Eucharist (Holy Communion), and consists of nine distinct sections linked by various short Litanies (repetitive, responsorial prayers). It generally lasts for two hours, from 10:30 a.m. to 12:30 p.m., or longer, depending on numbers attending.

Although this is not encouraged, people may arrive at different times, such as just before the reading of the Gospel or the start of Holy Communion. They will still light candles and honour the icons before finding a place to stand. This means that there can be quite a lot of activity, but everyone will be respectful and attentive. You may also notice people handing pieces of paper or small booklets to the deacon. These contain the names of people to be commemorated in the Liturgy. In some churches those names will be accompanied by *prosphora*, individual offerings towards the Eucharistic service, in the form of loaves of bread.

The service is led by the presbyter (priest), who will be assisted by a deacon and may have one or more lay helpers, such as an altar boy. As the majority of the service is sung or intoned rather than spoken, there will also be lead singers or a choir. No musical accompaniment is permitted as only the human voice is considered capable of praising God.

WHAT DO I DO?

❖ At an Orthodox service, dress modestly. This means no shorts, low necklines or bare midriffs. Women tend not to wear trousers to church, and in the Russian Orthodox tradition will cover their heads. If in doubt, take a shawl or stole with you. Remember to turn your cell phone off.

❖ In some countries, men and women sit separately, and it will be obvious where to sit.

❖ No Order of Service is given, and hymn or prayer books are not generally available as the emphasis is on prayer as a communal activity, and worshippers know the words by heart.

❖ It is usual to remain standing for the whole service, but as a guest you are welcome to sit down, except at moments of particular reverence, which will be indicated to you. It is fine to slip outside to stretch your legs.

❖ During the service the priest carries an ornate, golden, globe-shaped censer, suspended from four chains, with twelve bells representing the Apostles. The clouds of incense that are emitted have specific spiritual significance. When the priest walks through the church blessing icons and worshippers, just bow your head slightly. If you have any breathing difficulties, be warned that the air can become heavy after a while.

❖ At some point there will be an offertory (collection of money), so have some change available – £3 is an acceptable amount. The whole service will be intoned (chanted) or sung, with the exception of the sermon, which is read.

❖ At the Dismissal you might be invited to receive a piece of the blessed bread. This bread is not Communion bread, and is offered to everyone. It is possible to receive the bread and not kiss the cross, as others do (see below), but generally if you prefer not to do so, it is perfectly acceptable to decline the invitation politely.

WHAT HAPPENS?

◆ As a mark of respect, all stand and bow their heads as the priest enters and opens with the words 'Blessed be the Kingdom of the Father, and of the Son, and of the Holy Spirit, now and for ever, and from all Ages to all Ages'. This is followed by the Great Litany, which asks for peace, salvation and wellbeing, not only for those gathered but for Christians worldwide. The response is 'Lord, have mercy'.

◆ Whenever worshippers hear reference to the Father, Son, Holy Spirit, Theotokos (Virgin Mary) or the saints, or the word Glory, they cross themselves and may bend briefly to touch the floor with their right hand. The ending of each section is 'Amen'.

◆ The first part of the Divine Liturgy before the Gospel reading is interspersed with two Antiphons – sung responsorial verses. The third

Antiphon introduces 'The Little Entrance', where the priest processes around the church holding up the Book of the Gospels. All stand.

◆ The Trisagion hymn, 'Holy, Holy, Holy, Holy Immortal, have mercy on us' is followed by scripture readings from the Acts or Epistles (response, 'Alleluia') and the Gospel (response, 'Glory to You, O Lord, Glory to You'). In most instances, the priest will now read his sermon, although sometimes this may come later.

◆ Again after a short litany, the choir sings the Cherubic hymn before 'The Great Entrance', where the priest presents the gifts of bread and wine to the faithful. They are then carried through the Royal Doors to the altar. During the preparation of the gifts, the priest will be intoning responsorial prayers of intercession and the Prayer of Offering.

◆ Then the original Nicene Creed, the Orthodox Christian 'Symbol of Faith', is sung, and the Great Eucharistic Prayer is led by the priest. This leads to the consecration, the most sacred moment of the Divine Liturgy, and the congregation sing 'We praise Thee' as the priest prays in front of the Holy Table for the descent of the Holy Spirit to make the bread into the precious body of Christ and the wine into the precious blood of Christ. This prayer finishes in remembrance of the Virgin Mary and all those for whom the Liturgy is offered. All then recite 'The Lord's Prayer'. Generally, the door or curtain will now be closed and a candle is placed in front of the Royal Door.

◆ The clergy receive Holy Communion in the altar. Then the Communion Hymn is sung as the holy gifts are brought forward in the golden chalice. The priest calls the faithful to receive Holy Communion with the words 'With the fear of God, with faith and with love draw near'. As each communicant steps forward (some people cross their arms upwards across their chest) the priest speaks appropriate words and uses a long-handled narrow gold spoon to place a piece of the wine-soaked bread on the tongue of the communicant, who then briefly kisses the base of the chalice before moving away to receive a piece of blessed bread and returning to his or her place.

◆ Several more hymns might be sung before the formal ending, the Dismissal, which is marked by the priest holding up the cross, which each worshipper then kisses before receiving a second piece of blessed bread.

◆ Now people will begin to leave, but some may remain for a further service, perhaps in commemoration of someone who has died. This means that it can be quite difficult determining the formal ending of the Divine Liturgy.

◆ Other rituals might also be inserted during the main service, so bear in mind that this can only be a guide to what you might experience.

◆ Refreshments are often served after the service and you will be welcome to stay.

FESTIVALS AND HOLY DAYS

THE ORTHODOX CHRISTIAN CALENDAR

In Orthodox Christianity, as in Western Christianity, most festivals and holy days occur on fixed dates. Churches of the Greek tradition follow the Gregorian Calendar introduced by Pope Gregory XII in 1582, while the Slavonic tradition follows the Julian calendar of Julius Caesar, which means that everything on the fixed calendar occurs thirteen days later. The exception to this is that both these traditions celebrate the movable date of Easter on the same day. However, the difference in dates for Easter between Eastern Orthodoxy and Western Christianity can be anything up to five weeks.

Easter is the most important festival, and is considered to be the 'Feast of Feasts'. Additionally there

are 'twelve great feasts', with eight devoted to Christ and four to the Virgin Mary. The four canonical periods of fasting are Great Lent; the Apostles' Fast; the Nativity Fast and the Dormition Fast. There are also a number of single fast days on the Eve of Theophany; the Beheading of St John the Baptist; the

ABOVE Saints' days and special occasions, such as the installation of a new icon, are celebrated with processions of the cross through the streets.

Elevation of the Cross, and every Wednesday and Friday (with the exception of four fast-free weeks). Although fasting, which lasts from sunset to sunset, usually means abstinence from all food and drink (other than water), in the Orthodox Church it means excluding meat, dairy products, fish, olive oil and wine at different times according to various written authorities. Unlike Western Christianity, all fasting periods include Sundays. Every Sunday morning before Holy Communion is a period of fasting and abstinence, which includes abstinence from marital relations.

The following dates follow the Gregorian calendar and are ordered according to the Orthodox liturgical year, which begins on 1 September. Unless otherwise detailed, they are celebrated or commemorated in church with special Vespers and the Divine Liturgy.

NATIVITY OF THE THEOTOKOS (8 September)

('Theotokos', Greek, God-bearer.) This holy day is also known as the Nativity of the Virgin Mary.

THE ELEVATION OF THE HOLY CROSS (14 September)

This single fast day celebrates the recovery by St Helen (mother of the Emperor Constantine) of the true cross of Christ's crucifixion. It is also a celebration of the power of the cross as a spiritual phenomenon, and in churches the cross will be decorated with flowers. During the service the priest carries it in procession and then holds it aloft as the choir sings special hymns.

PRESENTATION OF THE THEOTOKOS
(21 November)

Also known as 'the Presentation of the Virgin Mary in the Temple', this commemorates the day when, at the age of three, Mary was offered to the Temple in Jerusalem in fulfilment of a vow made by her parents before her birth.

THE CHRISTMAS FAST
(15 November to 24 December)

In the Orthodox Church this is purely a time of fasting, unlike the period of Advent in Western Christianity, which is celebrated with candles, wreaths and special calendars. Christmas cards and presents are exchanged, however, and Orthodox Christians living in the West may be influenced by local culture and decorate their homes accordingly, as described in the chapter on Western Christianity.

CHRISTMAS EVE
(24 December)

In the churches there will be major services, both in the morning and in the evening. There will be no Christmas Carols, which are likely to be sung at home around the Christmas tree or as part of a community gathering, and will differ according to the country. After the church services there is usually a family meal with local food that fulfils the fasting requirements. The fast does not end until Holy Communion has been received.

CHRISTMAS DAY
(25 December)

Christmas Day is the beginning of the Christmas period, and will be celebrated with special prayers at the Divine Liturgy, which will be followed by a family meal according to local tradition.

HOLY THEOPHANY, OR THE
FEAST OF EPIPHANY
(6 January)

This marks the end of the Christmas period, and starts with a single fast day. The key emphasis in church is the service of the Sanctification of the Waters, a solemn service that commemorates Jesus' baptism by John the Baptist in the River Jordan, when the Holy Spirit descended in the form of a dove, and the voice of God the Father was heard, confirming Jesus' Divine Son-ship.

The faithful arrive with empty bottles and take home quantities of blessed water. In Orthodox communities

the water is contained in huge urns with taps, but in Western churches it can range from an elaborate container to a tub. Sometimes, priests visit parishioners and sprinkle their homes with the sanctified water. The blessing might also take place by the sea, a lake or a river.

IF YOU WISH
❖ If you are invited to this service and you would like some blessed water to take home, remember to take an empty bottle with you – plastic is acceptable.

ABOVE Epiphany Service of the Sanctification of the Waters in Ukraine.

PRESENTATION OF CHRIST IN THE TEMPLE (2 February)

Also known as 'The Meeting of the Lord', this commemorates the day on which, in accordance with Jewish law, Mary presented Jesus in the Temple at Jerusalem.

CHEESEFARE WEEK (February/March)

This is the week before the Great Fast of Lent. Meat is forbidden, and cheese and eggs are eaten as a way of starting the fast more gently. This week is also known as 'butter week' or 'pancake week', when *blinis* (similar to pancakes) made from butter, milk and eggs are eaten. Although it has nothing to do with Orthodox Christianity, a Russian folk tradition involves a colourfully dressed scarecrow, a pagan goddess called Lady Maslenitsa, being stripped of her finery on the Sunday evening, and as part of saying goodbye in winter she is burnt on a bonfire, along with any remaining blinis. Russian Orthodox communities in the West may well organise a celebration of some kind to mirror this folk tradition.

FORGIVENESS SUNDAY (February/March)

This day ends Cheesefare Week. At the evening service of Vespers, people ask forgiveness of one another for the start of Lent.

THE GREAT FAST OF LENT (February/March)

The Great Fast of Lent begins on the Monday seven weeks before Pascha (Easter), and includes all Sundays. The first day is also known as 'Clean Monday', since everyone has confessed their sins on the previous day. From now until Easter Day, all animal products, fish, wine and oil are forbidden, although the fast may be relaxed slightly at weekends. The main foods eaten during this time are vegetables, fruit, nuts and bread.

Owing to the penitential nature of Lent, the Divine Liturgy is not celebrated on weekdays, and the faithful can receive the holy gifts (bread and wine) in the beautiful evening service called the Liturgy of the Pre-Sanctified Holy Gifts.

THE CELEBRATION OF THE ANNUNCIATION (25 March)

This day marks the appearance to the Virgin Mary of the Archangel Gabriel with the announcement that she would conceive a son, Jesus, the Son of God.

PALM SUNDAY (March/April)

Palm Sunday celebrates the triumphal entry of Jesus into the city of Jerusalem, riding on a lowly donkey. It is the start of Holy Week, in which special services are held every day in the churches, in which are displayed palm leaves or other greenery tied into boughs. In Russia palms are replaced with pussy-willow leaves or branches, and Orthodox Christians in Jerusalem process with a cross carried by the Patriarch. In the Greek Orthodox tradition, the faithful receive a palm leaf after the Divine Liturgy.

IF YOU WISH
❖ **Easter cards are sent according to local custom.**

HOLY THURSDAY
(March/April)

This day commemorates the first Divine Liturgy (Holy Communion) and the institution of the Holy Eucharist, in a solemn service that usually takes place in the morning. In the evening is held the Service of the Twelve Gospels, at which all the Gospels recording the Passion of Christ are read in their entirety. This is possibly the longest service of the year, lasting between three and a half and five hours.

HOLY FRIDAY
(March/April)

This is a solemn and special day, which commemorates the crucifixion of Christ. During the afternoon before the Vespers service, the faithful bring quantities of flowers to the church and place them around a mounted icon cloth, which is a representation of the winding sheet used for Christ's burial, painted or embroidered with the figure of Christ. In the evening, to commemorate the taking of Christ's body from the cross to the tomb, everyone lights candles and the cloth is carried with great solemnity in a long procession around the outside of the church.

HOLY SATURDAY
(March/April)

The day between Holy Friday and Easter Day is marked in several ways. The Divine Liturgy has an air of mystical expectation, and there are often baptisms on this day. In the evening, before the start of the midnight service, in which the faithful spend the night chanting and praying, there is another long procession during which people remember the women who carried myrrh to Christ's tomb and found it empty. With lit candles they leave a darkened church and, led by the priest, process around it. Arriving back at the main doors, the priest proclaims 'Christ is Risen!' to which everyone joyously responds 'He is Risen indeed'. The doors then fly open and the faithful enter into a brightly lit church. The Easter hangings and vestments are white and gold, and there will be baskets of red painted eggs,

 symbolising the resurrection. This marks the end of the Great Fast of Lent, and after the service has concluded there is a community breakfast celebration with plentiful food, wine and laughter. There might even be dancing, and Greek communities celebrate with firework displays.

PASCHA (EASTER DAY)
(March/April)

After the start of the celebration on the evening before, there may be a Divine Liturgy in the morning, and there will always be a late afternoon 'Vespers of Love'.

BRIGHT WEEK
(March/April)

During this joyful following week, immediately after the resurrection of Jesus, all fasting has ended, and in the church the Royal Doors remain open until after Vespers on Sunday. All Easter services are repeated each day.

ABOVE Worshippers receiving the Holy Light from the priest at St George Greek Orthodox Church, Adelaide.

ASCENSION DAY
(May/June)

This, the fortieth day after Easter, marks the day when Jesus appeared to his disciples, telling them to wait for the descent of the Holy Spirit, and was taken up into heaven to sit at God's right hand. It is the culmination of his bodily life on earth.

PENTECOST
(May/June)

Pentecost (Greek, fiftieth day) falls on the seventh Sunday after Easter, and is also known as Trinity Sunday. For Orthodox Christians this is a two-day celebration. Trinity Sunday celebrates both the Revelation of God as Trinity, and the descent of the Holy Spirit on the disciples, causing them to speak in tongues. This was the beginning of the missionary work of the early Church, and the disciples were henceforth known as Apostles, from the Greek *apostolos*, 'one sent forward as a messenger'. Churches are decorated with masses of greenery, and the flowers that pack the church symbolise the giving of the Holy Spirit to the faithful. The celebration continues on the following day, the 'Day of the Holy Spirit'.

THE FAST OF THE APOSTLES
(May/June)

This begins eight days after Pentecost, and ends on 29 June, the Feast of Saint Peter and Saint Paul.

THE FEAST OF SAINT PETER
AND SAINT PAUL
(29 June)

This day commemorates the lives and missionary work of these two saints.

THE FEAST OF THE TRANSFIGURATION
(6 August)

An important day, this celebrates the appearance of Christ in his Divine glory to his disciples Peter, James and John. It is also the day when the faithful take large quantities of fruit to church for the 'Blessing of the Fruit' ceremony. As God's glory spills out into all of creation, so people celebrate the harvest of all natural things.

WHAT DO I DO?
❖ **If you are invited to this service, it would be polite to take some fruit and put it to be blessed. You will also be given fruit at the end of the service.**

THE FAST OF THE REPOSE OF
THE VIRGIN MARY
(1–15 August)

This is a fourteen-day fast before the Feast of the Dormition of the Virgin.

DORMITION OF THE VIRGIN
(15 August)

Also known as the 'Repose of the Virgin Mary', this commemorates the date of the Virgin Mary's 'falling asleep' (dying to this life before reawakening to eternal life in God).

THE BEHEADING OF
SAINT JOHN THE BAPTIST
(29 August)

This is an individual fast day, marked by local practice.

RITUALS AND CEREMONIES

BIRTH

The birth of a baby is a joyous occasion, and new parents will always appreciate a letter or card of congratulations. Traditionally a child was named after the saint commemorated on that day. Now it is usually left to personal choice, although culturally a Greek Orthodox name will be that of one of the grandparents.

BAPTISM AND CHRISMATION

An invitation to a baptism is likely to be verbal rather than written.

Baptism (from Greek, *baptizo*) means 'immersion into water for purification', and is the Holy Mystery (sacred service) that formally welcomes a person into

ABOVE Baptism in an Orthodox church, St Petersburg.

the Orthodox Christian Church. Traditionally, adults rather than babies were baptised, and early baptismal fonts were set low in the ground to allow full body immersion, in the way that Christ was baptised in the River Jordan. However, now it is generally babies who are baptised, from the age of three months, although this varies according to local practice. It is common for a baby to have three godparents, of whom at least one will be the same gender as the child.

The baptism ceremony for adults and babies is the same, and although it might be held as a separate occasion, it will usually take place with the congregation either before or after the Divine Liturgy. This means that the total service time will be approximately three hours, although in many instances guests attend only the baptism, and their hosts will instruct them about when and where to meet. When the baptism takes place before the Divine Liturgy, this will then also be the baby's first Holy Communion.

In the Orthodox Church, Chrismation takes place immediately after baptism, and the baby or adult is then a full Christian and receives Holy Communion, unlike in Western Christianity, in which confirmation takes place when a child is older and considered to be of an age to understand and confirm the Christian vows taken on his or her behalf at the Christening ceremony.

WHAT HAPPENS?

◆ The baptismal party is welcomed on arrival in the vestibule by the priest. Those presenting the child, who are usually the godparents, will be asked to renounce Satan. Prayers of Exorcism will be said and the Symbol of Faith, the Nicene Creed, will be recited three times.

◆ At the appointed time, the baptismal party will be invited to gather around the font, which might be a small tub, and given lighted candles. To the right will be a cloth-covered table containing the sacred items for the baptism and chrismation ceremony, and close at hand will be the baby's baptismal clothing.

◆ Either the mother or, preferably, a godparent will initially hold the baby, whose clothes are removed just before total immersion in the font by the priest, who says, 'The Servant of God [name of baby] is baptised in the name of the Father, Amen'. At the second immersion the priest says, 'And of the Son, Amen', and at the third and final immersion, 'And of the Holy Spirit, Amen'. The baby is then dried and dressed in special white baptismal clothes before the priest leads the baptismal party around the font three times as he sings a special hymn. The circling represents eternity.

◆ Next follows the chrismation, in which the baby is anointed on the brow, eyes, ears, nostrils, lips, chest, hands and feet, with Holy Chrism oil that has been prepared and blessed by a patriarch or bishop. This Holy Mystery seals the gift of the Holy Spirit on the newly baptised person.

◆ As it is likely that some of the chrism will be transferred to the baptismal clothes, the garments are treated with the utmost respect, and washed by hand. In the West they may be worn by future generations.

◆ Finally the priest leads the baptismal party around the font three times as he sings the hymn, 'As many as have been baptised into Christ, have put on Christ. Alleluia'. This procession represents the start of the Christian journey into eternity. After the Epistle and Gospel reading, the baby is wiped clean and four pieces of the baby's hair are cut in the sign of the cross. The service ends with a Final Blessing.

◆ There is likely to be a post-baptism celebration, probably at the family home or a hired venue. Gifts are often given, and it is best to ask in advance what would be acceptable. Godparents will usually give a cross.

MARRIAGE

Since marriage is viewed as a union with God rather than a legal contract, no vows are exchanged, and the couple will have undergone a civil ceremony beforehand to declare them legally married. The Sacrament of Holy Matrimony, which is rich with scriptural symbolism and mystery, consists of two parts: the Betrothal, and the Order of Marriage, also known as the Crowning. It is therefore unlikely that the couple will have an engagement party, although this, along with any pre-wedding celebrations, or a family dinner, is an entirely personal decision, which will be culturally influenced.

WHAT DO I DO?

❖ If you are invited to a Christian Orthodox wedding, you will receive a formal invitation.

❖ It is best to ask in advance if the couple has a wedding list, so that you can choose a present they will welcome.

❖ Dress smartly but modestly, as previously stated, and for a Russian Orthodox wedding women need to cover their heads.

❖ Although the wedding service was traditionally part of the Divine Liturgy, it is now more likely to be celebrated separately on a Sunday afternoon, or possibly on a Saturday. The length of the service is approximately an hour and three-quarters, during which you may sit down if necessary.

❖ On arrival at the church, find a place to stand (or sit if you need to). In some case there will be particular places for friends of the bride or groom, and you will be shown where that is. It is unlikely that you will be given an Order of Service unless a number of non-Orthodox guests are expected.

WHAT HAPPENS?

◆ The church will be beautifully decorated with fragrant flowers, and in front of the altar will be the marriage table, on which will be The Book of the Gospels, the priest's hand cross, or blessing cross, the common cup of wine, the wedding candles and the marriage crowns. In Greek Orthodoxy these will be circular wreaths of flowers, and in Russian Orthodoxy, golden crowns.

◆ The arrival of the bride and groom is likely to be culturally influenced, so they may arrive separately with their respective wedding parties, as in the Western Christian tradition, or together. While bridal attire might be culturally influenced, it is likely that the bride will wear white, and in all cases, rather than bridesmaids and a best man, the couple have attendants who assist them both and carry the matrimonial crowns.

◆ The first part of the ceremony, the betrothal, might be celebrated in the narthex (vestibule), and while you may not be able to see what is happening, you will be able to hear. On arrival, the priest comes to greet them and as the couple face him, he offers the opening blessing 'Blessed is our God always, now and ever, unto ages and ages'. This is followed by a special litany in which God is asked to bless the marriage with everything needed, including children.

◆ After a further prayer, the priest receives the wedding rings, which he uses to bless the couple three times with the sign of the cross. The rings then rest briefly on the ring fingers of their left hands, and the priest or attendant changes the rings three times between the bride and the groom before placing them on their right-hand ring fingers, on which Orthodox Christians wear their wedding rings. The priest then recites a long prayer before he chants the responsorial Marriage Psalm 28 as he precedes the couple with the censer, in a glorious procession to the centre of the church in readiness for the marriage ceremony.

◆ Here the couple are presented with lit candles to remind them of the light of Christ, and after the priest confirms that they are present of their own free will, and available to marry, a litany is chanted. Then follow the three Great Prayers of Marriage, and during the third prayer the priest unites the right hands of the couple.

◆ The next stage of the ceremony, the placing of the Marriage Crowns, is of particular significance, as the crowns represent both royalty and martyrdom. This means that the Grace of God bestows upon the couple the sovereignty needed to overcome their individual selfish instincts as they unite as one with God. The priest places the crowns on their heads; first the bridegroom and then the bride, as he repeats a blessing three times.

Two passages of Scripture are then read: the Epistle of St Paul to the Ephesians, and the Gospel of St John (Chapter 2). This is followed by another prayer and further responsorial petitions, which end  with everyone reciting the Lord's Prayer. The priest then blesses the cup of common wine, from which the couple drink. In the Greek Orthodox tradition, bread is dipped into the wine and given to the couple.

◆ As the choir sings hymns to the Virgin Mary and the Martyrs, the priest holds the hand cross. The couple join hands, and the priest covers their hands with his stole. He then leads the couple around the marriage table three times in a procession known as 'the Dance of Isaiah'. As the couple follow the priest, the congregation may shower them with handfuls of rice grains – an ancient symbol of fertility. The priest then removes the bridal crowns as he exhorts the couple to be exalted in the manner of biblical couples.

◆ The service concludes with two further prayers and a Final Blessing, after which everyone comes forward to congratulate them before they leave the church.

- ◆ The couple might now have photographs taken before leaving for the wedding breakfast (reception). Good luck confetti is rare at an Orthodox wedding, but may be used in Britain. Everything that happens after this is influenced by cultural background, but will usually include celebratory food and drink, speeches, music, dancing and the giving of gifts.

While the ideal is one marriage for life, divorcees are allowed to remarry. However, for a second or third marriage the service would be more penitential.

DEATH AND MOURNING

In the Orthodox Church, death is often called 'dormition' which means 'falling asleep', and is considered to be the gateway to eternal life. Orthodox Christians are buried, not cremated, as the body is regarded as the 'Temple of the Holy Spirit' (St Paul,1 Corinthians) and will be restored at the resurrection. Because of this respect for the physical body Orthodox Christians are often uneasy about organ transplants or genetic engineering.

When someone is sick, the community will pray for them, and they may receive Holy Unction (anointing the sick with special oil) from the priest. If they are dying, it is hoped that a final confession can be made and Holy Communion received. Special prayers 'for the departing of the soul' will be chanted.

After Death

When a person has died, if circumstances permit the priest, family and friends will gather around the bedside for the first, thirty-minute memorial service that in the Greek Orthodox tradition includes the Trisagion hymn of the Divine Liturgy. There will also be prayers for the repose of the soul of the departed. This service will be held again each day until the funeral. The body needs to be treated with the greatest respect, and may be washed in wine by women from the parish. Providing no post-mortem is required, it will be taken to a funeral home.

WHAT DO I DO?

❖ Letters or cards of condolence are welcomed, and flowers can be sent in advance to the funeral home. In some cases, donations may be requested, and these usually go to the church where the deceased worshipped.

❖ If you are invited to the memorial or funeral service, please wear black, as this is the colour of mourning for Orthodox Christians. For a Russian Orthodox service, women need to cover their heads.

The evening before the funeral there will be the final memorial service. Ideally this would be held in the church, but logistically, because it precedes the funeral service the following day, it is likely to be held at the funeral home. The funeral service, which will last about an hour and a half, is similar to Matins, with special prayers and litanies. Each person is given a candle symbolising hope in the resurrection. These remain lit throughout the service, for which everyone stands (unless they are unable to do so). Traditionally, *koliva*, a dish of cooked, sweetened wheat, is served at the end, as wheat represents resurrection.

The Funeral Service

The funeral service will be held at the church. It will include special prayers and chants, and may last two hours. There is unlikely to be a written order of service.

WHAT HAPPENS?

◆ The coffin is carried feet first into the church and placed in the centre, facing the altar. It is then opened and several sacred items – an icon, a wreath and a hand cross – might be placed inside. Each person receives a candle, which remains lit for most of the service. Towards the end people will move forward to say their final farewell by giving the last kiss on the forehead of the deceased.

◆ Following the Dismissal and the 'Memory Eternal' hymn, the coffin is closed, and the choir sings the Trisagion as it is carried out. If the church has bells, these will be slowly tolled. At the graveside the priest conducts a short service of Committal before the coffin is lowered into the grave, and mourners are offered earth to throw in if they wish.

◆ Afterwards there is likely to be a post-funeral gathering, to which you as a guest are welcome. Cultural influences will dictate what happens, but it is likely to be a modest, respectful occasion with refreshments.

There are further commemorations at the church on the third, ninth and fortieth days after death, and on the anniversary. These usually take place after the Saturday Vigil, or at the end of the Divine Liturgy on Sunday.

Ideally, a Christian Orthodox memorial stone is a crucifix, which is placed at the foot of the grave so that the deceased is facing it. However, local authority rules and cultural practice will dictate this. As and when the memorial stone is ready, family gather at the graveside and the priest performs a brief Rite of the Blessing of the Cross.

SOME USEFUL WORDS AND PHRASES

Chrism consecrated oil used in, for example, the ceremony of baptism and chrismation

Cross symbol of Christianity, representing the sacrifice of Jesus Christ, who was put to death on a cross

Eucharist Holy Communion, the ceremony commemorating Jesus Christ's Last Supper, at which bread and wine are consecrated and consumed.

Evangelists the four writers of the gospels of the New Testament in the Bible, Matthew, Mark, Luke and John

Gospel ('good news') separate written works in which the good news of Christian redemption was told; chiefly, the four canonical gospels of Matthew, Mark, Luke and John in the New Testament

Holy Bible the sacred texts of Christianity, divided into Old and New Testaments

Icon sacred image of a person, such as Jesus Christ, the Virgin Mary, or a saint

Iconostasis screen or wall across the church bearing icons and paintings and including doors to the altar; also a portable icon stand

Liturgy set form of worship for church services. Divine Liturgy is the term used for the Orthodox Eucharist service

Narthex outer hall or vestibule of a church, at its western end

Nicene Creed the profession of faith for Christians

Theotokos (Greek, God-bearer) the Virgin Mary, mother of Jesus Christ

Trebnik (Book of Needs) the book used in the Orthodox Church for services and prayers, including prayers and blessings for particular occasions

Trinity the Holy Trinity, God as Three Persons (the Father, Son and Holy Spirit) in One

Votive offering something, often a candle, that is offered in conjunction with a prayer, vow or vigil

Chapter 3

JEWISH
CEREMONIES

WHAT JEWS BELIEVE

Judaism is a monotheistic religion, believing in one Supreme Being – a merciful, just, all-seeing, all-knowing and all-powerful God who created and rules the world. It introduced a personal moral code and also the idea of free will, responsibility for choices made and individual accountability. The aim of Judaism is to sanctify life through education, prayer and observance of the ethical and ritual precepts of the Torah. By these acts Jews become partners with God in fulfilling His purpose.

Defined by their beliefs and actions, the Jewish people evolved from the biblical Canaanites and Israelites. In time Jewish communities grew up outside the land of Israel. The destruction of the Jewish Temple in Jerusalem by Rome in 70 CE had two major consequences: it reinforced this dispersal, known as the Diaspora (Greek, scattered seeds), so that the majority of Jews came to live outside historical Israel, and it gave rise to the system of law and custom still recognizable in modern Judaism. Jewish people, wherever they are, share the ceremonies, rituals, laws and commandments of their faith.

Jews do not believe that Jesus was the prophesied Messiah who would usher in an age of peace. This, it is believed, will only happen when the true Messiah from the house of David finally comes.

SACRED WRITINGS

The Jewish holy book is the *Tanakh*, an acronym for three sets of ancient Hebrew texts – *Torah*, *Nevi'im* and *Ketuvim*. Known as the Written Law, these texts contain God's instructions for living a good and spiritual life. The Torah consists of the Five Books of Moses (Genesis to Deuteronomy in the Old Testament of the Christian Bible) given to the Jewish people at Mount Sinai during their exodus from Egypt. It contains 613 *mitzvot* (commandments) whose purpose is the sanctification of creation – including the

PREVIOUS PAGE Lifting of the *Sefer Torah*, the handwritten scrolls of the Five Books of Moses, during the Shabbat service.

Ten Commandments, given to Moses on two stone tablets. Nevi'im (the Book of Prophets) contains direct prophecies from God, and Ketuvim ('Writings') records the wisdom of David and Solomon and includes the Books of Esther and Ruth.

Parallel to the Written Law was the Oral Law, the oral tradition passed down through the generations until after the destruction of the Temple, when it was compiled, edited and written down. This compilation is called the Mishnah, and the

ABOVE A *Sefer Torah* unrolled for reading in the former Glockengasse synagogue in Cologne.

THE NAMES OF GOD

God is called by many different names in the Bible. The Hebrew four-letter name of God – YHVH, revealed to Moses at the Burning Bush – is so sacred that it is never spoken by Jews. This name is used in the Torah when referring to God's relationship to the people of Israel, and by Jewish scholars when describing His attribute of mercy. The other most commonly found name of God is Elohim. This is used when describing God's relationship to the world generally, and according to scholars refers to His attribute of justice. Another frequently used name is Adonai ('my Lord'), and there are very many other, essentially descriptive, names for God. However, in conversation some religious Jews will refer to God as *Ha-shem* ('the Name') in Hebrew, and in English will write it as G-d.

various questions, discussions and decisions that arose from it are contained within a long Aramaic commentary called the Talmud (Hebrew, study), also known by the Aramaic name Gemara. These relate to the *Halakhah* (Hebrew, way or path) – Jewish law determining ritual practice and ethical behaviour.

BRANCHES OF JUDAISM

Like many religions, Judaism has different traditions, branches and sects. The main historical division is between Sephardim and Ashkenazim – Jews originating in medieval Spain and Germany respectively. Although the two groups differ in their culture, customs, pronunciation of

ABOVE Illuminated medieval *Haggadah*, the text read at the Passover supper.

WHAT JEWS BELIEVE

Hebrew and liturgical practices, there are no doctrinal differences.

Today the main branches of Judaism in the West are Orthodox, Conservative and Reform. The Orthodox believe that the written Torah and Oral Law are divinely given, without human influence, and live in strict accordance with this. The Conservatives accept the *Halakhah*, but look at it in a dynamic way – changes in practice are permitted if made in the spirit of the *Halakhah*. The Reform movement arose in nineteenth-century Germany with the aim of adapting Judaism to the modern world. Today its main centre is the USA. Emphasising the universality of Jewish values over Jewish particularism, it believes in 'progressive revelation' – each generation is granted different appreciations of the truth of the Torah.

Within each of these broad strands, however, there is a variety of approaches. Some more radical forms of Conservative, Reform and Progressive Judaism have introduced innovations such as ordaining women rabbis, promoting equality of gender

and the autonomy of individuals to decide whether or not to subscribe to a particular belief or practice.

There is also Judaism's ancient mystical tradition, the Kabbalah, which was embraced in the early nineteenth century by the Orthodox Hasidic movement. This has been brought to public attention in modern times by the New Age movement and, more recently, by celebrities attracted by the belief in numerology, astrology and reincarnation.

ABOVE Bronze *menorah* (candelabrum) once used in the synagogue in Moers, western Germany.

PLACE OF WORSHIP

The Jewish house of prayer is the synagogue (in Hebrew, *Beit Knesset*, House of Assembly). Even in the days of the Temple the synagogue was a place of prayer and Torah study and a community meeting house. Today it may also be referred to as a s*hul* (Yiddish, school) or Temple (by the Reform, mainly in the USA).

According to tradition, the Divine Presence can be found wherever there is a *minyan* (a quorum of ten Jewish adults – see below). There is no blueprint for synagogue architecture and the shapes and interior designs of synagogues vary greatly, reflecting local styles. They may or may not have artwork, and range from simple, unadorned prayer rooms to elaborately decorated buildings in every architectural style.

INSIDE THE SYNAGOGUE

Situated at the eastern, or Jerusalem-facing, wall is the ark, called *aron ha-kodesh* (the holy ark) by Ashkenazim and *hekhal (*palace) by Sephardim. This cupboard houses the handwritten parchment scrolls of the Law, the *Sefer Torah*. Its doors are covered by a richly decorated curtain, the *parokhet*. Above it hangs a lamp, the *ner tamid* (eternal light),which is a reminder of the presence of God. In front of the ark is a low platform, from which the sermon is preached and the priestly blessing is recited. The *bimah* (Ashkenazi) or *tebah* (Sephardi) is a raised, enclosed dais reached by steps, from which the *Sefer Torah* is read and prayers are led. In many Orthodox synagogues it is in the centre, and in many Reform synagogues at the end in front of the ark.

PLACE OF WORSHIP

In Orthodox synagogues men and women sit separately. There may be a screen or a women's gallery on the upper floor overlooking the *bimah* and the ark. In Reform they sit together.

The key people involved will be the rabbi (an ordained expert in Jewish law and spiritual leader) and the *chazan* (cantor), trained in the tradition of singing/chanting sacred text. In the Orthodox tradition, there will also be the *gabbaim* (singular, *gabbai*), two or more respected lay officials whose job during the service is to stand either side of the Torah when it is read, and who call honoured guests to the *bimah* for that purpose. They ensure that mistakes are not made in the reading of the Torah, or are corrected. Children are generally welcome, and bigger synagogues may have a crèche.

Two books are used regularly: the *siddur*, the daily prayer book, and the *chumash*, a printed version of the Torah, which is likely to have an English translation of

ABOVE Interior of the Orthodox Bialystocker Synagogue on the Lower East Side of Manhattan, New York.

the Hebrew on the facing page. Special prayer books called *machzorim* (singular, *machzor*) are used on the High Holy Days and festivals. The books, in Hebrew, are written and therefore read from right to left. Note: as books containing God's name, they should not be disrespected by being placed on the floor at any time.

SERVICES

There are three main daily services: S*hacharit i*n the morning, *Minchah* in the afternoon, and *Ma'ariv* in the evening, after sunset. In the Orthodox and Conservative traditions there is also an additional service, *Musaf,* which follows the morning service. A pious Jew will aim to attend each. For a complete service to take place, there must be a *minyan* (men only in the Orthodox tradition), with 'adult' defined as anyone over the age of thirteen plus a day. In Orthodox Judaism public prayer is always conducted in Hebrew; in Reform synagogues much of the service may be in English or the language of the land.

Men cover their heads during prayer, and visitors will be asked to put on a small skull-cap called a *kippah* (or, in Yiddish, *yarmulke*) when entering the synagogue. Married Orthodox women wear a hat when attending a synagogue service. Unmarried or widowed women do not cover their heads.

At a weekday early-morning service you might also see men wearing *tefillin*, two small cube-shaped leather

ABOVE Men wearing *kippot* inside the synagogue.

boxes attached to leather straps that contain the '*Sh'ma Yisrael*' declaration ('Hear O Israel, the Lord our God, the Lord is one ...', Deut. 6: 4–9) and other passages from the Torah, written by a scribe. One box is worn on the forehead, between the eyes, and the other is placed on the upper section of the left arm, adjacent to the heart. In rabbinic teaching they represent the balance between head and heart.

There are special services for festivals and holy days, at which specific prayers are said, and one of the most important of these is the Saturday morning Shabbat (Sabbath) service, which takes place from around 9.00 to 11.30 a.m.

WHAT HAPPENS DURING THE SHABBAT SERVICE?

◆ In Orthodox synagogues men and women sit separately, with women often sitting on the upper level. You will be shown where to sit.

◆ You will notice that all men cover their heads. If you are a man, you will be given a *kippah* to wear if you do not have one. In Orthodox congregations married women cover their heads, too, and bareheaded women will be offered a scarf. The men will be wearing a

ABOVE *Teffilin* worn by Hassidic Jews during morning prayers.

tallit, a striped prayer shawl with knotted tassels hanging from each corner. Non-Jewish men are not required to wear this.

◆ The service is led from the *bimah* by a *ba'al tefilla* (Hebrew, master of prayer), who is not necessarily a rabbi, and most of the liturgy is sung or chanted by the *chazan*. The service consists of well-defined sections. It starts with the congregation standing while several blessings and passages from the Mishnah, the Prophets and the Book of Psalms are read. This stage concludes with the recital by the *chazan*, and anybody who is in mourning, of *Kaddish*, a short prayer in Aramaic affirming God's greatness and holiness,

◆ The main section opens with blessings, including the '*Sh'ma Yisrael*'. There is then a period for silent recitation of the *Amidah* (Hebrew, standing), the central prayer of every service that is said standing with feet together facing in the direction of the Temple in Jerusalem. It concludes with a blessing for *shalom*, meaning both peace and completeness. After the *Amidah* has been completed silently by the congregants it is recited aloud by the *ba'al tefilla*. It is inappropriate to move around the synagogue while this prayer is being recited.

◆ There follows the central feature of the service – the reading of the *Sefer Torah*. The congregation stands as the *parokhet* is drawn back, the ark is opened and the Torah is removed and carried in procession to the *bimah*. It is important not to turn your back on the Torah as it passes you.

◆ While the ark is open, the congregation remains standing. Once it is closed, people are seated for the reading of the weekly portion, during which specially honoured persons are called up to recite the blessings before each reading. There is then another reading before the rabbi gives a sermon. In the Orthodox tradition there will be another silent recitation of the *Amidah*, followed by a public recitation by the leader. In non-Orthodox services, the *Amidah* is recited only once.

◆ Before the Torah is returned to the ark, the honour of *hagbahah*, where the opened scroll is lifted up to display at least three columns of text, including the portion just read, is given to a member of the congregation. It is customary for the congregation to stand and point towards the Torah as it is being displayed. Once the scroll has been viewed, another honoured congregant will come forward to perform *gelilah* (the ceremonial rolling-up and dressing of the scroll).

◆ The service concludes with another prayer, closing songs and synagogue announcements. It is then time for a communal *kiddush*, sanctification of the Sabbath over a cup of wine. Guests are not required to taste the wine, but some cake or biscuit is eaten before the socialising begins.

FESTIVALS AND HOLY DAYS

THE JEWISH CALENDAR

The feasts and fasts of the Jewish religious year follow a twelve-month lunar calendar, where each month begins with the new moon. This means that their dates vary in relation to the Western calendar. Because the lunar year is shorter than the solar year, an extra lunar month is added every two to three years in order to prevent the festivals slipping out of their seasons. The religious festival year begins in spring with the month of Nisan (March–April), which marks the time of the Passover.

Within the Jewish calendar the holidays fall on fixed dates, with the exception of Rosh Hashanah (the Jewish New Year). Somewhat confusingly, Rosh Hashanah is celebrated in the month of Tishrei, the seventh month of the ecclesiastical year. It is the civil new year, and the point at which the year number advances, and most Jews today consider Tishrei the beginning of the year. Specific dates and times of festivals can be found in

THE MONTHS OF THE YEAR

Nisan (March–April)	**Tishrei** (September–October)
Iyar (April–May)	**Cheshvan** (October–November)
Sivan (May–June)	**Kislev** (November–December)
Tammuz (June–July)	**Tevet** (December–January)
Av (July–August)	**Shevat** (January–February)
Elul (August–September)	**Adar** (February–March)

In a leap year the additional month comes before Nisan and is called Adar Sheni ('Second Adar').

Jewish newspapers, the synagogue and on various Jewish internet sites. The spellings of some months may vary.

There are three 'pilgrimage' or harvest festivals in the Jewish year, known as Shalosh Regalim ('three feet'), when in biblical times pilgrimages were made on foot to the Temple in Jerusalem. These are Pesach (Passover), Shavuot (Festival of Weeks) and Sukkot (Feast of the Tabernacles). The High Holy Days are Rosh Hashanah (Jewish New Year) and Yom Kippur (Day of Atonement). Other than Shabbat (the Sabbath) these are considered the most important dates in the calendar. All Jewish holidays begin at sundown on the previous secular day.

ROSH CHODESH ('HEAD OF THE MONTH')
The first day of each lunar month is welcomed with additional prayers and blessings both at home and in the synagogue.

TA'ANIT B'KHORIM/B'KHOROT ('FAST OF THE FIRSTBORN') (March–April)
Observed only by firstborn males if their birth was not by Caesarean section, this fast usually falls on the day before Passover, on 14 Nisan. It commemorates the firstborn Israelite boys miraculously spared the final plague in Egypt, who would otherwise have been slain. In Progressive Judaism the fast might also be observed by firstborn girls. It begins at dawn and is generally broken with a meal the following day, after the morning service.

PESACH, OR PASSOVER (March–April)
The festival of freedom lasts eight days in the Diaspora (15–23 Nisan) and seven days in Israel (15–22 Nisan). It

celebrates the protection and guidance of God, which enabled Moses to lead the Jewish people out of slavery in Egypt to freedom and points ahead to the final salvation of mankind. It was also the time of the barley harvest and the end of the rainy season. In many synagogues the Song of Songs is read on the Sabbath. For the mystics of the Kabbalah, Pesach symbolized the marriage of the male and female aspects of God.

The festival commences on the eve of 15 Nisan with the ritual family *Seder* (order) meal, at which the extended family gathers to recite the *Haggadah* – the text that recounts the events surrounding the exodus from Egypt, a story that has been told down the generations. The *Seder* reading includes four traditional questions posed by the children at the start of the ceremony, specific prayers, songs of praise and Psalms. No bread, flour or any other products containing leaven (yeast) may be eaten during Pesach, and bread is replaced by *matzah* (plural, *matzot*), a hard, flat cracker made of plain flour and water, the unleavened 'bread of affliction' eaten by the Israelites in Egypt.

ABOVE *Seder* table setting with the symbolic Passover foods.

WHAT HAPPENS?

◆ This is very much a family occasion, to which you may well be invited. Different symbolic foods are eaten in a specific order as historical reminders. On the table you will find a *Seder* plate containing six items. Three represent the harshness of slavery and are eaten during the first part of the meal, with the other three representing the resultant freedom. On a separate plate are three *matzot*, representing the unleavened bread that had to be eaten as there was no time for the dough to rise before leaving, and a dish of salt water, being the tears of slavery shed by the Jewish people. At the start of the ritual, the middle *matzah* is removed and one half is hidden for the children to find later, in return for a small reward. Called the *Afikomen* (Greek, dessert), it is then the last thing eaten.

◆ Traditionally some food is eaten while leaning to the left, signifying the relaxed posture of freedom. During the meal four glasses of wine or grape juice are blessed and drunk, with each cup representing the four expressions of deliverance promised by God – 'I will bring out', 'I will deliver', 'I will redeem' and 'I will take'. Wine on this occasion also symbolises the blood of the Passover lamb smeared on Jewish doorposts at the time of the tenth plague so that the Angel of Death 'passed over' and the Jewish firstborn were spared.

◆ At one stage, ten drops of wine are spilled on to the plate to recall the ten plagues visited on Egypt as part of God's plan to free the Jews, and symbolically to temper the joy of freedom with empathy for the suffering of the Egyptians.

◆ In some homes you may find an empty chair and always a full wine glass. These are left for the prophet Elijah, the precursor of the Messiah, for whom the Jewish people are still waiting. As part of the ritual, children will open the door for his arrival.

◆ The phrase that ends the *Seder* is 'Next year in Jerusalem,' expressing the eternal hope and expectation of the coming of the Messiah.

SEFIRAT HA'OMER ('COUNTING THE OMER') (April–May)

In the days of the Temple a sheaf, or *omer*, of new barley was offered up on the second day of Pesach (16 Nisan). For the next seven weeks each day was counted until the festival of Shavuot on the fiftieth day. Symbolically, this is a period of spiritual preparation for Shavuot, the occasion when Moses received the Torah on Mount Sinai. It is considered a period of semi-mourning and in more Orthodox traditions there are a number of restrictions relating to marriage and rejoicing during this time.

LAG BA-OMER (April–May)

The thirty-third day of Counting the Omer, 18 Iyar, is a festive break in the middle of the sombre Omer period. Restrictions are lifted for a day and celebrations break out! Weddings are allowed, music is enjoyed, and in Israel the devout make pilgrimages to the tomb of the second-century mystic Simon Bar Yochai at Meron in the Galilee. Bonfires may be lit to symbolise the light of the Torah, and schoolchildren may re-enact the historical revolt against the Romans with toy bows and arrows.

SHAVUOT
(May–June)

Falling fifty days after Pesach, on 6 Sivan, Shavuot, the Festival of Weeks, is a single-day festival in Israel, and two days in the Diaspora. Originally the festival of the wheat harvest, today it celebrates the receiving of the Torah at Mount Sinai. During the service the congregation stands for a reading of the Ten Commandments. Some communities decorate their synagogues with plants and branches, as tradition has it that Mount Sinai was green and fragrant when the Torah was received. It is customary to eat dairy foods, such as cheesecake and *blintzes* (thin pancakes) with cheese and other fillings on Shavuot.

SHIV'AH ASAR B'TAMMUZ
(June–July)

An important fast day, occurring on 17 Tammuz, this marks the beginning of the destruction of the First Temple in Jerusalem in 586 BCE and starts a three-week period of mourning for Orthodox and traditionalist Jews, during which time no weddings or other parties are allowed. It culminates on Tisha B'av.

TISHA B'AV
(July–August)

This, on 9 Av, is a solemn day of fasting and deep reflection, commemorating the destruction of both the

First and Second Temples in Jerusalem. The Book of Lamentations is read in synagogues.

THE MONTH OF ELUL (August–September)

This month, which precedes the Jewish New Year, is a time of review and preparation, in which people ask forgiveness from anyone they may have upset or wronged, and are willing to forgive others equally. It is a period of introspection and reflection, when services include special *Selichot* prayers (prayers for forgiveness). At the heart of these is recitation of the verse containing the Thirteen Attributes of Mercy that God is said to have taught Moses after the Israelites had committed the sin of idolatry (worshipping the golden calf), when redemption seemed impossible. In some communities, every day during Elul the *shofar* (ram's horn) is blown after morning prayers as a call to repentance.

ROSH HASHANAH ('HEAD OF THE YEAR') (September)

The Jewish New Year, 1 Tishrei, is a time for celebration and reflection. It marks the time when God created Adam and Eve. It is also known as Yom Hadin, or the Day of Judgement, on which it is said that God opens the books of Life and Death before sealing them again on Yom Kippur. The ten days of penitence between the two festivals are known as the Days of Awe, and are dedicated to *teshuvah* ('returning' or repentance) and to personal reflection on the meaning and purpose of life.

On these days the synagogues are full. People who normally don't set foot in a synagogue during the rest of the year are drawn to the High Holy Day services. Jews show their trust in God's compassion by dressing in their best for the festival and celebrating it in joy. In the synagogue the colour white, symbolising death and new beginnings, predominates.

During the afternoon before Rosh Hashanah, a festive meal is eaten that contains specific foods, listed in the Talmud as representing what is wished for the following year. After special blessings, bread is dipped into honey (not salt as on Shabbat), and following another blessing, an apple is dipped into honey to ensure a sweet and a good new year.

The liturgy on Rosh Hashanah features the themes of God as King and Judge. Penitential prayers are said, and the essential *mitzvah* is to hear the sounding of the *shofar*. This is a 'wake-up call' to make sure that we are really living life rather than just existing, so it also a time to make new resolutions for the year ahead. Traditional greetings are '*Shana Tova*' ('Good year') and '*Ketiva Tova*' (roughly, 'May you be written down for a good year in the Book of Life').

WHAT DO I DO?
❖ Families exchange gifts and New Year cards and e-mail messages before the holiday to friends and business acquaintances. If you have Jewish friends they will appreciate receiving a Rosh Hashanah greeting card.

YOM KIPPUR, OR THE DAY OF ATONEMENT (September–October)

This day, 10 Tishrei, is the most sacred day in the Jewish Year. It entails a complete twenty-five-hour fast, beginning before sunset the day before and ending with the appearance of the stars on 10 Tishrei. The fast is an act of penance, an exercise in self-discipline, a means of focusing the mind on the spiritual, and a means of awakening compassion. The five areas of abstinence are eating and drinking, washing, applying oils or lotions to the skin, marital relations, and the wearing of leather.

It was on Yom Kippur that Moses came down from Mount Sinai with the second stone tablets after God had shown mercy and pardoned the Israelites for worshipping the golden calf. It is therefore considered to be the day when all transgressions can be forgiven. It is an opportunity to achieve a high spiritual level and become almost angelic. Ultra-Orthodox believers wear white and spend all day in the synagogue.

The liturgy begins on Yom Kippur eve with the singing of '*Kol Nidrei*', a proclamation of the annulment of unfulfilled vows. The following day is spent in prayer, reciting memorial prayers for deceased relatives, confessing sins, requesting forgiveness and listening to Torah readings, to the Book of Jonah, and to sermons. The atmosphere grows intense as the prayers for forgiveness on a personal, communal and even cosmic level build up to the climax of the closing blast of the *shofar*.

After the service people gather at home to break the fast with tea followed by a meal.

SUKKOT, THE FEAST OF TABERNACLES, OR BOOTHS
(September–October)

Five days after Yom Kippur is the especially joyful autumn festival of Sukkot (15–24 Tishrei in the Diaspora,

ABOVE Ashkenazi style *shofar*, made from a ram's horn.

15–23 Tishrei in Israel). This is the last of the three pilgrimage festivals, and is a seven-day celebration of God's bounty and protection. It recalls the miracles of manna from heaven and the sending of seven large 'clouds of glory' during the forty years the Israelites spent in the wilderness on their way to the Promised Land. To commemorate this time, when the Israelites lived in temporary dwellings in the wilderness, many Jews build a *sukkah* at home – a makeshift open-sided shelter or hut with a roof of branches and leaves. All the family are involved in its creation and decoration and they will eat and may even sleep in it for seven days. The *sukkah* is essentially a reminder that it is not material possessions that make us happy – it is relationships, and in particular our relationship with God. So prayers are said, and guests may be invited to join the family for a meal.

During the festival morning services and in prayers in the *sukkah* there is also the symbolic rite of the waving the *arba minim* (four species). These are fronds of willow (representing the lips and speech), date palm (the spine), myrtle (the eye) and an *etrog* (a lemon-like citrus fruit – the heart) that are held together and shaken in the four

ABOVE The *arba minim* – wllow, date palm, myrtle and citron..

directions of the compass and towards heaven and earth in a motion that combines shaking and drawing in, so as to draw in the presence and beneficence of God.

SHEMINI ATZERET (THE ASSEMBLY OF THE EIGHTH DAY)
(October)

The festival of Shemini Atzeret falls on the eighth day of Sukkot in Israel (22 Tishrei), and the ninth (23 Tishrei) in the Diaspora. In Israel, and in Reform synagogues, it combines with Simchat Torah (see below), and the names are used interchangeably. These are two holidays on which work is not permitted.

SIMCHAT TORAH (REJOICING OF THE TORAH)

In Orthodox synagogues of the Diaspora, Simchat Torah takes place on the ninth day of Sukkot (23 Tishrei). A boisterous festival, it marks the conclusion of the annual Torah reading. The scrolls are removed from the ark and carried around the synagogue with singing and dancing. To signify the circular, never-ending nature of the Torah, the final portion of Deuteronomy is read, followed immediately by the first portion of Genesis.

CHANUKKAH, OR HANUKKAH
(November–December)

Starting on 25 Kislev, this eight-day Festival of Lights celebrates the victory of the Jewish revolt against the Hellenizing Seleucid rulers of Palestine in 164 BCE. Chanukkah (Hebrew, dedication) marks the restoration and rededication of the Temple after the uprising. The story is told that, wishing to rekindle the Menorah (candelabrum) in the Temple, the Jews found only enough ritually pure olive oil to last for one day, but it miraculously lasted for eight days! In honour of this event, in each household candles or oil lamps are lit in an eight-branched *menorah*, called a *chanukkiyah*. (This differs from the Temple Menorah, which had seven branches, representing the six days of creation and the day of rest.) Each day another candle is lit, starting from the right-hand side, using a *shamash* – a helper candle that is part of the *chanukkiyah*, meaning there are actually nine candles.

The lighting ceremony takes place after dark and is accompanied by blessings and songs, particularly the hymn '*Maoz Tsur*' ('Fortress of Rock'), and afterwards, traditionally, food fried in oil – potato *latkes* (pancakes), or *sufganiyot* (deep-fried doughnuts) – is eaten. Children

ABOVE Lighting the *chanukkiyah*.

may be given 'Chanukkah *gelt'* (Yiddish, money) or another gift, and traditionally play with a *dreidel* – a four-sided spinning top with a Hebrew letter on each side. This was originally used to keep the Jewish faith alive when regular religious practices were banned.

WHAT DO I DO?

❖ If you have Jewish friends, a Happy Chanukkah greeting card would be welcomed.

❖ The greeting for this as for most festivals is *'Chag Sameach'* ('Happy Holiday').

ASARA B'TEVET (December)

Also known as 'the Tenth of Tevet', this is one of four fast days in the Jewish calendar, and commemorates the beginning the siege of Jerusalem by the Babylonians, which led to the destruction of the Temple of Solomon. Subsumed within this date are 8 and 9 Tevet, which are equally sad days in Jewish history. Within the Orthodox tradition the Tenth is considered such an important day that it is observed even if it falls on Shabbat. Fasting, from sunrise to sunset, is undertaken only by healthy adults.

TU B'SHEVAT (THE NEW YEAR FOR TREES) (January–February)

This is celebrated on 15 Shevat, in the season in which the earliest blooming trees in Israel begin a new fruit-bearing cycle. It is significant both practically and spiritually, and is a day when Jews eat and give blessings for the 'fruits' associated with the Holy Land, especially those mentioned in the Torah. The festival is linked with ancient laws of tithing (giving fruit to the Temple), and its spiritual significance in the Kabbalah is the likening of humans to trees with strong roots, whose nourishment is taken from the Torah, the source of Jewish life.

TA'ANIT ESTHER (THE FAST OF ESTHER)
(February–March)

At a time when the annihilation of the Jews in Persia was planned, Queen Esther called on the Jewish people to fast with her for three days before taking the unprecedented step of asking her husband, the Persian king, for their deliverance, which he granted. This minor fast falls on 13 Adar, the eve of Purim, the celebration of that deliverance.

PURIM
(February–March)

Purim, on 14 Adar, concludes the annual festival cycle and emphasizes 'the hidden face of God' in world affairs. Sometimes called 'the Jewish Mardi Gras', it is a time of high celebration commemorating Queen Esther's saving of the Jews in Persia (see Ta'anit Esther, above). Apart from a lot of fun, there are also four important components to the day, which include the giving of money to charity in the form of three coins, symbolising the three half-shekels traditionally given in dues to the Temple of Solomon, giving mutual gifts of food and drink, and distributing alms to the poor.

At the evening and morning services the *Megillah*, the handwritten scroll of the Book of Esther, is read.

When Haman the villain's name is mentioned, the congregation hisses, boos and makes lots of noise with *graggers*, ratchet-style rattles, to blot out the name of evil.

Tasty treats are given to friends, including

hamantaschen, which are triangular pastries filled with prunes and poppy seeds that are sometimes held to represent Haman's ears. Traditionally, children and sometimes adults would dress up in fancy dress and put on plays for the community, perhaps a pantomime version of the Esther story, or go from house to house performing sketches poking fun at authority. Today there might be a fancy dress party for children. Finally there may be a festive meal in the late afternoon accompanied by much laughter and alcohol!

In cities that were walled at the time of Joshua, Moses' successor, Purim is celebrated on 15 Adar and is called Shushan Purim.

ABOVE Children on their way to give *Mishloach Manot*, or Purim food baskets.
TOP *Hamantaschen*, three-cornered Purim pastries with filling in the centre.

FESTIVALS AND HOLY DAYS

OTHER DAYS OF REMEMBRANCE

The following observances are not festivals or holy days, but are important national remembrance days.

Yom Hashoah (March–April)

This day, 27 Nisan, was established as Holocaust Remembrance Day by the government of Israel in 1951. It commemorates the victims of the Holocaust, and in Israel most public places will be closed. Sirens sound at 10:00 a.m. and people stand to attention and observe two minutes' silence. Jewish communities in the Diaspora will observe this day with special prayers, each in their own way.

Yom Hazikaron and Yom Ha'atzmaut (April–May)

Both of these days are important occasions in Israel. The first, on 4 Iyar, is a day of sorrow, when *yarhzeit* (memorial) candles are lit and prayers are said for those who have fallen in defence of Israel. This flows seamlessly into the second day, 5 Iyar, which celebrates Israel's independence in 1948, establishing a Jewish homeland once again.

International Holocaust Memorial Day (January)

In 2005 the United Nations designated 27 January an annual day of remembrance for victims of the Holocaust and of other genocides. This was the date of the liberation of Auschwitz-Birkenau, the largest Nazi death camp, in 1945. It is an international event, and each year has a different theme. Ways of marking it vary around the world and most will include special prayers, thoughts and a service.

RITUALS AND CEREMONIES

SHABBAT

Observance of Shabbat (Sabbath), the seventh day of creation, is at the heart of Jewish life. A festive day, it is observed by attending synagogue and with various home-based rituals, including three special meals. It starts very specifically at eighteen minutes before sunset on Friday evening (in Jerusalem, forty minutes) and ends on Saturday after sunset when the first three medium night stars are visible. Should you be invited to spend Shabbat weekend with an Orthodox family, the following is what you could expect during your stay. The Reform, Liberal or Progressive wings of Judaism would be more relaxed in their interpretations.

A traditional Jewish home is always one of welcome and hospitality, but Shabbat has the added sacred dimension. A very important element is that no work at all should be done, as it is believed that God created the world in six days and decreed that the seventh be a day of rest and reflection on the Torah. Among the strictly Orthodox this means no driving, phone calls, music, television or switching-on of lights, and certain appliances may be covered to ensure they are not used inadvertently. It also means no cooking, so all food will have been prepared in advance. However, this doesn't mean people will be eating only cold meals, as food may be kept warm in various ways. No washing up will be done until Shabbat is over. In the bathrooms, toilet paper may already be torn ready for use.

As a Jewish household is *kosher* ('fit' or 'suitable') – which briefly means that all food must be permitted and prepared according to Jewish dietary laws – there is no pork, bacon or ham, or any form of fish that did not start life with fins and scales, which includes, for example, oyster, lobster, clam, crab, crawfish and shrimp. Meat and dairy products are stored, prepared and eaten separately, with as much as a six-hour gap between. For example, a meat dish will not be followed by a dessert with cream, or coffee with milk; but there are many non-dairy alternatives.

At the front door and on some inner doors, fixed to the right-hand doorpost at an angle, there will be a *mezuzah*, a small decorative case containing a parchment scroll hand-inscribed with the first two sections of the '*Sh'ma Yisrael*'. This is done in fulfilment of the commandment to place the word of God on one's doorpost. It is customary for Orthodox Jews to touch and kiss the *mezuzah* as they enter and leave.

WHAT DO I DO?

❖ If you have any dietary or health restrictions, let your hosts know at least a week ahead. Because no cooking is allowed on Shabbat they'll need enough notice to plan and prepare the meal in good time.

❖ Part of the Shabbat observances may include a reading or discussion on an aspect of the Torah. This won't be expected of you, as a guest, although if you can and want to participate it

ABOVE *Mezuzah* containing the prayer '*Sh'ma Yisrael*', affixed to the doorposts of Jewish homes.

would be appreciated. It's worth remembering that conversations about movies, world affairs or sport are not generally appropriate to Shabbat, unless your host starts them.

❖ Smart casual clothing is safest. Having said that, Shabbat is a special occasion and families like to dress accordingly. For men, as ties are now worn less often, a plain white open-necked shirt would be acceptable. If in doubt, check with your host in advance – then everyone is comfortable! Male guests will be offered a *kippah* at the Shabbat table, but in an Orthodox home be prepared to wear it throughout your stay.

❖ Arrive three-quarters of an hour to an hour before Shabbat starts. This allows time to be shown where everything is and to get settled. If you wish to take a gift, flowers are always acceptable, but if your arrival time is close to the start of Shabbat make sure they are purchased already in water.

❖ The usual greeting on the Sabbath is '*Shabbat Shalom*' (Peaceful Sabbath). Unless you know your hosts well, it is better to address them formally as Mr and Mrs until they invite you to do otherwise.

❖ If you are carrying money, a mobile phone, a pen or a notebook, put these away for the duration of your stay as they are considered *muktzah* (needing to be set aside) and have no relevance during Shabbat.

❖ Reading about all the following rituals may lead you to think that it will be hours before you eat, but in fact they are concluded quite quickly, and in some households not all will be followed. Simply take your lead from the other people present. For a guest, the important thing to remember is that these ancient traditions honour the sanctity of Shabbat – so relax and enjoy!

WHAT HAPPENS?

The Friday Evening Shabbat Meal

◆ The evening may have started with attendance at the Friday evening synagogue service, during which psalms and the hymn 'L'Cha Dodi' are sung to welcome the Shabbat as an honoured guest or 'bride'.

◆ At home, the table will be beautifully laid in honour of the Shabbat with candles, *Kiddush* wine and traditionally two loaves of special bread, *challah*, made with enriched dough and honey, which are covered with an embroidered cloth. The commencement of Shabbat is signified by the lighting of the two white Shabbat candles, one for each *mitzvah* 'Remember the Sabbath Day' (Ex. 20.8) and 'Observe the Sabbath Day' (Deut. 5.12). Some families light additional candles to honour their children.

◆ In the home it is the woman who lights the candles, although in the Reform tradition it could be the man. A married woman may first cover her head with a kerchief, and women guests may also be offered one. Once the candles are lit, she will gather the light towards herself three times, drawing her hands over the  flames, finally covering her face and reciting a blessing. The candles won't then be moved or blown out for the duration of Shabbat. If they go out naturally this doesn't matter because the *mitzvah* will have been fulfilled.

◆ In traditional Jewish homes '*Shalom Aleichem*' ('May peace be upon you') – which is also a Hebrew greeting – might now be sung. Prayers of gratitude will be said, and '*Eishet Chayil*' will be sung by the men to acknowledge the strength of Jewish women. This may be followed by blessings for the children. All of these rituals reinforce the importance of everyone within the family, but some families may move directly from the candle lighting and blessing to the next ritual of *Kiddush*.

◆ *Kiddush* is a blessing that sanctifies Shabbat in remembering not only God's creation of the world in six days and his rest on the seventh, but also the Exodus from Egypt. A special goblet is filled to the brim with *kosher* wine or grape juice. The person reciting the blessing will stand. If others then stand, you do the same. *Kiddush* ends when the person leading the blessing drinks some of the wine, which may then be passed round the table for each person to take a sip. However, in the interests of hygiene, the wine for guests may be poured into individual glasses or already be placed in front of you.

◆ Other than saying 'Amen' at appropriate stages, generally no one speaks until after the blessing of the *challah*. There will either be one large loaf with two plaits, or two loaves, representing the double portion of manna that is said to have fallen from the heavens every Friday while the Israelites were wandering in the wilderness, saving them from starvation. The decorative cloth cover, and the board on which the *challah* is placed, are said to represent the dew that covered the manna.

◆ Hands are washed as an act of purification and a reminder that the Shabbat table is like a holy altar. This might only involve the host.

Between the washing of the hands and the eating of the bread there is no talking. Generally, between the blessing and the doing of an action there should be no interruption.

◆ The *challah* is then raised and the '*Ha-Motzi*' blessing (Grace before Meals) is recited. You may find that your hosts have printed a copy for you in English. The cover of the *challah* is then removed, and once the bread is cut, or broken, each slice is dipped in salt and passed around.  Salt, a preservative, is placed on the bread to symbolise something that is eternal. For those with an allergy, an alternative to the bread will be offered – it is the symbolism and ritual that are most important.

◆ Now it is time to eat, drink and enjoy the company. A traditional Friday night meal might include fish and there may be *lokshen* soup containing chicken, vermicelli-type noodles and vegetables. However, what makes this different from a regular dinner party is its sacred nature, which may be reflected in the discussion of the *D'var Torah*, literally 'words from the Torah', or the sharing of inspiring stories. Shabbat songs may be sung, for this is a time of celebration, and a wise saying is that 'song is the expression of an excited soul'.

Don't worry about not knowing the words –
just soak up the atmosphere.

◆ In the Jewish tradition, thanks are also given
after eating. On Shabbat and festivals, Grace
after Meals ('*Birkat ha-Mazon*', or '*bentschn*' in
Yiddish) opens with the singing of Psalm 126,
'*Shir Hama'alot*' (A Song of Ascents).

Saturday

◆ The second Shabbat meal takes place on
return from the Saturday morning synagogue
service, and will follow the same procedure as
on Friday night, except that no more candles
will be lit. In the afternoon some people might
have a nap, while others may go for a walk or
visit friends. This can also be a time for more
discussion or study of the Torah.

◆ The lighter third meal, the *Seudah Shlishit*, is
eaten in the late afternoon before sunset and
is really more of a snack with, for example,
bread, salads, fish and fruit. *Zemirot* (table
songs) are sung and Psalm 23 ('The Lord is my
Shepherd') is chanted.

◆ Shabbat ends when three medium-sized stars
are visible, and the farewell *Havdalah*
ceremony is performed. *Havdalah* means
'separation' or 'distinction', and refers to the
distinction between the sacred and the
everyday world. It starts with the lighting of a
double-wicked *Havdalah* candle. There are
then blessings over wine, fragrant spices and

the flame, after which everyone extends their hands towards the flame before the final prayer is read and the flame is extinguished in some wine spilled on to a plate.

♦ *Havdalah* can be followed by a festive meal called *Melaveh Malkha* (Aramaic, 'escorting the [Shabbat] Queen'). After entering regally on Friday night, she is escorted out in style with hymns to the Prophet Elijah, who will herald the coming of the Messiah. At the end there is a leisurely clear-up where everyone helps. Washing up is now allowed, although as a guest you won't be asked to help – it is up to you to offer enthusiastically.

BIRTH

The birth of a child is a cause for rejoicing, not just for the miracle of birth itself, but because it represents the continuation of Jewish life. A point to note here is that in Jewish law a child born to a Jewish woman is Jewish, even if she marries outside her faith. However, if a Jewish man marries outside his faith, his children will not be Jewish unless they convert later. This may be because the identity of the mother can be assured, but not necessarily the father.

Girls are considered special simply by virtue of being female, since Jewishness is passed on through the mother. Throughout Jewish history women have been instrumental in keeping the faith together. The birth of a daughter signifies the continuity of Jewish values, and the special ceremony to honour her birth is her naming. This takes place in the synagogue when her father can be called to the *bimah* on the Sabbath following her birth, and having announced her name to the congregation, a special '*Mi Sheberach*', a prayer for healing, is recited for the mother's health together with further prayers that the baby girl will grow into a Jewish woman of wisdom, goodness and understanding. There are variations on this ceremony.

On the first Friday night after the birth of a baby boy in some communities an informal gathering of family and friends, called *Shalom Zachar* ('peace be upon the male'), takes place. Essentially it is his first Shabbat. Although historically the gathering was meant to console the newborn for the Torah he has forgotten through birth, it is far from a sad occasion and is celebrated with a meal. However, it is not held when the Friday falls on Yom Kippur or the night of Pesach.

On the eighth day after his birth, provided he is in good health, the baby boy is circumcised. The ritual removal of the foreskin, called *Brit Milah* (Covenant of Circumcision), or *Bris* in Yiddish, fulfils the covenant between God and Abraham recorded in the book of Genesis and the ceremony is accompanied by a festive meal. In some homes on the eve of the *Brit Milah* older children are invited to recite the '*Sh'ma Yisrael*' in the belief that extra spiritual protection is needed, and children are untainted by sin.

WHAT DO I DO?

❖ Dress as for attending a synagogue service.

❖ Men wear a *kippah* during the reciting of prayers.

WHAT HAPPENS?

◆ The ritual of circumcision and naming may take place at the synagogue or in the home, and the baby will be dressed in white.

◆ Among Ashkenazim the first stage is to hand the baby to specially honoured guests, akin to Christian godparents, called the *kvatter* and *kvatterin*, usually a married couple who don't have children yet. They will pass the baby to his father, who takes him to the room where the *Brit Milah* will be held. Here he is placed on a special elevated chair – the 'Throne of Elijah', which could also be a beautiful cushion. Both men and women are present at the circumcision ceremony; in some communities women may be asked to stand at the back.

◆ The man given the honour of taking the baby and holding him across his knees in readiness, usually a grandfather or respected elder, is called the *sandek*, from a Greek word meaning 'companion of child'. The procedure is carried out by a *mohel*, who may be a rabbi or a religious scholar trained in the medical and ritual aspects of the *Brit Milah*. The rite starts with the singing of a welcome blessing, and after the circumcision and further blessings the child is formally given a Hebrew name and blessed again. This will be followed by a joyous, celebratory meal. It is worth noting

that some Reform Jews in the United States
do not practise circumcision and instead have
a welcoming ceremony called a '*Brit Shalom*',
meaning 'Covenant of Peace'.

COMING OF AGE
Bar/Bat Mitzvah

When a boy reaches the age of thirteen, he is
considered responsible enough to observe the *mitzvot*.
This is marked by the ceremony of *Bar Mitzvah* ('son of
the commandment'), held at the synagogue on the
Shabbat following his or her birthday. This is a serious
statement of faith, where the responsibilities for their
spiritual life now pass from their parents to them.

In recent times girls have undergone a similar
ceremony, a *Bat Mitzvah* ('daughter of the
commandment'), at the age of twelve – in Reform at the
age of thirteen.

WHAT DO I DO?
- ❖ Smart dress is usual, as for a wedding.
  Women wear hats.

- ❖ It is usual to bring a present for the boy
  or girl. In traditional families gifts might
  include a *tzedakah* box (a charity box to
  encourage generosity), or something that
  will further the learning of the Torah.
  However, it is increasingly popular
  nowadays to give the kind of presents
  that might be given for a birthday.

WHAT HAPPENS?

◆ The *Bar Mitzvah* is a public event and a social occasion, taking place within the regular Shabbat service. People dress smartly for it. During the reading of the Torah the young

person has an *aliyah* (is called to the *bimah*) where he (or, in some Reform communities, she) recites the *Maftir*, the last verses of the weekly portion, and, after a blessing by the father, chants the *Haftarah*, the reading from the Book of Prophets. This is a very important rite of passage, for which the child will have spent long hours practising.

◆ After the service everyone joins in the *Kiddush*. Family and friends then gather later at the house or chosen venue for what can be a lavish celebratory meal during which a speech of thanks is given by the *Bar/Bat Mitzvah* boy or girl. There is often music and dancing, both traditional and modern, and further speeches by the father, friends of the *Bar Mitzvah* boy, friends of the family, and anyone else whom the family invites to speak.

◆ The institution of *Bat Mitzvah* ceremonies for girls is a relatively new custom among the Orthodox, and the ways of marking it  vary from community to community. The girl may give a *D'var Torah* (a talk on topics related to a section of the Torah) in the synagogue on Shabbat or on a Sunday.

◆ Some communities have a ceremony for a group of girls in their thirteenth year called *Bat Chayil* ('daughter of valour'). After the girls have completed a *Bat Chayil* course, there is a special service for them in the synagogue, usually on a Sunday afternoon, with prayers, readings and a presentation. The girls do not read from the Torah, only from the Prophets or Writings, and may give an address on the subject of a valiant woman from Jewish history, such as Esther or Ruth.

MARRIAGE

A Jewish marriage is joyful, not only because it is one of the happiest and holiest days of a person's life, but also because it is hoped that the union will produce children to continue the Jewish tradition. Marriage is a sacred bond. However, although the ceremony may be moving, it is more a public statement of responsibility than a sacrament. The Hebrew for groom is *chatan* and for bride, *kallah*. It is important to note at this point is that traditions vary greatly, and if you are a guest you may not experience everything described here – it will depend very much on the branch of Judaism involved.

The Wedding Day

In strictly Orthodox communities the couple will not have seen each other for a week, and because it is believed that all their past mistakes will be forgiven when they become one united soul, both will fast from dawn on the wedding day until after the ceremony.

Meeting and Greeting

On the wedding morning, it is customary for the bride to host a pre-wedding reception for women guests, and the groom to do the same for male guests. This is known as *Kabbalat Panim*. Light refreshments are served at both. As bride and groom are likened to a King and Queen, it is not unusual to find them being treated like royalty, and the bride might well be seated on a throne-like chair. At the groom's reception songs are sung and there may be a reading from the Torah.

The Ritual of '*Bedeken*' (Yiddish, veiling)

Before the ceremony the male family members escort the groom to the bridal chamber to view his bride, after which he covers her face with a veil. There are several interpretations of this custom. One is that it signifies her character to be more important than her physical appearance. Another is that it stems from the incident in Genesis, when Jacob was tricked into marrying Leah instead of Rachel – so this is a way to check he will be marrying the right woman. In the previous generation the Torah says that when Rebecca saw Isaac, she veiled herself in a gesture of modesty. It can also be seen as demonstrating the groom's commitment to protect and clothe his wife. In Ashkenazi tradition neither will wear jewellery for the ceremony, to show that their commitment is not based on materialism. The bride is then blessed by both sets of fathers and grandfathers before they and the groom leave in readiness for the ceremony.

WHAT DO I DO?

❖ Everyone will be dressed very smartly for this occasion, and there are no restrictions as to choice of clothes, although if the couple are Orthodox visitors should err on the conservative side.

❖ There may be a wedding list at a particular shop or department store. Appropriate presents are household linens or other goods, or money. If you want to bring your present on the wedding day there will be someone designated to receive them, possibly the best man.

❖ If the ceremony takes place in a synagogue, when you arrive you will be shown where to sit and *kippot* will be provided for the men to wear. Women may or may not wear hats; so you may wish to take one with you to be on the safe side. At Orthodox weddings men and women will sit separately but on the same level, and in other denominations they sit together. You may or may not be given an Order of Service.

WHAT HAPPENS?

◆ Depending on the climate, the wedding ceremony could take place outside, or it could be held at the synagogue or another venue. The important thing is that it is conducted under a *chuppah*, an embroidered canopy supported by four poles that symbolises the new home the couple will build together, and which will sometimes be held by friends.

◆ Accompanied by music or chanting, the groom may be led to the *chuppah* by his family and friends to await his bride. She will wear white and, escorted by her parents, will arrive at his right. At a traditional Ashkenazi wedding the bride circles the groom seven times to signify the building of their new world together, but at a Sephardi wedding the groom will say a blessing over a new *tallit*, which is then briefly held over the heads of the bride and groom by four young men.

Blessings of Betrothal (*Kiddushim*) and the Giving of the Ring

◆ Wine is a symbol of joy, and after the rabbi has read the betrothal blessings, the couple drink from the *Kiddush* cup before the groom takes a plain wedding ring and places it on the index finger of her right hand (she will later move it to the left-hand ring finger). In the presence of two witnesses he then declares to his bride 'With this ring, you are betrothed to me according to the law of Moses and Israel'. They are then considered to be married.

The *Ketubah*

◆ At this point the *ketubah* (marriage contract) is read out by the rabbi. Written in Aramaic, it outlines clearly what the husband undertakes to provide for his wife, both materially and  emotionally, even in the case of divorce. Two witnesses may then sign this legally binding document, which remains the property of the wife. It is often beautifully illustrated and displayed in the home.

The Seven Blessings

◆ Then, over the second cup of wine, the rabbi and certain other honoured guests will recite the '*Sheva Brachot*', the seven blessings, after which the couple will again drink some wine.

Breaking the Glass

◆ A (wrapped) glass is then put down, and the groom shatters it under his foot. Although some joke that this will be 'the last time he gets to put his foot down', its deeper meaning is to recall the destruction of the Temple in Jerusalem, and to identify the couple with the continuance of the Jewish tradition.

- The end of the ceremony is marked with shouts of '*Mazel Tov*' ('Good luck'), enthusiastic applause and joyful music, as the bride and groom make their way briefly to a private *yichud* (seclusion) room for a few minutes alone. This is symbolic of their physical union and also gives them a chance to break their fast. It may also be the time when the groom gives his new bride a more decorative ring to go with the plain wedding band, and for both to put on any jewellery that may have been removed before the ceremony. They may also use this time to have some photographs taken.

- In the meantime the guests will have gathered at the wedding hall for the *seudat mitzvah*, the festive meal. Bride and groom may arrive at the reception in a specially hired form of transport such as a Rolls Royce, limousine, or horse and carriage.

- At the wedding feast there will be speeches and a lavish spread. After the meal, Grace is recited together with the seven blessings. There will then be much celebration with music, dancing and possibly live entertainment. In ultra-Orthodox communities there is dancing, but men and women dance separately. This is an opportunity for key relatives to say a few words about moral principles and to wish the newlyweds joy and happiness.

- The couple will stay until the end of the party, and may go on honeymoon later. Among the Orthodox this will be as much as seven days later.

Divorce

Judaism discourages but allows divorce, and either party can initiate proceedings. The husband will pay the maintenance laid down in the *ketubah*. Divorced partners can remarry, although there are restrictions on Cohanim (lineal descendants of the Temple priests) marrying divorcees. The Orthodox do not recognize the divorce proceedings of Reform Judaism.

DEATH AND MOURNING

In Judaism a terminally ill person should not be left alone, and a friend or family member will read or say prayers with them. When death occurs, the Chevra Kadisha, the Jewish Burial Society, is informed immediately and takes charge of all arrangements. They won't, however, move the body on the Sabbath. Only closest family will view the deceased, immediately after death. Autopsies are forbidden unless legally required, and Orthodox Jews are always buried in consecrated burial grounds, if possible within twenty-four hours of death. The belief is that the departing soul has returned to God, who will fairly judge his or her life.

WHAT DO I DO?
❖ It is important to note that flowers are not acceptable.

❖ It is customary to send a letter or card of condolence.

The Funeral Service

A Jewish funeral is simple in form, and lasts about an hour. Mourners gather at the cemetery at the appointed time. There are no rules about dress or colour, but common sensitivity dictates dark colours and modesty.

WHAT HAPPENS?

♦ There is a short service conducted by the rabbi at the hall of the cemetery, with prayers, a eulogy and more prayers, after which the body is borne to the grave in a procession. The body is buried in muslin, cotton or linen shrouds, and men are wrapped in a *tallit*. In the Diaspora it is placed in a plain coffin. In Israel coffins are not used.

♦ The procession may stop seven times on the way to represent the seven vanities in Kohelet, the Book of Ecclesiastes.

♦ At the graveside burial prayers are recited and the chief mourners – spouse, siblings, child or parent – will come forward first to shovel or throw earth into the grave. Each will shovel a few spades of earth, then anyone else who wishes can do the same. The mourners may return to the hall where the immediate male relatives recite *Kaddish*, a prayer of continuity.

After the Funeral

After the burial you may be invited back to the home of the bereaved family, who will be 'sitting *Shiva*'. This means that they will remain at home for seven days of intense mourning. In the house a seven-day memorial candle will be lit and mirrors will be covered. The bereaved sit on low stools and receive visitors, who offer condolences. Very close friends bring food and other necessary supplies. Prayers will be held at home each night except on Shabbat.

WHAT DO I DO?

❖ Stay for half an hour to an hour, or until the room fills up with visitors.

❖ Do not bring gifts or flowers with you.

❖ Offer condolences to each mourner, and wish them the traditional blessing of a long life.

❖ Sit only when the bereaved are seated.

❖ Don't attempt to strike up conversation; let the bereaved speak first. They may not feel like talking very much.

❖ Expect those present to talk about the deceased.

❖ When you leave, you are not expected to use the customary Jewish expressions for the occasion, but approach the bereaved and offer your condolences. You may wish to say 'I'm sorry for your loss' or wish them strength.

At the end of seven days a second, less intense period of mourning begins. Called the *Shloshim* ('thirty'), it lasts for thirty days, including the seven days of *Shiva*. In this period the Orthodox mourner does not shave, have a haircut, or enjoy entertainment, but otherwise most of the mourning restrictions are lifted. During the first eleven months the bereaved recite the *Kaddish* prayer in the synagogue services.

Approximately eleven months after death, and sometimes sooner, there will be a stone-setting ceremony, at which a headstone will be consecrated by close family members. This will be accompanied by readings of psalms and a special prayer – there might also be a eulogy. In Israel, this ceremony takes place at the end of the *Shloshim*.

SOME USEFUL WORDS AND PHRASES

Afikomen the piece of *matzah* that is hidden for children to find at the Passover *Seder*

Aliyah calling up to the *bimah* for the reading of the Torah

Aron ha-kodesh the holy ark, in the Ashkenazi tradition

Ashkenazi a Jew descended from followers of the medieval German rite

Bar/Bat Mitzvah boy's/girl's coming of age ceremony to mark adult membership of the Jewish community at the age of thirteen (boys) or twelve (Orthodox girls)

Beit Knesset 'house of assembly', synagogue

Bimah raised platform in the synagogue from where the service is led and readings made

Brit Milah 'Covenant of the Word', circumcision

Brit Shalom Covenant of Peace, ceremony performed by some Reform Jews in the US instead of circumcision

Chanukkiyah eight-branched candleholder, used at Chanukkah

Chazan cantor, trained in the singing or chanting of sacred text

Chumash printed text of the Torah

Chuppah wedding canopy

Diaspora (Greek, scattered seeds) Jewry outside Israel

Gabbai lay official of the synagogue, warden

Haggadah text telling the story of the exodus from Egypt, used at the Passover *Seder*

WORDS AND PHRASES

Halakhah 'the Way', Jewish law

Havdalah separation, distinction, short service which marks the end of the Sabbath

Hekhal 'palace', the holy ark, in the Sephardi tradition

Kabbalah the ancient mystical tradition within Judaism

Kaddish a short prayer in Aramaic affirming God's greatness, used in mourning

Ketubah marriage contract

Ketuvim 'Writings', scriptures including the wisdom of David and Solomon and the Books of Esther and Ruth

Kiddush sanctification of the Sabbath, over a cup of wine

Kosher 'fit', or 'suitable'. Kosher food is permitted and prepared according to the Jewish dietary laws

Machzor prayer book for use on special days

Matzah (plural, *matzot*) crisp, flat cracker, or unleavened bread

Menorah the seven-branched candelabrum of the Temple in Jerusalem

Mezuzah small case containing part of the '*Sh'ma*' prayer, affixed to right-hand doorpost

Minyan a quorum of ten adults, necessary for a service of prayer

Mishnah the first written compilation of the Oral Law

Mitzvah (plural *mitzvot*) commandment

Mohel man trained to perform circumcision

Nevi'im the Book of Prophets

Rabbi expert in Jewish law and spiritual leader

Seder (Hebrew, order) ritual Passover feast

Sephardi a Jew descended from followers of the medieval Spanish rite

Shalom peace, completeness. Also a greeting

Shiva seven-day period of mourning after a death

Shofar ram's horn, blown during the month of Elul, at the New Year and on Yom Kippur

Shul (Yiddish) synagogue

Siddur daily prayer book

Sukkah temporary shelter built with branches and leaves at Sukkot

Synagogue the Jewish house of prayer

Tallit a prayer shawl

Talmud commentary in Aramaic on the Mishnah

Tanakh the Jewish holy book, made up of three sets of ancient Hebrew texts, Torah, Nevi'im and Ketuvim, of which it is an acronym

Tefillin two cube-shaped leather boxes containing scriptural passages, attached to straps and worn on the forehead and on the upper left arm

Torah the five Books of Moses, Genesis to Deuteronomy.

GREETINGS

'Chag Sameach' 'Happy holiday', used for most festivals

'Chatima Tova' 'May you be sealed in the Book of Life' – Yom Kippur greeting

'Ketiva Tova' 'May you be written down for a good year in the Book of Life' – New Year greeting

'Mazal Tov' 'Good luck', or 'Congratulations'

'Shabbat Shalom' 'Peaceful Sabbath'

'Shalom' 'Peace'

'Shalom Aleichem' 'May peace be upon you'

'Shana Tova' 'Good year'

Chapter 4

MUSLIM
CEREMONIES

WHAT MUSLIMS BELIEVE

Muslim belief is shaped by the Islamic Creed, which consists of six Articles of Faith: in the unity of God (Allah); in Angels (the Prophet Muhammad* is said to have received his revelations through the Angel Gabriel); in Prophets; in books of Revelation (including the Torah, the Psalms and the Gospels); in an afterlife (the Day of Resurrection and Judgement); and in Divine Providence, or Destiny.

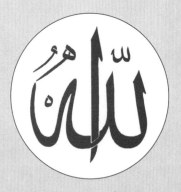

Islam means 'the peace that comes through surrender to God', and the Arabic word from which this comes also gives the universal Muslim greeting, *'Assalamu 'alaikum'* ('Peace be with you'). Allah is considered 'the formless one', and the beauty of Islam is reflected through intricate carvings, weaving and architecture. A true Muslim is defined as 'one who lives in peace', the belief being that peace is achieved through total focus and surrender to the will of Allah, who, as in other religions, has the key qualities of compassion, love, wisdom, justice and mercy. Ibrahim (the biblical patriarch Abraham, with whom Christianity, Judaism and Islam are all linked) is much revered in Islam because by being willing to sacrifice his son, Ishmael, he showed total surrender to the will of Allah. A common expression used by Muslims is *'Insh'Allah'* ('If Allah wills it').

Islam evolved in the seventh century in the Arabian Peninsula, against a backdrop of political, social and religious unrest. Although often referred to as a 'new' religion, it considers itself to be a final restatement of earlier revelations to the prophets Abraham, Moses and Jesus, and they and the

---

* When speaking or writing the name of Muhammad, it is customary for believers or followers of Islam to follow it with the words 'peace be upon him', which may be abbreviated to 'pbuh'.

holy books of Christianity and Judaism are all respected.

The Prophet Muhammad, who was born in Mecca (Makkah), on a central trading route between two warring empires, is said to have received the definitive word of Allah over a twenty-three-year period, thus correcting the distortions believed to have occurred in the earlier revelations and returning to the true word of God.

In the year 624, in the face of increasing hostility from his pagan compatriots, Muhammad migrated with his followers from Mecca to the city of Medina and became a respected and just leader, implementing many social reforms, including new and positive rulings about the rights and treatment of women. This migration is commemorated as Al-Hijra, the start of the Islamic New Year. Finally, in 630, after its peaceful surrender, Muhammad returned to Mecca, and Islam, the 'purified religion of Abraham', really took root. Muslims pray facing Mecca, and it is the place to which they are expected to make *Hajj*, a once-in-a-lifetime pilgrimage.

SACRED WRITINGS

The revelations to Muhammad were both recorded by scribes and memorised through recitation by his loyal followers, and Islam's holy book, the Koran

THE FIVE PILLARS OF ISLAM

Commitment to the Five Pillars of Islam demonstrates that Muslims are putting their faith first. It is the most important part of their lives. The Five Pillars are:

Shahadah (the declaration of faith: 'I bear witness that there is no God but Allah and that Muhammad is His servant and messenger.')

Salat (ritual prayers five times daily)

Zakat (annual charitable donation)

Sawm (fasting)

Hajj (pilgrimage to Mecca)

OPPOSITE ABOVE The name of God, 'Allah', in Arabic calligraphy.
PREVIOUS PAGE Hajj pilgrim praying at the Masjid al-Haram in Mecca.

(Qur'an), consists of 114 *suras* (short chapters). The Hadith is a separate collection of the Prophet's wise sayings. Both are written in Arabic, the sacred language of Islam. All Muslims, whatever their mother tongue, pray in Arabic, and are encouraged to learn the Koran by heart from a young age. Those who do so are known as *hafiz*.

SHARIA

Islamic Law (*Sharia*), where the emphasis is on ethical living, compassion to fellow humans and fairness to all, is based upon the Koran and *Sunna* (the living example by Muhammad of the revelations in the Koran). It governs all aspects of a Muslim's life, and deals with moral and personal issues as well as civil and criminal justice, although there are some disagreements between the different branches of Islam about the interpretation and application of the law.

BRANCHES OF ISLAM

The majority of the world's Muslims are Sunni (those who follow the traditions of the Prophet), and a smaller percentage, who have a large representation in Iran and the surrounding areas, are Shi'ites, or Shia. The difference between the two lies in disagreement about leadership of the Muslim community after the death of Muhammad. While he had not appointed a Caliph (successor), the Prophet had subtly implied that his chief supporter, Abu Bakr, should succeed him, and after his death Abu Bakr was chosen. Others felt that the succession should have passed to the Prophet's cousin and son-in-law, Ali. The name 'Shi'ite' is derived from *Shiat Ali*, which means Party of Ali.

ABOVE Al-Fatiha, the opening *sura* of the Koran. By the Ottoman calligrapher Hattat Aziz Efendi.

★ **MUSLIM CEREMONIES**   179

WHAT MUSLIMS BELIEVE

Shia Muslims believe that the direct descendants of Ali, known as the imams, provide the necessary guidance for people to live in accordance with the precepts of Allah. The twelfth and final imam, the Mahdi, is believed not to have died in the tenth century, but to be concealed by Allah from the physical world. Shi'ites believe in and wish for his return, which will herald a new age of divine justice.

The devotional and mystical strand within Islam is Sufism, in which individuals seek proximity to Allah. Drawing on the simple, ascetic lifestyle of the Prophet, believers experience Allah in the present through song, dance, trance and poetry, which take them to an inner world of ecstasy, love and intuition.

The revolving dance of the 'whirling dervishes', with their distinctive conical hats and long, flared, white skirts, is associated with the Mevlevi order of Turkish Sufis. The order is directly descended from two major Sufi poets of the twelfth century, Hafez and Rumi. Many Muslims do not acknowledge or agree with their mystical approach.

ABOVE In the centuries-old ritual of the Sema ceremony, the circling and revolving 'whirling dervishes' unify mind, emotion and spirit.

PLACE OF WORSHIP

The mosque (*masjid*) is the main place of worship, but Muslims may pray anywhere as long as they face the direction of Mecca's holy *Ka'bah*. Originally an ancient stone structure believed to have been built by Adam and later purified by Abraham, the *Ka'bah* later became the focal point of idol worship and was rededicated by Muhammad when he conquered Mecca and reinstated the worship of Allah.

Architecturally, many forms of mosque have been built, ranging from areas of open space and simple shelters to great domes and towering minarets, with variations in all the different areas of the Islamic world.

INSIDE A MOSQUE

A mosque is a simple house of prayer, where the focus of devotion is Allah. You will not see paintings, candles, icons or statues, but in rare cases there may be a display

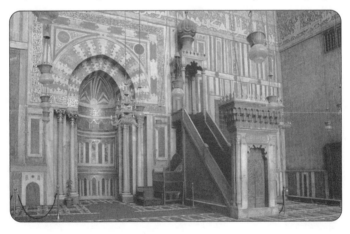

ABOVE Interior of the mosque of Sultan Hassan in Cairo, showing the *mihrab*, or niche facing Mecca, and the *minbar*, or pulpit.

of flowers and there is sometimes a chandelier. The only decoration on the walls might be a symbol of the moon and a star and/or geometrical designs of scriptural text, usually carved in wood and sometimes coloured green, blue or yellow. The floor will usually be laid with plain carpet, but some carpets are woven with a prayer section for each worshipper. In some countries, floors are marble or tiled. Muslims praying anywhere other than in the mosque have their own prayer mats, which traditionally incorporate in their design a *mihrab* (the niche in a mosque that shows the direction of Mecca). In using the mat during prayer, this niche is pointed towards Mecca.

Men and women pray in separate areas, so that their attention is not distracted from devotion to Allah. Women more frequently pray at home, however; they are excused *salat* (ritual prayers) during any kind of bleeding, but still continue to offer prayers of some form.

Some Muslim men wear traditional clothing, which will vary according to their country of origin, but others will be wearing Western clothing, with a brimless, knitted cap known as a *kufi*. As part of everyday life, many Muslim women choose to wear a headscarf, variously known as a *hijab, khimar, buknuk* or *niqab*, depending on the design and length. The guidance for modesty is often interpreted according to local traditions and customs, with some women choosing to wear an *abaya* (a full-length garment), or in more extreme cases but mainly in Afghanistan, a *burqa*, with total head and body coverage, leaving only a meshed area around the eyes. The idea for both men and women is that their body shape is not seen. The wearing of the *hijab* is controversial in certain secular countries that want to keep religion and state separate.

Wudu is the ritual washing that precedes prayers, and is the time of setting the intention for the prayer cycle that will follow. There will be a place for washing near the entrance to the mosque. The body parts that are washed a maximum of three times are the hands, the mouth, the nose (water is breathed in and out), the face, and the arms from wrist to elbow. Wet hands are then passed over the head and back before washing the ears inside and out. Washing both feet and ankles completes the cycle.

The key person in a mosque is the imam, a religiously educated scholar, who is fully versed in the Koran and Islamic Law. For Shia Muslims, the title of Ayatollah (the sign of Allah) is bestowed on a scholar with exemplary knowledge and understanding. For a small number of Shi'ites, the title of Imam has a different meaning, in that they believe an imam to be in direct contact with Allah, and therefore able to offer alternative interpretations of sacred text. As Islam considers that all have equal access to Allah, there are no ordained priests or ministers.

SERVICES

Islam is a devotional religion, and one of the Five Pillars of Islam is the call for Muslims to pray five times a day. In strong Muslim communities, the *adhan* (call to prayer) is chanted across the locality by a *muezzin*, or *muathan* (official) from the minaret of the mosque, but in smaller or mixed communities the call will be contained within the

mosque. The call starts with the *takbir* (declaration) '*Allahu Akbar*'. Often said to mean 'Allah is greatest', the nearest translation from Arabic is 'Allah is greater', that is, greater than you or I. The imam leads all

ABOVE The faithful praying towards Mecca in the Umayyad Mosque, Damascus, Syria.

prayers. Prayer times are governed by the position of the sun, and the number of *rakahs* (cycles of prayer) is determined by the time of day.

Fajr, with two *rakahs*, takes place before sunrise so as to start the day remembering Allah.

Zhur, with four *rakahs*, is said at mid-day.

Asr, with four *rakahs*, is said in the late afternoon and before sunset; both *Zhur* and *Asr* ask for Allah's guidance and greater meaning in life.

Maghrib, with three *rakahs*, is said just after the closing of the day at nightfall.

Isha, with four *rakahs*, takes place sometime before midnight, to remember Allah's presence in all ways.

Friday prayers may start at 1:30 p.m., and replace *Zhur* and *Asr*. The meeting starts with the imam's sermon from the *minbar* (seat on a raised platform facing the congregation). This is followed by two *rakahs* of special prayers. While on other days of the week worshippers will tend to say their prayers and leave, Friday is an opportunity to spend time with fellow Muslims in reading and understanding the Koran more fully.

Daily times are available on Islamic websites.

WHAT HAPPENS?

◆ The congregation stands behind the imam in rows, shoulder to shoulder, facing Mecca and having the firm intention to shut the world out and turn all attention to Allah. Praying and listening to the Koran are done with palms facing upwards, not together as in the Christian tradition.

◆ The *muezzin* will speak the *iqamah*, the second call to prayer of '*Allahu Akbar*', which the imam repeats after raising his arms with palms forward and fingertips to his ears (as if to hear more clearly). Worshippers will also raise their hands to their ears and repeat the words, either silently or quietly. The arms are then placed across the chest while a prayer is quietly recited. Two recitations from the Koran follow, one being the *Al-Fatihah* (opening chapter) and the other a personal choice. The imam will lead the prayers, which finish with '*Ameen*'. More verses of the Koran will then be read aloud by the imam, who after '*Allahu Akbar*' will bow in *ruku* (bending forward with the hands on the knees), followed by the congregation, who then return to *quiyam* (the standing position with hands at their sides) for another short prayer.

◆ This is followed by *sujud*, where worshippers kneel on the floor, lean forward to touch the forehead, nose, hands, knees and toes to the ground, and recite the '*Tashahhud*' (closing prayer). After pausing in an upright kneeling position with hands on knees, they repeat this action. This completes one *rakah*. Another *rakah* starts by standing and repeating the '*Allahu Akbar*'. Bowing and prostrating embodies the meaning of Islam, which includes surrender.

◆ The service ends with everyone sitting, palms upwards, as the imam invokes Allah with sectional prayers, to which all respond '*Ameen*'.

◆ After final blessings to all the prophets everyone stands and is invited to greet the person to their left and right. This may be a handshake or an embrace, after which people may stay a while to ask after family before returning home. There are no refreshments.

◆ Many Muslims live busy lives and may not always be able to perform prayers or go to the mosque at the required times. However, all prayers will be completed, wherever they can be said, before the end of day. On Friday all males over the age of ten will gather at the mosque for the obligatory and most important *salat ul-Jumuah* (Friday prayers).

WHAT DO I DO?

❖ If you are invited to a service, wear comfortable, modest clothing and ensure your head is covered at all times. As you enter a mosque, you are entering a sacred place of worship and need to remove your shoes. Socks are acceptable, and a good idea if you feel the cold.

❖ Remember to turn off your cell phone.

❖ As a non-Muslim visitor, you will be invited to sit at the back or to one side and observe. You will not take part in either *wudu* or the prayers.

❖ Note that no smoking is allowed anywhere in the vicinity of a mosque.

FESTIVALS AND HOLY DAYS

THE ISLAMIC CALENDAR

The Islamic year has twelve lunar months, which begin at sunset on the first day. This means that there can be considerable variation in the dates, according to the Western calendar, when certain religious observances and festivals occur. For example, Al-Hijra, the Islamic New Year, might be in October, November, December or January, so accurate dates and times in any year are best obtained from Islamic Internet sites or relevant publications.

THE MONTHS OF THE ISLAMIC YEAR	
Muharram	Rajab
Safar	Sha'ban
Rabia Awal	Ramadan
Rabia Thani	Shawwal
Jumaada Awal	Dhul-Qi'dah
Jumaada Thani	Dhul-Hijjah

Muharram, the first month, is one of the four holy months during which it is forbidden to fight. The second holy month is Rajab, when it is said that the Prophet Muhammad came into the presence of Allah. Ramadan is a month of fasting. The third holy month is Dhul-Qi'dah, and the fourth is Dhul-Hijjah – the month of Hajj, the annual pilgrimage to the holy *Ka'bah* at Mecca.

Essentially in Islamic law, there are only two major religious festivals: Eid ul-Fitr (Festival of Breaking the

Fast), celebrating the end of Ramadan, and Eid ul-Adha (Festival of Sacrifice). However, other days of historical note for Islam are acknowledged throughout the year.

AL-HIJRA
(Muharram)

The Islamic New Year starts by marking the migration from Mecca to Medina by the Prophet Muhammad and his followers. This event is regarded as the true start of Islam as a community, and also of the Islamic calendar, which is why we may see dates ending with AH, or H, representing 'After Hijra'. The New Year is not a high-profile celebration but, because of its nature as a new beginning, is considered a good time for resolutions.

YAUM ASHURA
(10 Muharram)

This day has different meanings for Sunni and Shia Muslims. For Sunnis it is a day of optional fasting introduced by the Prophet Muhammad to honour the Prophet Moses in leading the Exodus from Egypt.

For Shia Muslims this is a solemn day of mourning and remembrance of the violent death, in battle against the ruling Caliph Yazid I in 680, of Hussein, grandson

of the deceased Prophet and the third Shia imam. It has deep significance because they believe that a direct descendant of Muhammad should have been

ABOVE Musicians playing in an Ashura procession.

appointed Caliph upon the Prophet's death. The day is often marked with re-enactments of 'Passion Plays', and some Shia Muslims flog themselves in processions in memory of the pain suffered by Hussein (akin to some of the traditions of Good Friday in the Catholic Church). In Britain, large groups of Shia, distinguished by their red headbands, process through London for speeches at Marble Arch.

MILAD UN-NABI (BIRTH OF THE PROPHET) (12 Rabia Awal)

Ways of marking this occasion vary, with many communities gathering to tell the story of the Prophet's life, giving emphasis to his bravery, wisdom and compassion. Food is prepared and shared with the needy, who might also receive a charitable donation. Others will be more subdued in their remembrance because it also marks the anniversary of the Prophet's

ABOVE Re-enactment in Bahrain of the martyrdom of Ali, son of Imam Hussein, shortly before Hussein's death at Karbala.

death, and there are those who frown on any form of acknowledgement, because birthdays focus on the individual and not on Allah. Shia Muslims mark this date five days later than Sunnis.

LAILAT UL-MIRAJ, OR MIRAJ UN-NABI (THE NIGHT OF ASCENT)
(27 Rajab)

This falls in the second holy month, and is said to be the time when Muhammad, after a visit from the Archangel Gabriel, went on an extraordinary night journey on a wonderful winged creature, a Buraq. He ascended through the layers of heaven, discussing previous revelations with past Prophets, before coming into the presence of Allah, who told him that Muslims must pray fifty times a day. Through negotiation this was reduced to fives times daily and became *Salat*, one of the Five Pillars of Islam. Homes and mosques may be decorated with lights, and parents take their children to the mosque to pray and hear the miraculous story before celebrating with food and treats. A meal with neighbours, family and friends might be arranged, at which there would be more prayers. More devout Muslims may stay up all night to pray and read the Koran.

LAILAT UL-BARA'T (THE NIGHT OF FORGIVENESS)
(15 Sha'ban)

This is believed to be the night when, from sunset to sunrise, Allah is offering the seeker salvation, nourishment and healing. Some Sunni Muslims will spend their time praying and fasting through the night at home and in the mosques, asking for Allah's forgiveness and to be shown the way to lead good lives.

They believe that this night shapes their fate for the coming year, and in respect for the endless generosity and mercy of Allah, money is often given to charity.

For Shia Muslims, this is also the night that their twelfth and final imam, Muhammad-al Mahdi, was born. However, it is said that he disappeared at around the age of five, and it is believed that he will reappear at the 'appointed' time. This would seem to mirror Jewish and Christian beliefs in the coming of the Messiah.

RAMADAN

This is the Islamic month of obligatory fasting (*Sawm*), which is one of the Five Pillars of Islam. Fasting strengthens our will and teaches us to endure rather than give in to the usual human desire for instant gratification. It is a spiritual discipline, a time of physical purification, a reminder of how those less fortunate often feel and a time to give thanks to Allah for the blessings of life.

Fasting Muslims (those past puberty) will eat a protein-rich meal (*suhoor*) before fasting from dawn until *adhan* is heard at sunset. The fast is broken with *iftar*, a

meal that starts with the tradition of eating a date and drinking water or milk. Other traditional foods might be honey, nuts, milk, olives and figs. The general idea is just to 'break the fast' and keep the focus on Allah, so many communities eat this meal together and use the occasion to share food with those in need.

ABOVE Dates and milk to break the fast at sunset.

The last ten nights of Ramadan (*i'tikaf*, or retreat) are particularly important, with more devout Muslims actually residing in the mosque. Special prayers (*Tarawih*) lasting up to two hours are said and, while they are not obligatory, they are highly recommended for those who can participate. On the twenty-seventh of the month, during this time, is Lailat ul-Qadr (the Night of Power), when it is believed that Allah revealed the first verses of the Koran to Muhammad. Some Muslims spend the whole night in prayer and recitation of the Koran, because it is said that as the angels descend to earth, praying at this time is especially powerful.

Ramadan is also considered a particularly auspicious month because the gates of heaven are said to be open, while the devils are put in chains, and with the gates of hell closed it is easier to avoid temptation. Muslims will therefore try to give up bad habits, knowing that if they don't succeed, it's down to them and not evil influence.

It is a month said to be blessed by Allah, and Muslims believe that their good actions at this time will result in greater rewards. This is also why *Zakat*, the annual

ABOVE People gathered together for *iftar* in a mosque.

charitable donation, and another of the Five Pillars of Islam, is given during the last few days of Ramadan, because it gives a fixed point each year for the calculation, which is based on the wealth of the past year. *Zakat* provides money that will be given to those in need to ensure they have sufficient for the post-Ramadan celebration of Eid ul-Fitr. Giving money regularly is a reminder that true wealth and happiness come from the love of Allah, and not materialism.

Those who have to break the fast early for some good reason, such as needing to travel, can either make up the days up after Eid ul-Fitr or give a fixed charitable donation for each day missed. Those unable to fast will make a donation (*fidya*) instead. However, if the fast is deliberately broken for no good reason, there is a penalty (*kaffarah*) of fasting for sixty days; alternatively, a donation to feed sixty people can be given; there are strict rules governing this.

BEAR IN MIND!
❖ A point to note particularly during this month is that it is bad manners for people who aren't fasting to eat and drink in front of those who are. Because the fast also excludes water, you might notice that the breath of those fasting might not be so pleasant.

EID UL-FITR
(1 Shawwal)

This is a joyous religious observance, marking the end of Ramadan and the breaking of the fasting period. It starts with much anticipation of the first sighting of the new moon. If it is cloudy and the moon is not seen, the thirty-day cycle completes, and the fast is broken at the start of the new month. On the morning of Eid, there will be a special service, in which thanks are given to Allah for his blessings through the previous month and for his strength during the fast. Everyone wears new or their best clothes and gathers with family and friends to

eat a celebratory daytime meal, the first in a month. Warm greetings of '*Eid Mubarak*' ('Have a blessed Eid') will be exchanged, and children are given gifts. In some Muslim countries this is a three-day holiday.

WHAT DO I DO?

❖ Hospitality is an Islamic virtue, and you may be invited to join a family for this celebration.

❖ Alcohol is strictly forbidden, so don't take a bottle of wine as a gift. There are some lovely non-alcoholic alternatives available and, if in doubt, flowers are a good option.

❖ The traditional Muslim greeting is '*Assalamu 'alaikum*' ('Peace be upon you'), and the reply is '*Wa alaikum assalam*' ('And on you be peace'). The principle of using the right hand for eating also applies to shaking hands. If you are introduced to a Muslim woman, don't shake her hand unless she offers first, as it is considered modest for those of opposite sexes to avert their eyes, and avoid touch.

❖ Shoes are usually removed on entering a Muslim home, but if you are unsure whether this is necessary, just ask.

❖ In some more traditional cultures people still sit on cushions on the floor, but it is more likely that there will be Western-style seating.

❖ As with many cultures of Eastern origin, those Muslims who don't use cutlery will use only their right hand because food is, or was, taken from a communal bowl, and as the left hand is traditionally used for ablutions, it would be easy to spread infection. The best way to eat is to copy your hosts, and this might mean using pieces of flat bread to scoop food up, rather like using a fork or spoon. Any meat eaten will be *halal* (slaughtered in a certain way). Muslims do not eat pork, because it is considered *haraam* (unclean, as stated in Islamic law.)

HAJJ
(Dhul-Hijjah)

The *Hajj*, the pilgrimage to Mecca, is one of the Five
Pillars of Islam. It is a journey that all Muslims who are
financially and physically able must make at least once
in their lifetime, so as to offer prayers at the *Ka'bah*,
which is centred within the Masjid al-Haram, a huge,
open-air mosque, and represents a still point of focus
on Allah—a sort of symbolic spiritual anchor, and the
direction in which all Muslims face to pray.

Hajj Day (8 Dhul-Hijjah) is the start of the Hajj,
when those on pilgrimage make their way from Mecca
to the city of Mina, to find where they are staying and
to offer prayers.

In preparation for Hajj, there are a number of
preliminary rites. First, all pilgrims enter into *Ihram*, a
spiritual state of purity. To do this they shower and change
into special clothing, which for men is two large pieces of
white, unhemmed cloth, and for women a simple dress
and head covering. This ritual is a display of equality in

ABOVE Pilgrims performing *Tawaf*, circumambulation of the *Ka'bah*.

which a poor person could be standing next to a king. While in this state, they don't wash, shave or wash their hair, but can stand briefly under running water if they need to. They are also not permitted to quarrel, commit any act of violence to anyone or anything, or engage in sexual activity. Once in *Ihram*, two *rakahs* are performed.

Next is the recitation of the *Talbiyah* invocation that starts, 'Here I am, O God, at Your command'. This is followed by the *Tawaf* (ritual circumambulation) of arrival, which involves seven counter-clockwise circuits of the *Ka'bah*; completion of two *rakahs*, and performing the *sa'i*, in which pilgrims move with increasing speed between two rocks, Safa and Marwah, which are about 450 metres apart; they do this seven times, to enact the stories in the Bible and the Koran that tell of Abraham's wife, Hagar, desperately looking for water for her infant son, Ishmael. (Water miraculously appeared as a spring, the Zamzam, which is still in use). This ends the preliminary rites.

After *Fajr*, on 9 Dhul-Hijjah, the 'Day of Arafat', pilgrims journey a short distance to Mount Arafat and the Plain of Arafat, where it is said that the Prophet gave his final sermon before he died within the year. They stand near the Mount of Mercy until sunset, praying to Allah for forgiveness. This is a reminder of the Day of Judgement to come, and Muslims around the world will also fast and pray on this day.

EID UL-ADHA (FESTIVAL OF SACRIFICE) (10 Dhul-Hijjah)

This is the second religious observance of Islam. After spending the night in the Muzdalifa valley and collecting pebbles, those on Hajj return to Mina and throw them at Jamrat al-Aqabah, a pillar representing the devil, who had tried to tempt Abraham not to sacrifice his son. Because Abraham showed his faith in Allah, his son was spared and a sheep was sacrificed instead. This is what still happens on the pilgrimage, and in an act known as *qurbani* the meat is distributed to the poor.

At this point, after the sacrifice, men shave their heads and women cut off a lock of their hair. This act ends the state of *Ihram*, and the process of bathing and changing into regular clothing is symbolic of being reborn. All restrictions are lifted except that of sexual intercourse, which may not be resumed until after the *Tawaf Al-Ifadhah* is completed (see below).

For those not on Hajj, a sheep is also slaughtered, but in Britain the law insists that this be done in a proper *halal* slaughterhouse, and many Muslims now buy vouchers to cover the cost of a sheep and its slaughter. The meat is then distributed among the poor as well as used for a celebratory meal with family and friends. Muslims everywhere remind themselves of their own willingness to sacrifice anything to the will of Allah. In Muslim countries this is a four-day holiday.

At the end of the tenth day, many pilgrims choose to make the journey back to Mecca and perform the *Tawaf Al-Ifadhah*, which follows the same format as the preliminary rites outlined above. After this, all restrictions are lifted, and they then return to Mina for the remaining two or three days of Hajj. However, if they have not completed it on the tenth day, pilgrims will complete the *Tawaf Al-Ifadhah* before they finally leave Mecca, usually on the thirteenth day.

The final farewell ritual is the *Tawaf Al-Wadaa*, a last circumambulation of the Ka'bah, from which menstruating or post-natal women are exempt.

RITUALS AND CEREMONIES

BIRTH

Children are considered a precious gift from Allah, and the first words that will be whispered to a newborn child are the words of the call to prayer (*adhan*), which include the *Shahadah: 'La ilaha ilAllah'* ('There is no God but God').

Adoption is not permitted because every child must have a legal blood father. However, this does not stop couples fostering children in need.

BEAR IN MIND!

❖ Modern Muslims send baby congratulation cards, which often bear the word '*Mubarak*', which in this instance means 'Blessed one'. Any note or card of congratulation will be welcomed from non-Muslims. However, birthdays are traditionally not celebrated, as this turns attention to the individual and away from Allah, who should be the only focus of devotion.

The naming of a child (*tasmiyah*) can take place at birth, but is often done on the seventh day, and it is considered very important that the child be given a name with a beautiful and honourable meaning, which is why many male Muslims have Muhammad as one of their names.

Circumcision (*khitan*) for Muslims is recommended when a boy is seven days old, but cultural variations will dictate timings and can range from seven days to fifteen years. It is generally considered to be for reasons of health and hygiene, unlike in Judaism where it is a Covenant (an agreement between God and man).

In Islam coming of age is not marked by ritual. At puberty, which in the absence of any physical signs is early teens, a child is considered both formally and legally to be an adult, and is expected to observe all the obligations of Islam.

MARRIAGE

Marriage is a key part of Islamic life. The Prophet said that men and women were two halves meant to be joined together, and homosexuality is not accepted for this reason. Despite media stories of forced marriage, which are usually culturally related, the Koran very clearly forbids this. In Islam, marriage is a contract, not a sacrament, and parents usually work hard to ensure that their children marry someone of acceptable status.

An Islamic engagement is an official promise of marriage, and is the result of two families taking care to ensure that the couple have enough in common to create a solid foundation for their future. This decision will take into account their piety and modesty rather than focus on attraction and physical desire, which can fade over time.

Once the groom's family has received confirmation of acceptance by the bride's family, there will be a low-key celebratory meal for both families, at which a gift is given to the bride's family for the bride. However, this is not the 'marriage gift', which comes later. In some cases, engagement rings are exchanged, and if they choose to do this, gold is forbidden for the man. Until marriage, the couple is discouraged from spending time alone. Depending on circumstances, the engagement can be a day or several years, and no ceremonies will take place on either of the Eid Festivals, or during Ramadan or Yaum Ashura.

Before the signing of the marriage contract (the *nikah*), the marriage gift (*mahr* or *sadaq*) from the groom to the bride is offered and agreed upon. This can range from money to property, jewellery or clothing. In the case of money, half may be paid directly before the *nikah*, and the second half some time later, as agreed between the families. If the agreement is not fulfilled, this is dealt with under Sharia law.

In many cases, the first time the bride and groom meet is for the *nikah*, which is the formal bond that turns two individuals from 'strangers' to husband and wife. The ceremony is usually quite modest and attended only by the immediate families. It can take place either at the mosque with an imam or an appointed *qadi* (Justice), or can be held at the venue where the wedding feast will take place. However, the *nikah* and the wedding feast (*walima*) will often take place on different days, maybe even in different months, depending on when everyone can gather together for the celebration, as many people might be travelling long distances.

ABOVE An illustrated nineteenth-century Islamic marriage contract.

The *Nikah*

For the *nikah*, the groom will be sitting in the mosque or in a room at an outside venue together with two witnesses, one of whom may be the father of the bride, or her guardian (*wali*). The bride will probably be in another room, although this is not always the case—she might just be on the other side of the room with her immediate family. The imam or delegated 'other' will go with the two witnesses and ask the bride's family for permission for the *nikah* to take place. Once agreed, it will proceed, and both parties sign the documentation. When this is completed, the marriage is legal. There are no vows, no kiss, and any exchange of rings will be made privately between the couple.

Following the *nikah*, there may initially just be a dinner for the extended families; in small ways this may be similar to wedding receptions in other religious traditions, in that the bride and groom will sit at a table with their parents, both will be wearing their wedding

ABOVE Bride and groom in South Asian clothing at a *nikah* ceremony.

attire, and there might be a cake and a speech. However, friends will not be present, and an imam will give a short sermon, and, after ensuring they haven't changed their minds since the *nikah*, will pronounce them husband and wife.

The *Walima*

As we have seen, the wedding feast (*walima*) is often held later, and celebrations vary according to tradition and culture. Traditionally *walimas* are segregated, male and female. They may be held at the opposite ends of a large reception hall, divided by a partition or curtain, or in separate rooms. Many Muslims today, however, choose to have joint celebrations with family and friends, and in some cases these are very elaborate, with bride and groom seated at a central point on throne-like chairs. In any case there may well be people attending

ABOVE Friends and family celebrating the signing of the *nikah*.

who don't know the couple but who, as members of the community, have been invited to share the occasion.

Western visitors are sometimes disappointed by segregated celebrations, because women don't see the groom and men don't see the bride. The bride will probably wear her wedding dress and be accompanied by bridesmaids and possibly flower girls. Her dress might be elaborate, with lots of jewellery and flowers, or simple but beautiful, according to her origins. In the Arab tradition a bride wears a white dress and veil.

It is likely that during a celebratory night with female friends, the bride's hands and feet will have been painted in the *mehendi* tradition – the application of a beautiful (temporary) skin decoration using henna, a reddish-brown herbal substance – and guests might also have this done. This celebration, sometimes called a henna party, can be quite an elaborate event. In the Asian culture, the house or hired venue is decorated in themed colours of green and yellow, which friends also wear. The bride, though, will wear white and red.

WHAT HAPPENS?

◆ At a male *walima*, you will listen to recitations from the Koran and speeches about the Islamic principles of marriage. These may be given by the imam, a scholar or a senior relative of the groom, and it is becoming increasingly popular for the bride's uncle or brother also to say something. There will be food, but no alcohol. Depending on culture, the entertainment might include dancing to drums, or with no music. It is highly unlikely that there will be Western-style music.

◆ At a female *walima* there will also be food, and perhaps a table with a wedding cake and presents, but again, of course, no alcohol.

◆ The bride may sit under a flower-covered arch to listen to the speeches being given at the male *walima* via a loudspeaker system. There might be recitation of poems, then singing and dancing, perhaps accompanied by drums. At an Arabic or Egyptian women's *walima*, she might be greeted on her entrance with joyous ululation, a high-pitched wailing sound.

◆ As always, there are wide-ranging cultural differences. For example, at an Indonesian or Malaysian Muslim wedding, bride and groom would both be richly and colourfully dressed and seated on thrones like royalty. They would be expected to listen impassively to readings, despite some guests' best (and sometimes extensive) efforts to distract them!

WHAT DO I DO?

- ❖ If you are invited as a couple, you and your partner won't be together and will need to make prior arrangements as to where you will meet to leave – or you can just text each other.

- ❖ Revealing clothes are not appropriate, so make sure that your arms, legs and chest area are covered. For women, there may be occasions when you need to cover your head, so take a scarf or stole. Comfortable clothing is recommended, as in some communities there may be a requirement to sit cross-legged on the floor, which is difficult with tight clothes.

- ❖ If no wedding present list has been provided, money or gift vouchers are a good option.

- ❖ Do remember to turn off your cell phone.

- ❖ Remember, also, that no smoking is allowed in the vicinity of a mosque. The reception venue will have its own rules regarding this.

- ❖ It is important to note that some Muslims don't like having their photos taken, so if you want to use a camera do check first whether it will be acceptable.

- ❖ There will be a separate area for prayers, where shoes are not allowed, so make sure that you don't accidentally stray on to this area in your shoes.

A Muslim bride and groom will usually have a honeymoon of some sort, but they don't leave for this in the Western way amid cheering and clapping. Nothing is set in stone, however, so follow the lead of your hosts.

While marriage outside the Muslim faith is not encouraged, a male Muslim may marry a chaste Christian or Jewish woman as long as their children will be raised as Muslims. It is also possible for a non-Muslim to convert to Islam by reciting the *Shahadah*, after which time they are known as 'reverts' rather than 'converts'.

Polygamy (having more than one wife) is not restricted to Islam, but the difference is that the Koran (4.3) states that as long as a man can treat each wife justly, he may take up to four, although the Prophet exceeded this number. It seems that there are links between this decree and the historic Battle of Uhud in 625, in which a large number of men lost their lives and many women were widowed. Polygamy was seen as a way to care for them. Today, a first-time bride has the right to state whether she is prepared to accept this or not, and if her decision is against it, this is written into the marriage contract. Western Muslims are more likely to have only one wife.

DEATH AND MOURNING

In Islam, what counts with regard to the afterlife of heaven or hell is how well a life has been lived in devotion to Allah. Before death, family and friends will gather, and the dying person (*muhtadar*) will ask for forgiveness and blessings from both them and Allah. There will be prayers and readings from the Koran and it is hoped that before they die, they will be able to speak or hear the *Shahadah*, which they first heard when they entered the world.

As in the Judaic tradition, cremation is not permitted, and autopsies are only performed if absolutely necessary.

Where at all possible non-Islamic funeral directors are not involved, as they can unintentionally give offence by doing the wrong thing, such as sending men to collect a woman's body. In preparation for burial, preferably in a Muslim cemetery within twenty-four hours of death, the body will be ritually washed (*ghusl*), in accordance with Islamic rules, and wrapped in clean white cloth (*kafan*). If *Hajj* was made, the fabric worn during *Ihram* might be used. If the Muslim died a martyr, he or she will be buried in the clothes they were wearing at the time.

An Islamic funeral is a dignified but simple occasion that starts with the deceased being transported, usually by the family, to the mosque for funeral prayers led by the imam. Here, all family members and friends will be present, but only males then attend the actual burial. Where permissible the body will be placed directly into the grave without a casket, and turned to face the right – the direction of Mecca. Stones or wood will then cover the body, and three handfuls of earth will be thrown into the grave, each accompanied by a recitation of belief. Apart from these, the funeral will be silent. The removed earth will then be returned, and a small stone or marker may be placed on the grave. Muslim mourners, including relatives, then stay by the graveside for a while, as it is believed that the deceased is at this time being questioned by angels.

WHAT DO I DO?

❖ If you would like to send a card of sympathy, naturally avoid one with Christian or other religious images, and don't give flowers, as they are considered extravagant.

- ❖ Donations can be left after prayers at the mosque.

- ❖ It is not necessary to wear black, although Muslim mourners probably will, but it is not appropriate to wear brightly coloured clothes. Grey or navy blue are suitable alternatives to black. As always, clothing needs to be modest, and women need to cover their heads.

- ❖ Remember to switch your cell phone off.

After the burial, mourners and guests can return to the house of the deceased to offer their condolences to the bereaved, and food prepared by friends might be offered. In some cases, a separate memorial day might be arranged instead, in which case only family members would attend a post-funeral gathering.

Mourning is a time of mixed emotions because despite losing a loved one, it is hoped that they will have gone to a better place and be reunited with Allah, to whom their lives have been dedicated. The period of mourning is three days, during which the bereaved receive condolences from visitors. However, widows observe *iddat*, an extended period of four months and ten days, during which time they must not remarry, wear decorative jewellery or clothing, or move house.

Depending on tradition, some Muslims might return to the grave forty days later to say prayers but there will not be a headstone to mark the grave, for the same reason that birthdays are not celebrated.

SOME USEFUL WORDS AND PHRASES

Adhan call to prayer

Fidya compensation for missing a fast, in the form of food for the poor or a donation of money

Hafiz one who has learned the Koran by heart

Hajj pilgrimage to Mecca

Halal lawful; often used as a term for food permitted under Islamic law, which has been produced according to special rules, such as the method of slaughter of animals for meat

Iftar meal that breaks the fast

Ihram a spiritual state of purity

Imam for the Sunnis, the leader of prayers in the mosque; for the Shias, infallible guide to the inner meaning of the Koran and Hadith

'Insh'Allah' 'If Allah wills it'

Iqamah the second call to prayer

I'tikaf retreat

Ka'bah the House of God on Earth, the sacred sanctuary in Mecca containing the Black Stone

Koran God's revelation to Muhammad; the Muslims' holy book

Mahr gift of some significance, given to the bride by the groom on marriage as appreciation and protection

Masjid mosque

Mehendi the tradition of decorating the skin, especially the hands, with intricate patterns using henna paste

Mihrab niche or arch in a mosque, and also on a prayer rug, indicating the direction of Mecca

Muezzin man who makes the call to prayer

Mubarak blessed, or blessed one

Nikah marriage contract

Qadi judge or magistrate

Quiyam standing prayer position

Qu'ran The Koran, the holy book of Muslims

Qurbani distribution of sacrificed meat to the poor

Rakah cycle of prayer

Ruku prayer position, bending forward with the hands on the knees

Sadaq marriage gift

Salat ul-Jumuah Friday prayers

Shahadah the declaration of faith: 'I bear witness that there is no God but Allah and that Muhammad is His servant and messenger.'

Sharia Islamic law

Suhoor meal before a fast

Sujud prayer position, kneeling and leaning forward to touch the forehead, nose, hands, knees and toes to the ground.

Sura chapter of the Koran

Takbir the declaration of 'Allahu Akbar'

Talbiyah prayer used by those on Hajj

Tarawih special prayers in last days of Ramadan

Tashahhud closing prayer

Tasmiyah the naming of a child

Tawaf ritual circumambulation

Wali guardian

Walima wedding feast

Wudu ritual washing preceding prayers

GREETINGS

'Assalamu 'alaikum' 'Peace be upon you'

'Wa alaikum assalam' 'And on you be peace'

'Eid Mubarak' 'Have a blessed Eid'

Chapter 5

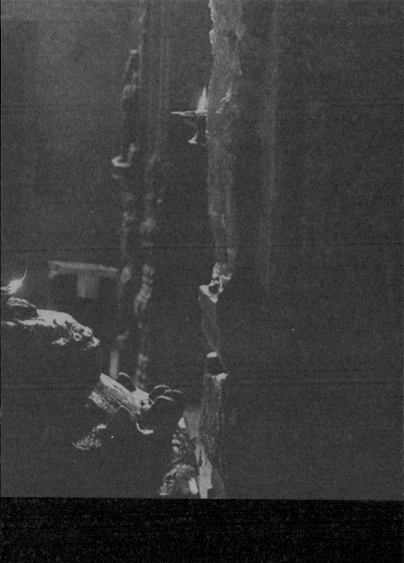

HINDU
CEREMONIES

WHAT HINDUS BELIEVE

Hinduism has evolved over millennia, with roots going back to the civilizations of the Indus Valley in the third millennium BCE. The spiritual path and way of life that emerged in India became the *Vedic Dharma* (the Divine Knowledge), also known as *Sanatana Dharma* (the Eternal Law) and later as Hinduism. Today India and Nepal are, formally, secular countries, but the majority of Indians and Nepalese are Hindus, and there are Hindu communities around the world.

Hinduism is a complex religious system, but, contrary to appearances, is a monotheistic faith, with belief in a Supreme Being. This universal spirit, or ultimate reality, is Brahman, or Nirguna-Brahman, meaning 'without attributes', sometimes referred to as 'That'. The visible manifestations of Brahman are called *saguna*, meaning 'with attributes'. Three forces arise out of Brahman. Known as the the *Trimurti*,

these are often depicted as a three-headed image. They are Brahma, the creator; Vishnu, the sustainer; and Mahesh or Shiva, the destroyer. The female principle of Shiva is Shakti, worshipped in her own right, and sometimes known as *mata* (mother) or *devi* (goddess).

Their respective consorts – some say, the representations of their feminine attributes – are Saraswati, goddess of learning, knowledge and the arts; Lakshmi, goddess of beauty and prosperity; and Parvati, goddess of love and devotion, although her darker sides are represented in Durga, goddess of overcoming difficulties, and Kali.

The incarnations of the *Trimurti* are known as *avatars*. Vishnu has had numerous mythical avatars, the best known being Lord Krishna, whose consort is Radha. Followers of Vishnu, also known as Narayan, are called Vaishnavites, and sometimes wear sandalwood

PREVIOUS PAGE Woman praying in the Meenakshi Amman Temple dedicated to Shiva in the holy city of Madurai, Tamil Nadu, India.

paste in vertical stripes on their foreheads. Two of Shiva's incarnations are Pashupati, champion of animals, and Nataraj, king of the dance. Shaivites wear ritual ash in horizontal stripes on their foreheads.

Another key aspect of Hinduism is the Jivatman, the soul, or divine consciousness residing in each individual. This is part of the eternal Atman, the Supreme Self – with a capital 'S', to distinguish it from the Ahamkara, the small 'ego-driven' self that experiences human suffering. This concept is what makes Hinduism a non-dualist religion, believing as it does that we are Brahman (God/Atman) and Brahman is ourselves, that is, there is no separation: we are 'one'. The goal of meditation, chanting and devotion to spiritual practice is therefore to reconnect with the Supreme Self that we always have been and always will be.

ABOVE Statue of Lord Krishna revealing the *avatars* of Vishnu.

SAMSARA, KARMA, DHARMA, MOKSHA

Hindus believe in *samsara*, or the transmigration of souls, and life is lived with awareness of *karma*, the law of cause and effect. This means that what you do in this lifetime will be stored up as *sanskaras* (imprints in the non-physical body) that return with each rebirth and influence how well, or otherwise, your life goes next time round. It is said that each lifetime brings the opportunity to burn past *sanskaras* by living a righteous life of *dharma* (truth) and following spiritual practices. It is hoped that this minimises the number of rebirths, or improves their quality, and ultimately leads to *moksha* – freedom from the cycle of life, death and rebirth.

'DEITIES'

Human beings seem to need a focus for devotion, and Hinduism accommodates this by including human attributes in that focus. For example, Hindus might pray to Saraswati, the goddess of knowledge and learning, for a good outcome in an exam; to Lakshmi, the goddess of prosperity, for financial abundance; and to Ganesh, the popular elephant-headed god, and son of Shiva and Parvati, 'the remover of all obstacles and Lord of auspicious beginnings' at the start of a new venture. Thus Hinduism could be summarised as 'one reality, many paths', which makes Hindus very tolerant of other religions and beliefs.

PURUSARTHA: *THE FOUR GOALS*

The four aims of a Hindu's life are:

Dharma, following the path of righteousness and adhering to social and religious law

Artha, concerned with worldly success in the pursuit of work, wealth and possessions

Kama (not to be confused with *karma*), enjoyment in life, desire and the pursuit of pleasure

Moksha, liberation from the cycle of life, death and rebirth

SACRED WRITINGS

While there is no single holy book that can be considered a final authority, the scriptures known as the *Vedas*, which stretch back some eight to ten thousand years, form the foundation of all Hindu belief, and are believed to have been divinely revealed to *rishis* (visionaries) as *sruti* ('that which is heard'). For thousands of years the *Vedas* were an oral tradition, and those who held this knowledge, and transmitted it from father to son, became the Brahmin, or priestly, caste. All other scriptures, such as the later *Puranas*, which contain mythological accounts of ancient deities, are considered *smriti* ('that which is remembered').

In time, they were written down in Sanskrit, the classical, sacred language of Hindu literature, and contain the *Upanishads*, the philosophical texts at the end of the *Vedas*. Probably the two most famous and extensive teachings that evolved from the Vedic texts are contained in the epic spiritual poems of the *Mahabharata* (telling of the rivalry between two families, and the pending battle of Kurukshetra). This includes the *Bhagavad Gita* (the dialogue between Vishnu's incarnation, Lord Krishna, and his devotee, Prince Arjuna, before the battle), and the *Ramayana* (the story of how Lord Rama, said to be an incarnation of Vishnu, rescues his kidnapped wife, Sita, from the evil, ten-headed King Ravana, with the help of Hanuman, the monkey god). All three poems are deeply philosophical and contain guidance for righteous living.

CASTE

A sometimes controversial aspect of Hinduism is that of the caste system, a social hierarchy originally consisting of four *varnas*, or colours. This does not refer to skin colour, but has been likened to a diamond that reflects light in different colours; the diamond is the Divine, and the radiated lights are the different reflections of divinity created as social orders, of which the most influential were the Brahmin priestly families. The second level, the Kshatriyas, were the warrior, or ruling class and the third, the Vaishyas, were artisans and traders. The Shudras, as servants and unskilled labourers, formed the fourth and lowest level, but below them were the Untouchables, who were literally 'outcaste'. Mahatma Gandhi, of the Vaishyas (Gandhi means 'greengrocer'), renamed the Untouchables *'Harijan'* (children of God), and they have now been reclassified as Panchama, the fifth *varna*, with some of them fighting for their rights in groups calling themselves Dalit (oppressed). While the caste system is now illegal in India, it persists in practice, particularly in regard to marriage.

SCHOOLS OF YOGA

Yoga means 'union' (with Brahman). Within Hinduism four different paths of yoga have emerged that seem to meet the needs of different personality types.

Raja yoga is a very disciplined and classical yoga, also known as Ashtanga (eight limbs) yoga. Patanjali, a respected author, wrote in the *Yoga Sutras* (c.150 BCE), that practice of the eight limbs of yoga – *yama* (restraints); *niyama* (observances); *asana* (posture); *pranayama* (breath control); *pratyahara* (detachment); *dharana* (concentration); *dhyana* (meditation) and *samadhi* (union, wholeness) – would lead to the ability to cease the fluctuations of the mind, and to the discovery of the real Self.

Jnana yoga is the yoga of knowledge, using the mind to transcend the mind, and includes reading and reflecting on sacred text, so as to understand its deeper wisdom and profound meanings, and gain insight and inner 'awakening'.

Karma yoga was quite radical as it was open to everyone, regardless of caste, placed an emphasis on improving social and economic conditions, and embraced an interest in the exploration of science and medicine. It promotes a holistic approach and believes that the ability to live fully in the present, rather than the past or future, comes with the recognition that the constant cycle of desire does not bring fulfilment. It is the path of selfless action and service, as embodied in the life of Mahatma Gandhi. Hatha yoga, which focuses on posture and breathing, comes from this path.

Bhakti yoga is a path of love and devotion to a chosen deity, or to a *guru* (spiritual teacher, from the words *gu*, dark, and *ru*, light). A guru helps a devotee to evolve from the dark of ignorance to the light of truth, through various spiritual practices that include reading sacred texts, chanting and meditating. Outside India the best-known followers of Bhakti yoga are the saffron-robed Hare Krishna movement, whose constant chant of devotion is '*Hare Krishna*' (*Hare* is a Krishnaivite term for God).

Modern Hindu movements that have popularised yoga as a form of body/mind balance in the West include those of Transcendental Meditation of Maharishi Mahesh Yogi; Osho; Mother Meera; Sai Baba and Ramana Maharshi.

ABOVE A 65-foot high statue of Lord Shiva meditating in the lotus position. Kempfort Shiva Temple in Bangalore, southern India.

PLACE OF WORSHIP

A Hindu temple is generally referred to as a *mandir*. A purpose-built *mandir* is designed according to guidelines laid down in the priests' manual *Vastu Shastra*, which includes instructions on space, direction, allocation of areas – much like the Chinese Feng Shui – and when to build, but in the West many *mandirs* are adapted from existing buildings, including redundant churches.

Generally, a *mandir* outside India will have been created and funded by the local community, and will have a full management structure, from chairperson to caretakers. The key religious person is likely to be a *swami* (the respectful title for a Hindu monk) or a *pandit*, a scholar of sacred Hindu text. Their role is to lead *satsang* (collective prayer), give readings and discourses, counsel worshippers and conduct rituals and ceremonies. *Swamis* are sometimes called *sadhus*. Although this term is usually associated with the holy men with matted hair who gather in India every three years for the sacred Khumb Mela pilgrimage, *sadhus* are holy men and women who follow an ancient tradition of never remaining in one place long enough to become attached.

Other places of worship are *ashrams* – retreats following Hindu monastic tradition where devotees go for varying periods of time to deepen their *sadhana* (spiritual practice). Part of this is *seva* (selfless service). *Seva* can range from administration to cleaning bathrooms, but, regardless of the task, the emphasis is on the spirit of willing service.

At home, Hindus will also have a shrine or altar for daily *puja* (devotion) and while this might just be a simple fabric-covered shelf with an image of a favourite god or goddess, incense and a candle, it could also be a dedicated room containing a *murti*, or statue of a deity. Meditation is a strong focus of devotion, as it is believed to be the inward path of reconnection to Atman, and will usually include the silent repetition of the universal and most ancient *mantra* (sacred Sanskrit sound syllable) '*Aum*', or '*Om*' (pronounced to rhyme with 'home').

INSIDE A *MANDIR*

Each *mandir* is unique, and while some have simple welcome areas with wooden floors, others have carpets and a few have grand marble halls. On entering, however, you are always likely to find a calm atmosphere, a smell of incense and a great many pictures of the different deities, together with framed writings, Sanskrit verses and other sacred images.

Within the prayer area are a number of colourfully decorated *garbhagrhas* (shrines) with oil lamps, incense sticks, flowers and plates or bowls of food, such as fruit and nuts, placed in front of a *murti*. Key deities will usually be grouped in twos or threes at the front; some *murtis*, such as Ganesh, will be contained within individual shrines at different locations in the temple. If the temple follows a particular guru, there will usually be a *murti* of that guru. Above each shrine will be a *sikara* (tower symbolising a mountain), as it is believed that this directs the deity into both the shrine and the devotees. At large *mandirs*, such as the Neasden Temple in London, a *sikara* is part of the outer roof structure.

A *murti* is specially made to detailed rules, and once consecrated by a Brahmin priest is considered to embody the deity represented. It is therefore treated with the utmost reverence, which includes daily bathing, clothing (in colourful and majestic garments) and the offering of food.

WHAT DO I DO?

❖ If you are invited to a *mandir*, wear comfortable, modest clothing covering your whole body, arms and legs; there is no need to cover your head.

❖ Depending on the size of the *mandir*, you may be security-checked, and often only very small (postcard-sized) bags are permitted, though this is not normally an issue in smaller temples.

❖ If you want to use a camera or camcorder, it is polite to seek permission before entering.

❖ Once inside, you are required to remove your shoes and leave them in the designated area. If your feet are likely to get cold, take or wear socks. This is also a good idea if you are not used to sitting cross-legged on the floor, as they can help to cushion the sides of your feet.

❖ There will be restrooms, somewhere to put your coat and an area where refreshments are served after some services – this is always the case on major holy occasions.

❖ Make sure that your cell phone is switched off.

SERVICES

Mandirs vary in how they arrange their services, but *satsang* is held every day of the week, sometimes both morning and evening. Because most people live busy lives, Sunday is the day when the greatest numbers are likely to gather at the *mandir* to meditate, chant and listen to readings or teachings from sacred texts. In some temples on certain Sundays, perhaps the first of each month, devotees come together to sing *bhajans* (hymns), which are sung in every language of India, including Sanskrit. After oil lamps are lit, the *pandit* or the elders will lead the singing, accompanied by a floor-level harmonium and other musical instruments.

In the shrine area, silence is maintained, apart from chanting, to respect those who might be meditating or reflecting. When not standing, both men and women sit cross-legged on the floor, sometimes in separate areas.

WHAT DO I DO?

❖ Remember that it is deeply offensive to direct the soles of your feet towards the *murti* or the guru.

❖ This means that you won't be able to stretch your legs out if you are uncomfortable sitting cross-legged. Although you won't be sitting the whole time, if you feel unable to hold this position for about an hour, you can sit on a chair at the back (on the appropriate gender side, where applicable).

WHAT HAPPENS?

◆ *Satsang* usually starts with *murti darshan*, a
time when the deities can be viewed and
honoured; respects are paid by standing in front
of them, slightly bowing the head and adopting
the *namaste* greeting gesture,
with the hands held closely
together at heart level, with
palms and fingertips touching and
facing upwards. A worshipper
might also kneel and touch the
forehead to the floor, or perform a
full body prostration.

◆ There will then be time for private prayer and
mantra meditation and you might notice some
devotees using a *mala* (a string of beads, like
a rosary) to count the recommended 108
repetitions. Some will also sit on an *asana*, a
small portable meditation mat (an *asana* is also
a yoga position), and wrap themselves in a
special shawl, both of which are said to absorb
and increase the *shakti* (sacred energy) with
each meditation.

◆ The *pandit* then conceals or covers the key deities
and leads the seated congregation in a chant, after
which there may be prayers, a reading, a talk and
more quiet time for contemplation.

◆ This ends with *arati*, a particular ritual of
devotion and worship. Again, different temples
have their own approach, and the following is

offered as a guideline. The *pandit* (or *swami*, or appointed member of the community) reveals the deities again, and devotees stand. The ceremony may start with the sounding of the sacred conch shell, the banging of a drum or the chanting of '*Om*' three times. The *pandit* walks to a particular shrine, bearing a tray of oil lamps and other offerings, and devotees follow.

◆ In front of the deity being honoured, the 'flame of truth' is lit and the *pandit* leads a chant (chant sheets are often provided), while ringing a bell with the left hand and ritually waving the lamp before the deity with the right. Another deity is then honoured in the same way, and the devotion culminates in honouring the key deities, during which the *pandit* will turn towards devotees and wave the flame towards them.

◆ When the chanting finishes and the lamps are placed in front of the deities, there is a chance to receive a purificatory blessing from the sacred flame; moving forwards, devotees pass their palms over the flame, drawing it towards them by touching their forehead and eyes with their fingertips. You will see that some devotees also touch their lips and their heart area. They might then have a *bindi* (red mark) put on their forehead by the *pandit* before bowing or kneeling in front of the deities in a final act of reverence.

WHAT DO I DO?

❖ Once people are seated again, *prasad* (blessed food), which might be fruit, nuts or sweets, is distributed. To receive this sacred gift, put your cupped hands in front of you with the right palm slightly covering the left, and give thanks with a slight bow of the head.

❖ While the food might be placed on your left palm, it is only eaten using the right hand because the left hand was traditionally used for ablutions. After *prasad*, some people might stay a little longer for quiet reflection.

❖ You will also see that in front of the deities, there are donation boxes for *dakshina* (monetary thanks). You can choose whether to contribute, bearing in mind that temples are non-profit-making and generally depend on the generous support of the community.

❖ If you are invited to the *mandir* (or other venue) to chant and hear teachings directly from a guru, it is usual for there to be *darshan* afterwards. *Darshan* means to be in the presence of a holy being, and devotees move forward in line to pay their respects to the revered spiritual teacher.

❖ If there is a very long line, it is best not to speak to the guru unless he or she addresses you first, but they usually offer a blessing by brushing you briefly with peacock feathers, although some will touch, or even hug.

❖ It is customary for devotees to bend forward with their hands in the *namaste* position, and some might make a deeper bow. Depending on the circumstances, it may be possible to speak with the guru after *darshan*.

ABOVE Performing evening *arati* with incense smoke at a ghat on the River Ganges in the holy city of Varanasi, northern India.

FESTIVALS AND HOLY DAYS

THE HINDU CALENDAR

The Hindu calendar uses the sun and moon, the brightest objects in the sky, as time markers. The sun heralds the return of each of the six *ritus* (seasons), while the new moon marks the start of each month, which is divided in two. Amavashya is the auspicious night of the new moon, and Purnima is the night of the full moon. The months therefore do not coincide with the Western calendar.

THE MONTHS OF THE YEAR	
Caitra (February–April)	**Asvina** (August–October)
Vaisakha (March–April)	**Karttika** (Sept–Nov)
Jyaistha (April–June)	**Margasirsa** (Oct–Dec)
Asadha (May–July)	**Pausa** (November–January)
Sravana (June–August)	**Magha** (December–February)
Bhadrapada (July–September)	**Phalguna** (January–March)

The names of the months may be spelt in different ways, depending on the region. Months are divided into *Shukla paksha* (SP) – the first, 'bright' fortnight of the waxing moon, considered auspicious for births, marriages or the commencement of tasks – and *Krishna paksha* (KP) – the second, 'dark' fortnight of the waning moon

Festivals and holy days are very important in Hindu culture, and there are a great many of them. Those listed here are the main festivals celebrated both in India and by Hindu communities around the world. All these celebrations are greatly influenced by cultural context, but have certain fundamental elements in common.

The use of the lunar calendar means that, year by year, the dates of the festivals and holy days change in relation to the Western calendar. Here we give the date within the relevant Hindu month and whether it falls in SP or KP. Dates for each year can be found on Hindu websites.

If you visit a *mandir* or *ashram* during festivals and holy days, you might see a *rangoli*, an elaborate and colourful *mandala* (sacred geometric design) made from sand, powder or flowers, on the ground outside. It is known by different names in different traditions, and its designs might include the Hindu symbol for the universal mantra '*Om*'; the sacred lotus flower (the national flower of India), whose unfolding petals represent purity and suggest the expansion of the Self, growing as it does from the mud into the light; and also the *swastika* (not to be confused with that used by Nazi Germany). The *swastika* represents the four goals of Hinduism and the four directions; the centre point represents creation, the centre being the mystical point of neither creation nor non-creation, and the lines emerging from it the movement of creation from that centre. The bent arms extending from these lines signify our movement from one goal to the next in an eternal flow of birth and rebirth.

People also create *rangolis* outside their homes on special occasions, as symbols of welcome and hospitality. One might also be painted permanently on the floor of a temple as an auspicious *yantra* (picture of power) to which prayers would be directed.

Every month there are two important and auspicious dates for visiting the *mandir*. These fall on the eleventh day after both the new and the full moon, and are called the Ekadashi (which means one plus ten). For those who are able, these are often waterless fasting days, on which grain and beans are avoided from sunrise to sunset.

NAVARATRI
(Spring: February–April)

Navaratri means 'nine nights,' and there are two festivals of this name. The first falls in spring, in the month of Caitra, which in northern India is the beginning of the Hindu calendar, and the second, considered to be the more auspicious, in the autumn month of Asvina. Both festivals are also known as Durga Puja and the Festival of Joy.

On each successive night at the *mandir*, which will be brightly decorated with coloured lights and flowers, all forms of the three major goddesses, Saraswati, Lakshmi and Durga, are worshipped and their exploits recounted from the *Devi Mahatmaya* (the Great Story of the Goddess). This celebrates the power of the divine feminine, and women will be dressed in bright clothes and jewellery, much of which will be newly bought for the occasion.

In Gujarati communities, from western India, women perform the traditional *Garba* and *Dandia* circle dances, clashing short sticks in time to foot-tapping music.

RAMNAVAMI
(February–April)

Falling on 9 Caitra (SP), Ramnavami celebrates the birth of Lord Rama, the first human incarnation of Vishnu, and a ruler associated with a peaceful and righteous reign. This is a day of fasting, which begins in the early morning with a prayer to the sun, and is followed at noon, said to be Lord Rama's time of birth, with a special prayer or chant.

In parts of India, especially in the north, there is a grand procession with a richly decorated chariot and four people dressed as Lord Rama, Sita, his queen, his brother Laxman, and his devotee, Hanuman, the monkey god.

Hanuman symbolises strength, selfless devotion and energy, and is worshipped in his own right with temple prayers, fasting, chants and readings, particularly on his *Jayanti* (birthday) which also falls in Caitra, although this month varies in different regions.

Ramayana Week

This precedes Ramnavami and, in a few Hindu communities, is the time when the whole of the *Ramayana*, the life story of Lord Rama, will be recited, together with *Ramlila*, a dramatic reenactment of the ten-day battle between Lord Rama and the evil Ravana, who had abducted his wife, Sita. This is a favourite with children, who join in wholeheartedly, and is a powerful way of bringing this sacred story alive. The temple will be colourfully decorated, with *prasad* and additional food being donated by different families each night.

RAKSHA BANDAN, RAKHI BANDAN (June–August)

This falls on 15 Sravana, at the full moon. *Raksha* means 'protect', and *bandan* means 'tie', and this home-based ceremony sees the sister tie a *rakhi* (red and gold thread) around her brother's right wrist for protection, and to symbolise her love for him. A *mantra* is chanted, and the brother gives his sister a small gift in appreciation. Today this tradition has expanded, and more elaborate *rakhis* are often exchanged within communities, or offered as a sign of friendship with a prayer for good fortune and happiness.

KRISHNA JANMASHTAMI (June–August)

Falling on 8 Sravana (KP), this celebrates the birth of Lord Krishna, the eighth avatar of Vishnu, and one of the most popular Hindu deities because of his many brave,

wise and down-to-earth qualities. He is frequently shown with his childhood devotee and consort, Radha, and is often worshipped by the name Radha-Krishna. He is alternatively known as Gopala, from his friendship with the *gopi*s (female cowherds), and many images show him dancing and playing the flute. Krishna's wisdom is reflected in the sacred *Bhagavad Gita*, the epic seven-hundred-verse dialogue between himself and Arjuna that is part of the even longer poem, the *Mahabharata*.

Lord Krishna is said to have placed great emphasis on keeping righteous company, and after a day of waterless fasting, devotees gather at the *mandir*. A special shrine will have been created in which the child Krishna is placed in a small rocking crib, and devotionally offered his favourite childhood food of curd or buttermilk.

During the evening there might be lengthy readings from the *Mahabharata,* and some temples stage plays. As always, there will be plenty of singing, and around midnight, the time of Krishna's birth, there will be a special *arati* and chant followed by *prasad* of *panchajiri* (there will be regional variations), made from a mix of five savoury and sweet ingredients. Celebratory food, contributed by the community, will then be shared.

GANESH CHATURTHI
(July–September)
This is a ten-day festival from 4 to 14 Bhadrapada (SP), which honours the hugely popular elephant-headed god, Ganesh, the remover of all obstacles and lord of

ABOVE Lord Krishna, hero of the *Mahabharata* epic, and his beloved wife, Radha.

auspicious beginnings. He is prayed to at the start of any ceremony, new venture or project, so that it might prosper. His name comes from *Gana* (followers of Shiva) and *Isha* (lord). He is also the god of learning and of letters and scriptures, as it is said that his broken trunk was used as a writing tool to scribe the *Mahabharata* as it was created.

On the first day of this globally popular festival, clay images are made of Ganesh, and his presence is invoked in temples and homes. The images are often gigantic and elaborately painted. Devotees might fast each day of the festival, and will visit the specially decorated *mandir* for *aratis*, prayers and Ganesh chants. Every day until the fourteenth, Ganesh is worshipped with red sandalwood paste (which after *arati* is placed on a devotee's forehead as a blessing) or red flowers, and offered traditional *prasad* of chopped cucumbers and *laddus* – sweet balls of wheat flour, *ghee* (clarified butter) and sugar.

In some countries, the tenth day can be spectacular. In Paris, for example, Ganesh is carried through the streets on a chariot, amid singing, dancing, drumming and chanting. Similar processions take

ABOVE The immersion of Ganesh signals his departure after helping his devotees. On another level, it symbolises the cosmic law of cyclical change.

place in other parts of the world, and the culmination by *visarjan* (immersion) of Ganesh in the sea, a river or any other body of water, is to say goodbye for another year to the god who is taking away with him all the obstacles and troubles from the lives of his devotees.

NAVARATRI
(Autumn: August–October)

This is the second festival of nine nights, taking place from 1 to 9 Asvina (SP), and as the goddess Durga is believed to remove the miseries of life, it includes fasting, music, joyous dancing, rituals and feasts that reflect local customs, as well as visits to the *mandir*, as in the spring festival.

DUSERA, DHUSSERA
(August–October)

This takes place on 10 Asvina (SP), and again is celebrated according to the customs of the region. Those communities who created images of Durga at the start of Navaratri will ceremoniously immerse them in water, in the manner of the Ganesh Chaturthi described above, while others burn effigies of the evil Ravana, King of Lanka, to celebrate Lord Rama's victory in killing him and rescuing his beloved Sita. Overall, it is considered to be a day of good triumphing over evil, a theme that flows into the next festival.

DIWALI, DEEPAWALI, DIVAL
(September–November)

The 'Festival of Lights' takes place over five days, and is probably the most famous festival celebrated by Hindus, Sikhs and Jains (the last two having their own meanings for the celebration). Starting on the last day of Asvina and ending on 2 Sud in Karttika, for those following the Gujarati calendar, this is also their New Year, and you could well find yourself invited to join in.

For some Hindus the occasion celebrates the triumphant return to the city of Ayodha of Lord Rama and Sita, twenty days after the defeat of Ravana. It is said that they arrived to find *avali* (rows) of *deepa* (lamps) displayed in people's houses in honour of their return – hence the name Deepawali.

While the form, and reason for celebrating, will again vary according to region and culture, common to all preparations are a thorough cleaning of the house, decorating throughout with strings of lights and lamps, wearing new clothes and drawing *rangolis* at the front entrance – although for convenience these may now be replaced by elaborate stickers. One of the most popular designs for Diwali is that of the lotus flower, because of its association with Lakshmi, the goddess of beauty, wealth and prosperity, who it is hoped will enter the houses displaying lamps in the window to light her way.

Such is the belief in the auspiciousness of this time, that special Lakshmi shrines might be created containing pictures of desired material possessions, and prayers will be offered for blessings on new businesses and a successful year. In India, this marks the end of the harvest season, and thanks are given for the prosperity it has brought.

Another aspect of Diwali is that of gambling, which has its origins in the legend that tells of Parvati playing cards with her husband Shiva, and declaring that anyone who gambled at this time would be lucky. However, for those who aren't, there is always the opportunity to consider that perhaps there is more to life than materialism, and the deeper spiritual meaning of Diwali is to celebrate an awareness of the inner light that shines through the dark of ignorance and fear.

WHAT DO I DO?

❖ Often likened to the Christian celebration of Christmas, the custom for Hindus is to send Diwali cards, wish others 'Shubh Diwali' (Happy Diwali), have firework displays and exchange gifts, which makes it a time of great excitement for children. You might choose to join in with these customs.

❖ Hindu friends may offer you a googra, a popular Diwali pastry of sweet coconut.

❖ Hindu friends might invite you to join them for a celebratory meal, in which case it could be helpful to know that as part of the ahimsa vow (adopted by Mahatma Gandhi) of not harming other living creatures, a majority of Hindus are vegetarian. They might also not eat garlic or onions (so if you invite Hindu guests, check their preferences). One thing you can be sure of is that you won't be offered beef, because the cow is the sacred representation of Mother Nature.

❖ When you arrive at a Hindu household, it is customary to remove your shoes, and if older members greet you with the traditional *namaste* bow, just briefly do the same in return.

❖ If cutlery is not used, there may be a *chapatti* (flat bread), which you can use to scoop the food up, or otherwise make small, neat bundles of the food on your plate with just the tips of your fingers. Unless you are left-handed, remember to use only your right hand. Although it can seem a bit tricky at the start, you will soon get used to it and no one will be offended if a guest does not manage perfectly.

❖ Although Hindus are not forbidden to drink alcohol, many choose not to do so, so check with your hosts beforehand and don't take wine unless you are sure they will welcome it.

❖ As with everything so far, there are vast cultural differences, so the best policy is: 'if in doubt, ask'. Otherwise, just enjoy the warmth and hospitality that you are sure to experience. Tradition teaches that a guest should always be offered sweet words, somewhere to sit, and refreshments.

MAHA SHIVARATRI
(December–February)

This means 'The Night of the Great God, Shiva'. Sometimes called 'Shiva's Mystical Night', it falls annually in KP during Magha, and is considered one of the most sacred nights in the religious calendar.

At the *mandir*, the key focus is the *Shivalinga*, the holy symbol of Shiva. Varying in size, this can be made of different substances, but a natural, round-topped stone is favoured, resting on a circular pedestal with a narrow drainage channel. This symbolises Shiva as the centre of creation, and during Maha Shivaratri it might be adorned with flowers, garlands and offerings of incense and fruit. There may also be a special altar with a statue of Shiva.

> **DON'T GET IT WRONG**
> ◆ Suggestions that the *Shivalinga* represents the male and female sexual organs as creative energies would not only give offence to most Hindus, but would be an injustice to the highly intricate philosophy and practice known as *Tantra*.

The day will start with prayer and fasting. In Western countries, devotees are then likely to gather for evening worship and while singing sacred verses and chanting 'Om Namah Shivay' to honour Shiva, they will take it in turns to anoint the *Shivalinga* with a mix of honey, milk and special *tulsi* leaves. Although some communities will continue to worship and fast through the night, others will complete with *arati* and break their day-long fast with *prasad*, followed by communal food.

HOLI, DHULETI
(January–March)

This is the very lively 'Festival of Colors' on 14 and 15 Phalguna (KP). It is a light-hearted festival, which in

India marks the start of spring, and gives people a chance to let off steam and drop their social barriers for a short time. It starts with Holika Dahan, which commemorates a triumph of good over evil.

The story tells how the evil demon Holika's murderous plan was thwarted, because of her young victim's devotion to Lord Vishnu. The result was her own death by fire, so large bonfires are lit and great delight is taken in calling Holika rude names.

On the second day (in the West, the two occasions might be combined) coconuts and fruits are likely to be offered in the large fire created outside the *mandir*. In some areas, there are street processions with drumming, dancing, and various forms of entertainment. Young people are allowed to get drunk and jokingly behave badly; friends and family are visited with gifts of *thandais*, a chilled, almond-based drink sometimes laced with *bhang* (from the cannabis plant) and *ghujias* (sweetmeats), and then family members are sprinkled with coloured powder and water by the eldest male. This is just the beginning, because then everyone takes to the streets and covers each other with coloured powders and water.

WHAT DO I DO?

❖ If you are invited to join in, don't wear your best clothes, and if you take a camera to record the fun, make sure you cover it first with clear plastic!

❖ If this sort of event doesn't appeal to you, avoid it!

RITUALS AND CEREMONIES

In Vedic philosophy, for the first three *varnas* –
Brahmins, Kshatriyas and Vaishyas – there are four
stages of life leading towards *moksha*, or liberation
from the cycle of life, death and rebirth. How these
stages are lived will influence the outcome.

Brahmacharya, the educational stage, is when a
student is encouraged to learn whatever will be needed
for later life, and to stay celibate during that period, so
as to not to distract from the learning.

Grahasta (householder) is the stage when the
main emphasis is on family life.

Vanaprastha is effectively retirement, when a
husband and wife minimise their personal possessions
and probably move to live with a married son.

Sannyasa (renunciation) is when, usually after the
death of the spouse, an individual gives up everything and
becomes a 'forest dweller', a hermit whose only attention
is on Brahman (this is not much adhered to now).

There are also sixteen *samskaras* (sacraments or
rites of passage) that cover the lifespan of those in these
varnas, and traditionally not to observe them might
have meant a fall in status. However, particularly in the
West, not all of these are observed, and the following
will focus on the most universal, with brief mention of
a few others for context.

BIRTH

Of paramount importance is the birth of a male heir to
continue the family line, and also to perform the last
rites for parents. The pre-natal *samskaras* are:

Garbhadhana (purification of the womb), to prepare the couple spiritually and mentally for a soul to be received, and make sex a conscious act rather than purely for gratification; *Pumsavana* for a healthy, and hopefully male child, and *Smantonnayana*, to ward off evil spirits.

Smantonnayana

Today, this ceremony is probably reflected in the women-only 'baby shower' party that is held on an auspicious day in the seventh month of a first pregnancy. This is a great celebration: everyone dresses as if for a wedding and has a thoroughly joyous time. Mothers bring their own children, tie good luck *rakhis* around the right wrist of the mother-to-be and impart lots of tips on birth and child rearing. Food is brought, and gifts of good omen such as jewellery and money are given. Some cultures hold a celebration after the birth instead, when visitors can admire the new baby.

IF YOU WISH
❖ The safe arrival of a baby is a cause for celebration, and the new parents will be delighted to receive a congratulatory card.

Jatakarma

After the ten days of ritual impurity after birth, the *pandit* will probably visit with gifts of fruit and sweets or even baby clothes; the father places a small amount of ghee and honey on his baby's tongue, and speaks sacred words in his or her right ear. This brief ceremony is the first of the childhood *samskaras*.

Nama-karana

Traditionally, the very important *Nama-karana* (naming) ceremony is held on the twelfth day. In the West, however, it may be a little later and combined with two other *samskaras* – *Niskramana,* which is the baby's first outing to see the sun and moon and visit the temple, where prayers are offered for safety in life, and *Annaprasana,* which is the baby's first feeding with solid foods, which are prepared during recitation of Vedic verses.

WHAT HAPPENS?

◆ For the naming ceremony, family and friends gather either at home or at a hired venue, which will be decorated with flowers, bunting, flags, candles and incense. As the star of the occasion, the baby will be beautifully dressed. The baby's name will probably have been chosen according to the position of the moon in his or her astrological chart. A *havan* (sacred fire) might be lit and the ceremony, which includes chanting and three or four prayers, will be led by a priest or *pandit*, who might use a gold ring to write the chosen name in a plate of rice. Then the eldest member of the family will speak the name into the baby's right ear. There will be joyful songs, and celebratory food, probably a buffet prepared communally.

WHAT SHALL I GIVE?

❖ Ask what kind of gift would be appropriate. Otherwise, money is always welcome.

Chadakarana

Chadakarana is the shaving of a male child's head, usually between the ages of three and five (but this can be up to the age of eleven), so as to promote strong hair and remove impurities. The religious component of offering prayers for a safe outcome came into being because of the historical dangers of doing this with sharp implements. Today this ceremony would probably just involve either a boy or a girl having their first haircut, and might be combined with *Karnavedha*, the piercing of the nose or ear, which must be done before primary school starts. In some cultures this happens as young as thirteen days, and is a cause for much celebration.

Vidyarhamba

Vidyarhamba starts the educational *samskaras*, and originally came with the learning of the Sanskrit alphabet. Today it is the start of primary school, when prayers are offered to Saraswati, the goddess of education, learning and the arts.

COMING OF AGE
Upanayana

Upanayana, one meaning of which is 'sitting close by', is one of the most important *samskaras*. It marks official acceptance into the *varna* through the receiving of a sacred thread, representing the cycle of life and death and consisting of nine white cotton threads ritually woven together.

The thread is worn constantly. When it is replaced, once a year, the new one must be in position before the old one is ritually taken off and burnt. In traditional cultures, this stage marked the beginning of the male's segregation from the women of the household, by whom he would now be served.

Originally this *samskara* applied to all *varnas*, but now it is often only undergone by Brahmin boys – and today, increasingly, girls, although they don't actually wear the sacred thread. It took place between the ages of eight and sixteen, at the time when a male child left the family home to receive spiritual education from a guru, hence the meaning of *Upanayana*. Now, in a rite of passage similar to that of a Jewish *Bar* or *Bat Mitzvah* or Christian Confirmation, it is takes place at the age of puberty, around twelve or thirteen.

WHAT HAPPENS?

◆ The ceremony, which lasts around three hours and involves many people from the community as well as family and friends, is led by a *pandit* and includes chanting and prayers. The *havan* will be lit and as the pandit recites the ancient *Gayatri Mantra* from the *Rig Veda*, the sacred thread is placed over the left shoulder (the boy's upper body will be bare) and runs under his right arm (when a close relative dies, it is reversed).

◆ This ritual is accompanied by special prayers to strengthen the recipient for life ahead, and signifies that not only is he *dvija* (twice-born), this time spiritually, but also that he is now ready to take seriously his responsibilities as a man.

◆ In a light-hearted part of the ritual the boy tries to run away and is brought back by his maternal relatives, who lavish him with presents including smart new clothes and money, although, also as part of the ritual, he has to playfully beg for money to support his studies – usually from his mother or aunts, as he knows they won't refuse! The occasion finishes with the customary celebratory meal.

WHAT SHALL I GIVE?
❖ If you want to give a gift, a small amount of money, no more than a few pounds or dollars, will be gratefully received.

The boy is meant to remain celibate until the next *samskara* of marriage. Traditionally he was also considered to be ready for the *Vedarambha samskara* of learning the *Vedas*, and reciting the *Gayatri Mantra* three times a day for 108 repetitions, often using a *mala* made of rudraksha berries – sometimes called 'tears of Shiva'. Today, the focus is likely to be on his general education.

Samavartana

Samavartana marks the end of education, and was traditionally the time of deciding whether to continue the spiritual life or to marry. Today, it recognises the end of formal education, probably university, after which the individual is free to make choices about the next stage of life, which will ideally include marriage and children.

MARRIAGE

In Hinduism, *Vivaha*, the marriage *samskara*, is considered to be a sacrament, not a contract, and marks the second stage of life as a householder (*Grahasta*). Despite Western influence, many marriages are still arranged by parents, and in more orthodox traditions, once suitable partners have been identified, their astrological charts will be checked to determine compatibility. A meeting will then be arranged so that the couple can decide if they agree with the choice; all being well, a *vagdana*, an oral agreement by both families of the couple's intention to marry, and a *lagna-patra*, a written agreement, consolidate the engagement.

Where the couple have met through work or friends, the *vagdana* is made when the two sets of parents first meet, and the *lagna-patra* is likely to be the official registering of the marriage, with the parents signing as witnesses. Many couples today choose to buy engagement rings and have a celebratory party with music, singing and dancing, often including Western music. As always, food will be plentiful and blessings on the marriage will be sought from Ganesh.

In traditional families, an auspicious date for marriage is advised by the astrologer, which historically would not take place between the second half of the months Asadha and Kartikka (generally the second half of July–November), when it is said that Lord Vishnu sleeps for four months. The reality these days, though, is that couples marry when a suitable time is available.

Celebrations Before the Wedding

Traditional Indian weddings can extend over weeks and would include a *sangeet sandhya*, an evening of musical entertainment hosted by the bride's family, and an ideal opportunity to introduce, before the wedding, those who hadn't met previously. However, as time is often more limited, a number of celebrations are likely to be consolidated into one, and on the day prior to the wedding, family and friends will gather at each partner's home in the morning for prayers and *Ganesh puja*, after which the bride's family takes wedding gifts, which might include money and jewellery, to the groom's family, where another celebration will take place in the form of a meal.

This day will end with separate parties for the bride and groom. The rooms will be brightly decorated, and everyone one will dress up in colourful clothes. There will be music, dancing and singing of traditional wedding songs, and plenty of food, which may be vegetarian – it will probably be a buffet. During the bride's party she will have her hands and feet painted in the intricate and beautiful *mehendi* tradition, using henna paste. Her friends and family will have only their hands painted. (Sometimes the groom is also decorated in this way.)

ABOVE A Hindu bride during a traditional wedding ceremony.

TRADITIONAL INDIAN DRESS

Before we come to the wedding itself, it is worth noting what the bride might wear. The *sola singaar*, a form of dress code for women laid down in ancient Sanskrit texts, prescribes sixteen items: a lower and upper garment, traditionally a *sari*, a long piece of richly coloured fabric wrapped several times around the waist, with the final section placed over the chest and shoulder, and worn over a *choli* (short, tight-fitting blouse) of the same colour; a *bindi* (the red dot made from vermilion and placed between the eyebrows at the seat of the *ajna*, the third *chakra* (point in the ancient energy system) said to relate to vision, memory and intellect; gold necklaces; earrings; flowers for the hair; rings (fingers and nose – although a nose pin is more popular currently); bangles; silver anklets with bells; silver toe rings (gold is sacred and only for the upper body); upper arm bangles, often with a snake design for protection against evil; natural oil perfumes (rose, jasmine, lemon and amber); sandalwood paste for the skin; thin chain waistbands with minute bells; henna for hand/feet painting and colouring hair, and *kohl/kajal* (black eyeliner).

Today, the only time that a Hindu women is likely to be adorned with all of these is her wedding day, because men and women often wear Western clothes, and traditional dress is influenced strongly by region and community. However, a popular form of clothing is the *salwaar kameez* (thin, pyjama-like trousers covered by a long, loose tunic) draped with a *dupatta*, a long rectangular scarf that reaches below the waistline if worn over the shoulder, but is often worn draped around the chest and over both shoulders.

Be prepared for the celebrations to continue well into the early hours, despite an early start the next day.

The Wedding Ceremony

In India, a wedding is often an elaborate and lengthy ceremony, performed by Brahmin priests in Sanskrit, and lasting up to three days or more; in the West most ceremonies now last no longer than two or three hours, are mainly in English and are followed by a wedding feast reception.

The ceremony itself will probably be held in a hotel, or other suitable venue, but not at the *mandir*, unless there is a separate hall. All Hindu marriage ceremonies are performed according to Vedic ritual, but as it would be impossible to include all the variations of different regions and cultures, what follows are some of the main customs – although even these can vary, so just go with an open mind and heart ready to enjoy the experience.

ABOVE A Hindu wedding ceremony in Rajasthan, north-west India.

There is not usually an Order of Service, although some couples provide them now, because they have so many Western friends who appreciate knowing what is happening and why.

You are certain to see a selection of the fashions mentioned above, and one thing you can guarantee is that they will be elaborate and richly coloured. Traditionally, different regions have their own colour preferences for bridal wear, but again Western influence means that many couples will choose according to their personal preference.

Traditional wedding attire for the groom would typically be a *sherwani* (a long Nehru jacket, with side splits and a stand-up collar), *churwidars* (tight-fitting ruched trousers) and *mojhris* (Indian shoes), and this is what is usually worn even for more Westernised weddings. Depending on his *varna*, he might also be wearing an elaborate turban with a pleated fan and brooch at the front and a length of material at the back.

Instead of the traditional sari, the bride may wear a sumptuous *lengha*, or full skirt, and she will probably be wearing all the accessories mentioned above, together with a *mangatika* or *tikli* (a small pendant on a tiny chain which is secured in the hair parting and rests on the forehead). The idea is that she represents the goddess Lakshmi, bringing prosperity and beauty to her new home.

The key central feature is the beautiful four-pillared *mandap* (sacred canopy) under which the ceremony is held. Traditionally this would have been made up of whole banana plants, *tulsi* leaves, marigold flowers and coconuts, but now is likely to be covered in fragrant flowers, lights and draped fabric. At really big weddings, this will be set up on a raised platform.

Within the pillars will be the means to create the *havan* as well as perhaps a statue of Ganesh, and depending on culture either two throne-like chairs or a stylish wedding stool.

WHAT DO I DO?

❖ You'd be well advised to start the wedding day with a good breakfast, as it is likely to be a long time before the next meal!

❖ As a guest your clothing needs to be smart, such as you would normally wear to a special occasion of this kind. If the ceremony is being held at a temple, cover your upper arms, legs and chest. Women are welcome to wear saris if they choose, and heads needn't be covered.

❖ Arrive at the requested time, and you will be shown where to sit. Keep any presents you have brought until later.

ABOVE An outdoor *mandap*, or wedding canopy, with royal chairs for the bride and groom.

WHAT HAPPENS?

◆ The ceremony might commence with the music of a *nadaswaram*, an Indian wind instrument, and once the groom has arrived, escorted by members of his family, he will be greeted not only by other family members and friends, but by the bride's family too, with blessings being exchanged.

◆ At this point, he might stamp on a clay pot (contained within a cloth for safety), to demonstrate that he has the ability, strength and determination to overcome any obstacles that the couple might face in married life, and a *sutra bandhan* (protective thread) might be tied to his right wrist with the blessings of Durga, the goddess of power.

◆ Escorted by her parents, his bride will then join him, and the *pandit* will invoke the blessings of Ganesh. The *Kanyadanam*, when the father places his daughter's hand in that of the groom, is one of the most important moments of the ceremony, after which they make an oath to each other to be together as one, and the groom places a *sindhur bindi* (a red dot to symbolise marriage) on his bride's forehead, and she a *tilak* (red dot) on his.

◆ Today, many couples exchange wedding rings, but traditionally the groom ties a *mangala sutra*, a necklace made of black beads with a gold disc-shaped pendant at the front, around her neck. After showering yellow rice on each other's heads, to symbolise health and prosperity, they exchange garlands of flowers, and loose ends of their clothing are tied together to show their firm and lasting commitment to each other.

◆ As with all Hindu ceremonies, the sacred fire is a key component, and even though this may be very small if indoors (it could just be a candle in a container), it is still crucial. Once it is lit, the couple perform *Agnipradakshina,* an offering of prayers and other ritual items, such as ghee, rice and sandalwood, to Agni, the god of fire, around which four stones might be laid to signify the four goals of life: *dharma, artha, kama* and *moksha.* The couple will then walk round the fire clockwise, touching each stone as their sign of commitment to all four.

ABOVE During the wedding ceremony *mantras* are recited. At the end of each *mantra* some clarified butter is poured into the sacred fire.

◆ With the ceremony drawing to an end they perform the most important act, which is to take seven steps, *Saptapadi*, hand in hand clockwise around the fire, making a vow with each step. In some traditions, the *pandit* then directs the couple to look towards the morning star, or Arundhati, to whom they pray for the highest blessings, following which friends and family place flower petals, rice or confetti on their hair by way of blessings for a happy life before everyone leaves for the wedding feast and reception.

ABOVE The bride bids farewell to her family at the end of the wedding ceremony.

The Feast and Reception

There is unlikely to be a formal greeting line when you arrive. For the feast, there will be a 'top table' for the couple, their families, the best man, and the maid of honour. During the evening there will be a number of speeches before the music and dancing begin. Often there is no wedding cake, but if there is, it will be cut by the couple and shared as part of the dessert.

The couple will generally lead the first dance, and the high-spirited celebrations may last long into the night. Traditionally, the couple do not leave before their guests, although they might do so at more Westernised weddings. Generally, the honeymoon is started some days later.

WHAT DO I DO?

- ❖ As with all couples starting in life, wedding presents are welcomed, and if you have not seen a gift list, it would be suitable to give an item for the home.

- ❖ Take it to the reception and on arrival place it in the designated area. (It won't be opened for several days.)

- ❖ There might be a seating plan, so check where you will be.

DEATH AND MOURNING

Antyeshti, the cremation sacrament, is the most important of all the rites of passage, and many Hindus near their death are taken by their relatives to Varanasi (Benares) on the sacred River Ganges, because it is said that in the holy city the cycle of rebirth is ended, and *moksha* is achieved. If not in Varanasi, it is hoped that most Hindus will die at home. A dying person is laid with the head towards the east, and a *diva* (lamp) is lit next to it. He or she will be encouraged to focus on silently repeating their *mantra*, while family members will chant, pray and read sacred texts. This would also take place in a hospital, and if the person is unconscious before death, the *mantra* will be softly chanted into the right ear, as it was at birth.

WHAT DO I DO?
❖ A sympathy card and flowers are welcome. Flowers can be sent to the funeral directors.

Before the Funeral

If a person has died at home, the lamp remains lit, incense is burned, mirrors may be covered and religious pictures turned to the wall, as a period of mourning – usually twelve to fifteen days – commences. Where possible, in preparation for washing the body, a fire is lit and a funeral priest blesses a *kumbha* (clay water pot). In the absence of a priest, the chief mourner (usually the eldest son for a male, and the youngest for a female) will perform *arati* over the body, which is then washed, anointed with sandalwood, wrapped in white cloth (the colour of purity) and adorned with flowers. Children with lighted sticks chant as they circle the body, and women offer *pindas* (sesame seed and rice balls) for the onward journey. If the body was initially taken to a funeral parlour the family will have it brought back to the house, and if this is not possible, even in a funeral parlour or before a post-mortem, the family will still arrange to perform these rites themselves.

WHAT HAPPENS IN INDIA?

◆ Within twenty-four hours of the death, the male relatives carry the body to the funeral pyre. They circle the pyre three times, anti-clockwise, before placing the body on it.

◆ As the principal mourner again circles the pyre three times with the clay pot on his shoulder, *mantras* are chanted and other relatives knock holes in the pot, releasing the water that symbolises life passing away.

◆ The mourners then turn away from the body as the chief mourner lights the all-important *agni* (consecrated fire) to release the soul. Without facing the body again, the mourners then leave.

WHAT DO I DO?

❖ There is no particular dress code for funerals, but it is usual, of course, to dress modestly.

❖ If you are invited to the crematorium, stay in the waiting area until the main funeral procession arrives and has moved ahead.

WHAT HAPPENS IN THE WEST?

◆ This ritual is almost impossible to carry out in the West, because cremations are currently only permitted at licensed crematoria, where the body must be contained in a coffin, and waiting time for a cremation can be longer than a week. Also, because of timing issues, many coffins are not released to the flames during the farewell services, but kept on conveyor belts to be burned at a later date. Hindus consider this very bad indeed for the deceased, whose soul needs to start its next journey as soon as possible, to avoid becoming a ghost – a soul without a home.

◆ Because of the limited time allowed at a crematorium, sacred rituals will usually be performed at the home of the deceased before cremation.

◆ As the coffin is carried in, feet first, to a specially prepared room, a priest or elder leads sacred chanting; if the necessary rituals are not complete, these will take place now, and will include placing a *tilak* (red mark) on the forehead of a deceased man, or a *sindhur* at the hair parting of a deceased woman.

◆ Flowers might then be scattered over the body, together with other ritual items, before a *pandit* says prayers and gives relevant readings. The family members will then place the coffin in the hearse.

- Where possible the funeral cortege will pass the temple, which in effect has to take the place of the *kumbha* ritual described above.

- When the coffin arrives, male members of the family will carry it in, followed by the women (in some cultures women don't attend) and then the other guests. There may be a photograph of the deceased near the coffin. The short service will be led by a *pandit* or Brahmin, and will include prayers, chanting and a brief eulogy on the deceased, probably given by a family member.

- The chief mourner will then push the button, either to conceal the coffin or, where possible, release it to flames, which in most instances might involve going to another area of the crematorium to ignite the cremator. If this is not possible, a block of camphor fuel may be lit in an earthenware pot to represent the fire god Agni. If they can, the immediate family will walk reverentially around the coffin.

- There will usually be a post-funeral gathering at the house of the deceased. Before entering, the guests are sprinkled with water by the chief mourner, in an act of ritual purification (which in some communities would involve showering at another house and a complete change of clothing). This will happen even if the gathering is at an external venue.

- Because of the length of time it can take for the cremation to be executed, additional rituals that would normally take place over the period of mourning now often have to be combined, and it is likely therefore that the *sapindikarana* ritual – extremely important as it is seen as the final goodbye – will take place on the same day. This involves cutting a *pinda* (dough-like substance) in half, one piece representing the deceased and the other the previous three generations. The priest carefully cuts three pieces from one half and blends them seamlessly with the other – so signifying that the deceased is now an ancestor.

◆ Refreshments will be provided, either supplied by outside caterers or brought to the house by neighbours and friends.

Afterwards

The ashes are generally collected three days later, and may be flown back to India to be scattered in the sacred River Ganges. The sooner the ashes are scattered, the better for the soul of the deceased, and water from the Ganges has been used to 'anoint' three major rivers in Britain for use as credible alternatives.

At the end of the mourning period, the house is thoroughly cleaned, and the ending of the ritual impurity means that temple visits are permitted, as is attendance at functions such as weddings.

On the anniversary of death, a male heir will perform the *shraddha* rites, offering to the ancestors. This is one of the reasons for the importance of a male heir – so that the *antyeshti* rites can be performed.

SOME USEFUL WORDS AND PHRASES

Agni consecrated fire

Agnipradakshina prayers and offerings to the god of fire

Ahamkara the identification or attachment of one's ego; the small, ego-driven, illusory self

Antyeshti cremation rites

Arati ritual of devotion and worship in which light from burning wicks is offered to one or more deities

Artha concerned with worldly success

Ashram a Hindu retreat

Atman the Supreme Self, or world soul, including *Jivatman*

Avatar (Sanskrit, 'descent') incarnations on Earth of a being from a higher spiritual realm

Bhajan Sanskrit hymn

Brahman the Supreme Being, the Absolute without form, the source of all existence, the universal spirit

Dakshina monetary donation

Darshan being in the presence of a holy person

Dharma truth, following the path of righteousness

Guru spiritual teacher

Jivatman the individual soul, one's true self, part of the Supreme Self

Karma the law of cause and effect; the belief that what you do in this life affects your subsequent lives

Mahabharata epic spiritual poem containing the *Bhagavad Gita* and the *Ramayana*

Mandap sacred canopy, under which the marriage ceremony takes place

Mandir Hindu temple

Mantra repeated prayer

Moksha liberation from the cycle of life, death and rebirth

Murti image of a deity

Namaste greeting ('I greet God in you'), said while bowing the head, with hands held together, palms and fingertips touching

Pandit scholar of sacred Hindu texts

Prasad food that has been blessed

Puja devotion

Puranas scriptures containing mythological accounts of deities

Sadhana spiritual practice

Sadhu holy man

Saguna Brahman 'The Absolute with qualities', the visible manifestations of Brahman

Samsara transmigration of souls

Samskara sacrament, or rite of passage

Sanskara the imprints left on the subconscious mind by experience in this or previous lives

Sapindakarana funeral ritual

Satsang collective prayer

Seva selfless service

Shradda rites performed on the anniversary of a death

Swami Hindu monk

Trimurti the three aspects of Brahman – Brahma, Vishnu and Mahesh (Shiva)

Upanishads philosophical texts at the end of the *Vedas*

Vedas the Sanskrit scriptures that form the foundation of Hindu belief

Yoga traditional Indian mental and physical disciplines, including meditation; one of the orthodox schools of Hindu philosophy

Chapter 6

SIKH
CEREMONIES

WHAT SIKHS BELIEVE

The Sikh religion is strictly monotheistic, believing in one Supreme Being who created the universe, who is present everywhere. Everyone is equal before God, the ultimate, eternal Guru, whose grace is available to all who set their hearts on finding the truth. Because Creation is good and life is a gift from God, Sikhs do not renounce the world. They aim to work honestly, share with others and lead a truthful life within their community. They believe in reincarnation and the law of *karma*, and that by finding God in this life – through meditation, work, charity and service to others – it is possible to break the cycle of birth and death and attain spiritual liberation. They reject empty religious ceremony and avoid pilgrimages and statues.

Sikhism was founded in the fifteenth century in the Punjab, which now straddles the border of Pakistan and north-west India. This was a time of increasing tension between Hindus and their Mughal rulers, who were seeking to convert them to Islam. Its founder, Guru Nanak, was born in 1469 to a high-caste Hindu family. From an early age he displayed a radical streak by questioning and arguing with both Hindu and Muslim religious sages, with whom he studied. It is said that at the age of thirty-one he disappeared while bathing in the river near Sultanpur. Reappearing three days later, after a mystical experience, he declared that he would follow neither Hindu nor Muslim, but only God.

Guru Nanak then embarked on an extensive period of journeying and study, during which he wrote down his spiritual insights in poetic prose, which were set

ABOVE The phrase *Ik Onkar*, 'One God', written in Punjabi Gurmukhi script.
PREVIOUS PAGE Sikh initiates leading a procession in Wolverhampton, England.

to music by his travelling companion, Mardana, a Muslim childhood friend and professional musician. Radically he wrote them in Punjabi, the language of the ordinary people, rather than Sanskrit, an exclusively scriptural language and the preserve of Brahmin priests. His new and refreshing ideas attracted various disciples, and led to the foundation of the Sikh religion. The word *sikh* means student, or disciple, and a *guru* is the spiritual teacher who leads the student from *gu* (darkness) to *ru* (light).

THE TEACHINGS OF GURU NANAK

Guru Nanak taught that there is only one God, Akal Purakh, meaning 'a timeless being that never dies' (also known as Waheguru and Satnam), to whom everyone can have direct access. This, combined with the other bedrock teachings of Sikhism – that everyone is equal regardless of race, colour, ability, religion or gender – was extremely controversial, and in complete opposition to the Hindu faith with its extensive rituals, priests, Sanskrit texts and hierarchical caste system, which he denounced.

While Guru Nanak still believed in reincarnation, he believed that spiritual progress and *mukti* (liberation) from *awagaun* (the cycle of life, death and rebirth) came through living a productive and moral life in service to God and the community. He rejected the notion that being celibate and living the ascetic life of a *sadhu* (a holy man who relies on others for food and shelter) was a quicker path.

He taught that the aim of a Sikh was to overcome his *haumai* (ego) by meditating on God's name. Far from renouncing life, this meant living among people and being an agent for change. Earth was a place to practise *dharmsal* (righteousness) and move away from being *manmukh* (self-centred) with the negative human temptations of *lobh* (greed), *kam* (lust), *karodh* (anger), *ahankar* (pride) and *moh* (attachment), towards becoming *guru-sikh* (guru-oriented). This in turn would create harmonious living with *hukam*, the Divine Will that shapes everything, while accepting that we also have free will to create our destiny both in this life and in the lives to come.

DEVELOPMENT UNDER THE TEN GURUS

Guru Nanak gathered around him a small group of disciples. This fellowship of believers grew in number until the Sikhs became a distinct community. He was succeeded by nine gurus, each chosen by his predecessor, who further evolved and developed the institutions of Sikhism. The last in the line of living Gurus, Gobind Singh, who died in 1708, transferred his activities to the Sikh community itself, and to the collection of sacred scriptures.

In 1573, Guru Arjan Dev (the fifth Guru) commenced the building of the rectangular Harmandir Sahib (Temple of God), and it was intentionally built with four entrances, facing four directions, rather than the traditional single entrance. This made a strong statement that all are welcome regardless of caste, colour, nationality, gender or religion. Resting just above the water line, it is sited in the Amrit-Sarover, a holy reservoir, where worshippers perform ritual bathing before entering the temple and religious musicians sing *shabads* (hymns) for twenty-one hours a day. In English, the Harmandir Sahib is known as the Golden Temple because of its gold-plated domes.

Situated in the holy city of Amritsar (Lake of the Holy Nectar) in the Punjab of north-west India, it is the spiritual and cultural centre

ABOVE Guru Gobind Singh (with bird) encounters Guru Nanak Dev. An eighteenth-century painting of an imaginary meeting..

of the Sikh religion. As a place of learning and worship for Sikhs, it welcomes millions of visitors annually, and following Guru Nanak's *guru ka langar* tradition (community kitchen in the name of the Guru), it feeds everyone free of charge.

After the martyrdom of Guru Arjan Dev at the hands of the Emperor Jahangir in 1606, his son Guru Hargobind Sahib (the sixth Guru), established the Akal Takhat (eternal throne), a separate building in the Golden Temple complex that was reserved for the political and military aspects of Sikhism. At his investiture, he wore two *kirpans* (swords) to symbolise *miri*, temporal authority, and *piri*, spiritual sovereignty. These interlocking swords form the outer part of the *Khanda*, the Sikh emblem, with the inner symbol being a double-edged sword (the ability of truth to cut through *maya* (illusion), encircled by a *chakar* (a weapon made from a flat metal disc) symbolising the oneness of God.

Following the execution in Delhi of Guru Tegh Bahadur (the ninth Guru) on the orders of the Emperor Aurangzeb, his son Guru Gobind Singh (the tenth Guru) created the Khalsa Panth (the collective body of initiates).

During the festival of Vaisakhi in 1699, Guru Gobind Singh called for a volunteer to give his life as a sign of devotion. Even though it appeared that the first volunteer had been killed, four more offered themselves for sacrifice. Finally, all five emerged alive, having gone through an initiation ceremony that involved drinking *amrit* (water of immortality), a mixture of water and sugar (for human kindness) that the Guru had stirred with a double-edged sword (for valour), while reciting prayers.

Known as the *panj piyare* (the five beloved ones), these were the first Amritdhari (initiates) and as *sant sipahi* (saint soldiers) they were devout followers of the Gurus' teachings. These Amritdhari Sikhs agreed to live by the *Rehat Maryada* (strict code of conduct), always to wear the five emblems collectively known as the *panj kakaar* (or the Five Ks) and to be prepared to defend themselves and fight oppression. They were given new names of Singh (lion) for men and Kaur

THE FIVE KS

Kesh: uncut hair (purity)

Kara: a steel bracelet worn on the right wrist, unless left handed (God – no beginning, no end)

Kanga: comb worn to keep hair tidy (clean body; clean mind)

Kacha: special knee-length undershorts (comfort and chastity)

Kirpan: a small ceremonial sword (soldier/saint)

(princess) for women. Although a turban is not part of the Khalsa (pure path) requirement, a male Sikh is required to wear one in public as a sign of devotion to God. Thus for Amritdhari Sikhs the Five Ks became a core part of their lives.

All Sikhs are encouraged to undertake the Amrit Sanskar ceremony, which initiates them into the Khalsa brotherhood.

Non-Khalsa Sikhs who keep their hair uncut and don't wear the Five Ks are known as Kesdhari; those who cut their hair and may be on their way to becoming a Khalsa Sikh are called Sahajdhari (which means 'slow adopter' of the Khalsa).

SACRED WRITINGS

The Sikh holy book is the Siri Guru Granth Sahib, also called the Granth Sahib, which

ABOVE Kanga, Kara and Kirpan – three of the five articles of faith.

contains the spiritual poetry of the historical gurus. The first version of the Granth Sahib, known as the Adi Granth (first book), was compiled by Guru Arjan Dev, the fifth Guru. He brought together the *bani* (sacred writings) of the first four Gurus together with those of various Hindu and Muslim saints and his own inspired *bani* in a single volume. The Adi Granth was installed when the Golden Temple was completed in 1601.

The final version, embodying the authority and spiritual knowledge of all ten Sikh Gurus, together with significant contributions from other devotional writers, was prepared by the last Guru, Guru Gobind Singh, who after an unbroken line of two hundred and thirty-nine years, declared that there would be no more human Gurus, and that guruship would pass to the sacred text, becoming respectfully known as the Siri Guru Granth Sahib (Sahib means Lord).

Written in Gurmukhi, a special form of Punjabi script meaning 'from the mouth of the Guru', it has 1,430 pages, is organised into thirty-one sections, and is the core inspiration for the practical and spiritual life of every

ABOVE Siri Guru Granth Sahib, the sacred book of Sikhism.

ABOVE Frontispiece of a Dasam Granth maunuscript, dating from the early nineteenth century.

Sikh. A second scriptural book, the Dasam Granth, was written by the tenth Guru, Gobind Singh, and apart from containing his autobiography has a number of popular *shabads* (hymns) that are sung on certain festival days.

BRANCHES OF SIKHISM
The Udhasi
One of the oldest sects, the ascetic Udhasi, was founded by Guru Nanak's eldest son, Siri Chand. Being more aligned with the *sadhu* (renunciate/holy man) tradition, and focused on the path of non-attachment, it separated from mainstream Sikhism after his death and continued as a separate spiritual tradition.

The Namdhari
The Namdharis, while fully accepting the Sikh scriptures, believe in the continuity of living gurus. They believe that the tenth Guru, Gobind Singh, did not die in 1708 but lived on under a different name and bestowed the succession on Balak Singh in 1812. His

disciple Ram Singh founded the Sant-Khalsa (Saintly Khalsa), which became a powerful socio-political force in the Punjab. Namdhari Sikhs wear a *sidhi-pagri* (flat white turban), white clothing, are strict vegetarians, and tend to arrange marriages within their own sect.

The Neeldhari

Guru Balak Singh also gave rise to a sect that emphasized meditation through a particular form of breathing. Founded by his nephew, Kahn Singh, the Neeldharis acknowledge only Baba Balak Singh's spiritual authority, and not that of Baba Ram Singh, and are distinguishable by their free-flowing blue turbans.

The Nirankari

The Nirankari movement was founded by Baba Dyal Singh (died 1855), a Sahajdhari (clean-shaven) Sikh, in reaction to the rituals and superstitions he believed were polluting the original teachings of Guru Nanak. He promoted a return to the worship of God as 'the formless one' and the purification of Sikh practice.

The Sanatan

A splinter group to emerge from classical Sikhism were the Sanatan Sikhs, who accept aspects of Hindu and Muslim teachings. Their particular pluralistic perspective is not accepted by mainstream Sikhs.

The Radhasoami Satsang

This faith is a synthesis of Sikh and Hindu traditions. Founded by Shiv Dayal Singh in 1861, its current spiritual leader, Gurinder Singh Dhillon, has attracted interest in the West. He has established two hospitals. One is based at the Beas Ashram and gives free treatment, and the other is the Majarah Sawan Singh Charitable Hospital, a thirty-five-acre complex near the Dera at Beas. Here international doctors spend a few weeks annually, giving their services free.

The 3H Organisation

One of the newest movements is the 3H Organisation (standing for Happy, Holy and Healthy), also known as the Sikh Dharma Brotherhood, which evolved in North America in the 1970s. It consists mainly of initiated Western Sikhs who wear white clothing, and strictly follow the Khalsa code.

PLACE OF WORSHIP

Wherever there is a Sikh community there is a *gurdwara* (literally, the doorway to the Guru), distinguishable by the *nishan sahib*, the orange/saffron-coloured flag displaying the Khanda emblem (except the Namdhari Sikhs, who don't display the flag). The Golden Temple in Amritsar is the largest, and one of five historical *gurdwaras* that today are controlled and managed in the Punjab by an elected central body, the Shiromani Gurdwara Parbankhak Committee.

Other *gurdwaras* can be purpose built, a converted house, or just a room dedicated for such use. It depends on the size of the community, who all contribute to the creation and upkeep of their *gurdwara* through the

ABOVE The Harmandir Sahib, known as the Golden Temple, in the holy reservoir of Amritsar.

appointment of a management committee. It was Guru Nanak who introduced the ideal of *vand chakna* – sharing what you earn with others – and the fifth Guru introduced *daswandth*, a one-tenth-of-income contribution to the Sikh community (now given as a voluntary sum). Apart from being a place of worship, the *gurdwara* is a centre for social activities, which include classes for children to learn Punjabi, and where important issues are discussed. Central to every *gurdwara* is the Siri Guru Granth Sahib, and some devout Sikhs also keep a copy at their homes in a special room dedicated to daily family reverence and *satsang* (a gathering of devotees for inspirational worship and meditation).

Based on the ethics of sharing, community and inclusiveness, the *langar* (free kitchen) is an integral part of every place of worship, where donated food is cooked by *sewadars* (volunteers). Preparing food for the *sangat* (congregation) is an act of devotion known as *sewa*, or *seva*, meaning selfless service, and is a core value and commitment for Sikhs, who are renowned for their hospitality and generosity. Preparing and cooking the food is very much part of the service, and devotional songs are often sung to create a sacred atmosphere.

The key people at a *gurdwara* are the *granthi* and the *giani*. The *granthi*, apart from ceremonial reading of the holy book, arranges daily religious services, as well as taking care of the overall smooth running of the *gurdwara*. As a Sikh's relationship is directly with God, and inspired by the wisdom contained within the Siri Guru Granth Sahib, there are no priests. However, the *giani*, a person who is well versed in the Sikh religion, will usually lead a service. These days, the *granthi* and the *giani* are often the same person.

INSIDE A *GURDWARA*

A typical *gurdwara* contains a Diwan Hall (the main hall and worship area), a room where the Siri Guru Granth Sahib is placed at night, a *langar* and eating area, a shoe room and a schoolroom/community meeting room.

At the front of the hall will be an area covered with a *palki* (canopy), which in larger *gurdwaras* may be very ornate and colourful. This contains the Siri Guru Granth Sahib, which rests on large cushions placed on a low table known as the *manji sahib*. The *giani*, or person delegated by him, sits next to the *manji sahib* and throughout the service waves a *chaur* (a whisk-like feather fan) over the book to signify its sovereignty.

To one side of the *palki* will be a ritually prepared, covered bowl of thick, sweet paste made from wheat flour, sugar and water. Once it has been infused with recitations from the holy book, and a Khalsa member has inserted his *kirpan* blade into the mixture several times during the *Ardas*, the special opening and closing

ABOVE The interior of Singh Saba, a *gurdwara* in Poland.

prayer, it is known as *karah prashad* (blessed food). There is also a portion of food from the *langar*, which, once blessed, will be added to the community meal.

In larger *gurdwaras* there may be presentation screens displaying the words that the *giani* is reciting, and it is likely that these will include an English translation. As *shabad-kirtan* (hymn singing) is a key part of Sikh worship, *ragis* (religious musicians) will face the *sangat* to play the harmonium and *tabla* (small drums).

SERVICES

Each day there is a short ritual (*prakash*), when the holy book, the Siri Guru Granth Sahib, is opened for the day. A similar ceremony (*sukhasan*) takes place before it is removed or formally closed at the end of the day.

Worship consists mainly of singing passages from the Siri Guru Granth Sahib. There are various daily prayers, the general format being similar to that of Sunday, the main day of worship, when a service lasts approximately three hours, from around 11:00 a.m. to 1:00 p.m.

The main service is held in the Diwan Hall, and although it is not a religious requirement, men and women may be seated separately. As the service is very much a community occasion, people tend to come and go at different times and usually kneel and bow each time towards the holy book. They might also greet each other respectfully and quietly share a few words before settling to worship.

ABOVE The *giani* reading from the Granth Sahib.

WHAT HAPPENS?

◆ On entering, Sikhs walk to the Siri Guru Granth Sahib and, generally with their right hand, place a donation of money in the container provided, or perhaps a gift of food or cloth to the side. They then perform *matha taykna*, kneeling and touching their foreheads to the floor towards the holy book, in honour of the wisdom it contains. They never turn their back on the holy scriptures.

◆ The service opens with the *giani* singing Guru Nanak's hymn, the '*Asa-di-Var*'. Everyone then stands with folded hands (palm to palm) to sing a special verse, before the first *Ardas* prayer is recited. Another short verse is sung before the Sikh salutation '*Waheguru ji ka Khalsa, Wahe guru ji ki Fateh*' ('The Khalsa belongs to God, Victory is gifted by God') is recited. With the congregation seated again, there will be more readings. Towards the end of the service everyone stands for the second, closing *Ardas* prayer. Following the *Ardas* the *giani* covers the Siri Guru Granth Sahib in a fine coloured cloth, known as a *ramalla*, before he opens the holy book at random and recites the first hymn on the left-hand page. This is known as '*Hukamnama*' (Divine Will), and provides a daily contemplation.

◆ Everyone is then given a portion of *karah prashad*, which is accepted in cupped hands to symbolise taking the sweet blessing into the heart. You might notice that some people have a piece put into a small plastic bag, as well as receiving their portion. This is to be given to family members who could not attend the  *gurdwara*. This marks the end of the formal service, though the musicians will often continue to play.

WHAT DO I DO?

❖ If you are invited to the *gurdwara*, wear comfortable, modest clothing to cover your arms, legs and chest, and keep your head covered at all times.

❖ Sikh men generally wear turbans, but some younger men cover their heads with a *patka*, a piece of cloth tied at the back of the neck. Younger boys have their hair wrapped and covered in a knot, and women cover their heads with a *chunni*, the scarf from their clothing. As a male visitor you would be offered a *patka*, but women require a stole or scarf, which can also be obtained from the *gurdwara*.

❖ Initial entry will be to the communal hall area. Shoes are not worn in the presence of the holy scriptures, so you remove your shoes here and leave them in the designated place. If you think your feet might get cold, you can wear socks. This is also a good idea if you are not used to sitting cross-legged on the floor, as they can help to cushion the sides of your feet.

❖ As a visitor, you are not required to give a donation when you arrive, or perform *matha taykna*, but if you wish to offer a donation before you leave, £1 is an acceptable amount.

❖ You will either be shown where to sit, or it will be obvious. If you feel unable to sit on the floor for up to two hours, sit near the back of the hall, so that you can slip out if you need to. Some larger *gurdwaras* have a few drop-down chairs attached to the wall.

❖ Cameras and videos are not allowed; also ensure that your cell phone is switched off.

❖ You are likely to hear the traditional Sikh greeting, '*Sat Sri Akal*', meaning 'God is true and timeless'. As in the Hindu tradition, people often greet each other with hands held at chest level in the *namaste* position (with palms and fingertips touching), and a bow of the head.

❖ It is very important to remember that it is discourteous to point your feet towards the holy book, or, as you walk out, just to turn your back. It is appropriate to bow slightly first and take a few steps backwards before turning to leave the room.

❖ During the service, take your lead from your neighbours as to when to stand or sit.

❖ The *prashad* is eaten with the right hand, and, as it is very greasy, it is a good idea to have a tissue or wet wipe with you.

❖ It is customary to stay for the free community meal, which is strictly vegetarian and contains no eggs. This has been prepared by devotees, who either recite *gurbani* (sacred text) while preparing it, or have been listening to the transmitted service. You may now put your shoes on again, but remember to keep your head covered at all times.

❖ The food might be either served to you in moulded, portioned trays as you line up, or placed in front of you once you are seated in *pangat* (rows) at tables or, more traditionally, cross-legged on the floor.

❖ Food is generally eaten with the fingers, but a spoon is likely to be provided for you to scoop the curry or *dhal* into a *roti*, a flat, doughy bread that is a good fork substitute. Although it can seem a bit tricky at the start, you will soon get used to it – just watch others. Unless they are left-handed most people will use their right hand to eat the food, although there are no strict rules regarding this.

❖ When you have finished your food, take your tray to the designated washing-up area.

FESTIVALS AND HOLY DAYS

THE SIKH CALENDAR

Since 13 March 1998, Sikhs have used a specially designed solar calendar, the *Nanakshahi*, named after Guru Nanak, to determine the dates of the majority of their festivals. The exception is Guru Nanak's birthday, which follows the Hindu lunar calendar and falls in the month of Katik at *Poornamashi* (full moon). The dates of those Sikh festivals that are celebrated at the same time as Hindu events – such as Diwali and Hola Mohalla – continue to be set by the Hindu Vikrami calendar. As the Sikh calendar is less variable, it links more easily with the Gregorian Western calendar, and both are shown.

THE SIKH YEAR

The names of the months of the year in Punjabi are as follows, with their starting dates.

Month	Begins on	Falls in
Chet	14 March	March–April
Vaisakh	14 April	April–May
Jeth	15 May	May–June
Harh	15 June	June–July
Sawan	16 July	July–August
Bhadon	16 August	August–September
Asu	15 September	September–October
Katik	15 October	October–November
Maghar	14 November	November–December
Poh	14 December	December–January
Magh	13 January	January–February
Phagan	12 February	February–March

Sangrand, when the sun enters a new zodiac sign each month, is marked in the *gurdwaras* with the hymn of '*Bara Maha*' (the hymn of twelve months). Written by the gurus, it consists of calendar poems that speak of the mood of that month for devotees to reflect on.

Festivals are occasions for Sikhs to rededicate themselves to the faith. Essentially there are four key *gurpurbs*, or Gurus' remembrance days, and three *melas*, or fairs – Holi, Vaisakhi and Diwali.

The *gurpurb* ceremonies are very similar, but there are different hymns and readings specific to each occasion. In the Punjab the celebrations can last for three days, but in the West they usually start at sunrise and span a period of forty-eight hours, starting with Akhand Path (continual readings from the holy book), the singing of '*Asa-di-var*' (Guru Nanak's hymn) and general devotions.

In large Sikh communities there is likely to be a parade, in which the Siri Guru Granth Sahib is carried through the streets under an ornate canopy to the

ABOVE Festival parade of the *panj piyare* on Hola Mahalla.

accompaniment of music, hymns and sacred chants. The procession is proudly headed by five Sikhs dressed in *kurta* or *shola* (traditional uniform) and representing the *panj piyare*, the beloved five – the five Sikhs originally initiated by Gobind Singh in 1699 – while teams of *gatka* (weapons-based martial arts) display their skills of swordsmanship. *Sharbat*, traditionally a mix of chilled milk, sugar and water but now usually orange juice, is offered to those watching, and traditional *langar* is served continuously at the *gurdwara*, which will be beautifully decorated and lit, as will Sikh homes.

Around sunset, a special devotional night program that includes singing, poetry, lectures and readings takes place, continuing until the early hours of the morning. Where there is no *gurdwara*, this will happen in Sikh homes.

HOLA MAHALLA, OR HOLA MOHALLA (March–April)

This festival, usually just called Hola (masculine of Holi), takes place in the month of Chet on the day after the Hindu festival of Holi. However, it has a different

ABOVE Demonstration of the martial art of *gatke* at the head of a procession in Bedford, England.

significance for Sikhs. It was established by Guru Gobind Singh at a time when Sikhs were subjected to increasing aggression from Mughal rulers, and is therefore an occasion where Sikhs display their military prowess (*hola mahalla* means 'mock fight'). At Anandpur Sahib, in the Punjab, it is a three-day festival that includes military-style processions with war drums and standard bearers, mock battles, exhibitions, martial art displays and bareback horse riding, together with devotional songs, religious readings, music and poetry competitions. *Langar*, free food, is provided for everyone. In the West, this will be equally spectacular but is likely to be condensed into one day, with *gurdwara* communities parading through town centres carrying their *nishan sahibs* (Sikh flags).

VAISAKHI, OR BAISAKHI (April–May)

This important festival falls on 13 or 14 Vaisakh, and in the Punjab is the Sikh New Year. Traditionally it was associated with the wheat harvest. It has particular significance as the time that the tenth Guru, Gobind Singh, created the Khalsa Panth with the *panj piyare*, and is when the Amrit Sanskar ceremony is held for those Sikhs who are offering themselves for initiation. It is during this festival that the cover of the *nishan sahib* (Sikh flag) is ritually replaced, and *gurdwaras* elect new presidents and management committees.

Akhand Path (continuous reading of the Guru Granth Sahib for forty-eight hours) commences two days earlier and is completed on the morning of Vaisakhi. This is followed by hymn singing and sermons, and is the occasion for *amrit* ceremonies. There are competitions involving sports and martial

poetry and essay writing on the festival theme. All generations take part in *sewa* (selfless service to others) in *langar*, which continues over three days.

MARTYRDOM OF GURU ARJAN DEV (June–July)

This *gurpurb*, on 16 Harh, commemorates the fifth Guru, who was tortured and put to death for his faith by the Mughal Emperor Jahangir in 1606.

BIRTH OF GURU NANAK (October–November)

This *gurpurb*, at the first full moon in the month of Katik, celebrates the birth of the founder of Sikhism.

DIWALI, OR BANDI CHHORH DIVAS (October–November)

The Hindu Festival of Lights, in the month of Kartik, has a different significance for Sikhs as it coincides with Bandi Chhorh Divas (Prisoners' Release Day). The

ABOVE *Langar* being served during Vaisakhi in the Keshgarh Sahib *gurdwara* in Anandpur Sahib, the second holiest Sikh city.

sixth guru, Hargobind Sahib, had been imprisoned by the Emperor Jahangir; this day marks his triumphant return from prison, together with fifty-two Hindu princes, whose release he had also cleverly obtained. To honour his return to Amritsar, the Golden Temple was lit with hundreds of lamps and today *gurdwaras*, homes and businesses are brightly decorated with candles and rows of lights. There are also street processions, mainly in the Punjab. Evening services with special hymns and prayers last between two and three hours, after which delicious *mateyia* (sweets) are shared and firework displays light up the skies.

Diwali is also the occasion when Sikhs say special prayers at the *gurdwara* to commemorate the martyrdom of Bhai Mani Singh, a scholar and transcriber of the final version of the Siri Guru Granth Sahib. Having uncovered a Muslim plan to slaughter the Sarbat Khalsa, the powerful collective body representing and making policy decisions for all Sikhs, who were due to gather for their twice-yearly meeting (Diwali and Vaisakhi), he sent a successful message of warning, but paid with his life.

MARTYRDOM OF TEGH BAHADUR (November–December)
This *gurpurb*, on 24 Maghar, commemorates the martyrdom of the ninth Guru, who was tortured and beheaded at the hands of the Mughal Emperor Aurangzeb in 1675.

BIRTH OF GURU GOBIND SINGH (December–January)
This *gurpurb*, on 5 Poh, celebrates the birth of the tenth and last Guru.

RITUALS AND CEREMONIES

BIRTH

As life is considered a sacred gift from God, the birth of a child is eagerly awaited. Traditionally it is hoped that the firstborn will be a boy, so that he can eventually perform the funeral rites for his parents. The birth of a son is the occasion of much celebration, and when the baby boy is five weeks old the ceremony of *chhati* is held. This takes the form of a feast, hosted by the father's family, during which gifts are given.

In the West, congratulations cards are always welcome, whether for a boy or for a girl.

Although some Sikhs observe a forty-day impurity period, as it is believed that during this time the mother is susceptible to evil spirits, this is not a religious requirement, and generally, as soon as the mother is

ABOVE *Hukamnama*, taking a verse at random from the Siri Guru Granth Sahib. This is seen as the order of God for that particular day.

able, the family and relatives will visit the *gurdwara* either taking *karah prashad* with them or having it made there. Hymns are then recited in the presence of the Siri Guru Granth Sahib, before the holy *hukamnama* (a random selection from the holy book) is taken. The name of the child will then be created by using the first letter of the hymn at the top of the left-hand page. Following the *hukamnama*, a special prayer is recited, the *Ardas* is said, and *karah prashad* is distributed in the usual way.

Once a name has been decided on, it is then announced to the *sangat*, usually a week later at the Sunday service. A boy's name will include Singh and a girl's Kaur. Sikhs do not perform circumcisions as they are considered to be mutilation of the body, as is any form of body piercing.

Some devout Sikhs ensure that their newborn baby receives *amrit*, the water and sugar mixture that is stirred while the *granthi* recites 'Japji Sahib', the first five verses of the morning prayer. Using a *kirpan*, the *granthi* gently places some of the *amrit* in the baby's mouth. This is the first part of initiation into the Khalsa, and full initiation will take place later, at varying ages.

COMING OF AGE

Essentially boys start to wear a turban at around the age of eleven or twelve, and to mark this the family may arrange a turban-tying ceremony. This will usually take place at the *gurdwara*, where after the *Ardas* the *granthi* will tie the *pagri* (turban, which is five yards long) while the *sangat* recites a special chant of joy and approval. The family make generous donations to the *gurdwara*, and the boy is given gifts.

MARRIAGE

The family is the foundation of Sikh society, and the wedding ceremony, *Anand Karaj* (blissful event, or occasion), is seen as uniting two souls into one, and is a partnership of equals. In the West today, many young Sikhs find their own partners through their community or workplace, and tend not to marry as soon as their education has finished. However, traditionally and still in many families, it is the parents who find suitable partners for their children, either through family connections or using the services of a *bichola* (matchmaker). Once the appropriate inquiries and matching are complete, the couple will meet and add their approval. Again in more traditional families, this might not happen, and the couple might not meet until the wedding ceremony.

The Engagement Ceremony

When the match is agreed, a date for the wedding ceremony is fixed. From the purely religious point of view there are no inauspicious days. Invitations will be prepared and distributed by both sets of parents, and a *Kurmai* (engagement) ceremony is held in which male relatives of the bride visit the groom and his family to present gifts of Indian sweets and fruit. If this is held at the *gurdwara*, after *Ardas*, a special *Kurmai shabad* will be sung from the holy book and a *hukamnama* is read. A *joli*, a pink scarf created into a container shape, will then be placed in the groom's lap ready to receive seven handfuls of fruit from the bride's father, who then places a *chhuara* (date) into the young man's mouth to confirm acceptance by everyone of the forthcoming marriage. In return the groom's family send gifts of *chunnis* (long scarves) and sweets to the bride's family.

Before the Wedding
Mayian

Mayian is a joyful occasion that takes place in the respective homes of the bride and the groom, generally two days before the wedding ceremony. Family and friends gather together and the bride or groom sits on a wooden stool. Four female relatives will hold a red cloth over his or her head, while a paste containing turmeric is rubbed into

face, arms, legs and any other accessible areas of the body. It can be a messy ritual, which is said to purify the skin and make it look smoother, but everyone has great fun as traditional songs are sung, food is prepared and the women are given gifts of specially prepared Punjabi sweets.

Chura

Chura is the occasion on the day before the wedding when the bride's maternal uncle visits with gifts of clothes and red bridal bangles that have been dipped in milk as a sign of her purity. He places the bangles on his niece's wrists as the women sing traditional songs. Later the women will gather for what is essentially a Sikh 'hen night', during which there is lots of singing, dancing and food, and applying of the *mehendi* (henna paste) to the bride's hands and feet in a beautiful and elaborate pattern. Other members of the wedding party will also have this applied to their hands, but the bride's will be the most intricate. These 'rituals' are essentially cultural, and are not given importance in the *Rehat Maryada*, the Sikh code of conduct. Sikhism is usually simple rather than ostentatious.

Milni

There are two *Milni* ceremonies. The first, on the morning of the wedding day, is the ritual meeting of the heads of both families. This takes place at the *janigarh* (wedding hall) or the *gurdwara*, and the *baraat* (party of the groom's relatives) is greeted with hymns of welcome. After the reciting of *Ardas* by the *granthi*, immediate male family members on each side exchange gifts of turbans, cash and garlands of flowers with their counterparts, and then everyone enjoys a Punjabi breakfast of tea and savoury snacks, such as *samosas* and *bhajis*, before the wedding ceremony. The second *Milni* takes place the next day.

The Wedding Ceremony

The ceremony will take place in the Diwan Hall of the *gurdwara*. The points to remember are essentially the same as for attending any *gurdwara* service.

WHAT DO I DO?

❖ Even though you will want to look particularly smart, and you will be surrounded by vibrant colours, clothing should be modest, covering upper arms, chest area and upper legs. It should also be comfortable, as you will almost certainly be sitting cross-legged on the floor, or with your legs to one side – never point your feet towards the holy book. Your head must be covered while you are in the *gurdwara* and the surrounding area.

❖ Remember to turn your cell phone off before entering the building.

❖ Shoes are removed before entering the Diwan Hall.

❖ Men and women will generally be seated separately, although non-Sikh visitors may usually stay together.

WHAT HAPPENS?

◆ Guests, friends and family take their places in the Diwan Hall while *ragis* (musicians) play and sing *kirtan* (devotional songs).

◆ Once everyone is settled the groom will enter with his parents, and make donations of money and new cloth for the Siri Guru Granth Sahib. His wedding attire is likely to be cream or white and will be a form of *salwaar kameez* (pyjama-like trousers covered by a long, loose tunic) with a *dupatta*, a long, rectangular scarf, which might be saffron like the Sikh flag, placed around his neck. In some cases, before leaving the house his sister might have adorned his turban with a *kalgi* (draped beads with a central decoration), but again this is cultural and not religious, and must be removed before his bride joins him. If he is Khalsa (Amritdahri Sikh) he will be carrying a large ceremonial sword.

◆ The bride will be richly dressed, typically in red, and adorned with her wedding bangles (which may have *karliras*, small golden ornaments hanging from them), a necklace, earrings and in some cases a *mangal tika* or *tika* (a small pendant on a tiny chain secured in the hair parting and resting on the forehead). Carrying flowers, she will be escorted by members of her family to a special hymn, and will sit to the left of the groom in front of the Siri Guru Granth Sahib.

◆ While any Sikh officiate can conduct the ceremony, it is usually led by the *granthi*, who will ask the couple and their parents to stand for a brief opening *Ardas*. A *hukamnama* specifically for the couple will then be selected and recorded, before a short hymn is sung and the officiate delivers his sermon, in which he outlines the duties and responsibilities of married life. Their acceptance of this is shown by bowing before the holy book, after which they stand.

◆ In a moving ritual known as *palla pharana* (scarf joining), the bride's father takes one end of the groom's *dupatta* and gives it to his daughter, and his future son-in-law holds the other end; this signifies that the father is transferring his daughter's care to her future husband.

◆ Then, as they sit, they listen to the reading by the *granthi* of the first of the four stanzas of the *Lavan* wedding hymn. This hymn, which is the core religious element of the ceremony, was composed by the fourth Guru, Ram Das, and outlines the sacred nature of marriage and the formula for its success.

◆ Then *ragis* sing the same stanza while the couple rise and bow before the holy book and the groom leads his bride in a clockwise circumambulation around the Siri Guru Granth Sahib. These are the first steps that the couple take together, and must be timed to finish when the *ragis* finish singing the

stanza, at which point they sit down and again bow in reverence.

◆ This is repeated a further three times for the remaining three stanzas, and in an act of supporting her leaving their family for another, the bride's immediate family, particularly her brothers, might help her complete the rounds.

◆ When the *Lavan* is completed, the *granthi* declares them to be married and if, as is increasingly the custom, they are to have wedding rings, these may now be exchanged at this point. The ceremony is concluded by the singing of the hymn '*Anand Sahib*', part of the *nitnem* (daily prayers) that all Sikhs say three times a day, followed by everyone standing for the closing *Ardas*, and hearing the randomly selected *hukamnama* and receiving *karah prashad*.

◆ Everyone will then leave to attend the reception.

The Wedding Banquet

The reception will usually be held at a community centre or hotel. It is very unlikely that it will be at the *gurdwara*, because there will be strict rules prohibiting smoking, alcohol and meat. Occasionally, the ceremony might be held at home, but then the same will apply because you will still be in the presence of the Siri Guru Granth Sahib. While the groom and family members might change, the bride will remain in her wedding attire all day.

WHAT HAPPENS?

◆ Presents are given and the celebration starts with the bride and groom cutting the wedding cake and then leading the first dance. Before the main course of the banquet is served, the couple will eat a few mouthfuls first – but not the whole meal! During the evening there will be a great deal of singing and dancing, and the bride's sisters might be given rings by the groom as an acknowledgement of the family connection.

◆ Traditionally at the end of the celebrations the bride would be transported to the groom's house in a *doli*, a palanquin or covered litter carried by four bearers. This ritual symbolised the change in status of the bride from daughter to daughter-in-law. Today it is likely that a decorated car will take the couple to the bride's former home, where she will say goodbye to her family and sprinkle rice in four corners of the room as a blessing, and then on to the groom's house, where she will be ceremoniously greeted by his family and given gifts of money or jewellery (Sikhism does not condone the giving or receiving of dowries). The next day, the couple will return to the bride's family for tea, and then may depart on a honeymoon.

◆ Apart from the actual ceremony itself, there are wide cultural variations in what happens before and after it, so this description is only a general guide. Whatever happens, you are sure to enjoy the experience.

DEATH AND MOURNING

Death is regarded as a transition from one state to another, where the physical body dies but the soul lives on. Like Hindus, Sikhs are cremated as soon after death as possible. As an act of purification, the body will be ritually washed in a ceremony called *antam-ishnan* before being taken by the immediate male relatives for cremation.

WHAT HAPPENS?

❖ In India, the body will be carried by male relatives on a wooden bier in a ritual known as *modha-dena*, and after the *granthi* recites *Ardas* for the soul of the deceased, the chief mourner, the eldest son, will perform *agni-bhaint* by lighting the funeral pyre.

❖ However, in the West, the body may be taken to a funeral parlour where facilities are often available for the ritual washing of the body, after which it might be returned home or taken to the *gurdwara* for people to pay their respects.

❖ The coffin will then be closed and taken by hearse to the crematorium where it will be carried into the chapel by male relatives and followed by mourners, including women but not children. A special prayer, the '*Kirtan Solah*', usually a night-time prayer said before sleep, will be recited to signify the final sleep.

❖ As in the Hindu tradition, it is imperative that the body is given to Agni, the sacred fire, so that the soul can be released, and in the absence of a funeral pyre the eldest son needs to push the coffin into the cremator – which might be located in a different area of the crematorium – or at least press the button. (Women are never involved in this aspect of the funeral.) However, if even this is not possible, at the end of the chapel service, the son will press the button to close the curtains that conceal the coffin from mourners.

WHAT DO I DO?

❖ As a guest you would wear subdued colours, but many Sikh mourners will wear white, the symbol of purity. Flowers and sympathy cards are both acceptable. After the cremation, the funeral party will return to the *gurdwara* for a service that follows the previously outlined format, followed by *langar*.

Ashes are generally collected three days later, and may be flown back to India to be scattered in the sacred River Ganges. Often this will be at Haridwar, where records of previous generations are kept according to the region of ancestral origin, and the most recent death can be recorded. Alternatively, they might be scattered in the River Sutlej at the *gurdwara* of Kirtapur Sahib in the Punjab. In Britain, water from the Ganges has been used to 'anoint' three major rivers for use as credible alternatives.

The period of mourning has cultural variations, but is generally between ten and thirteen days, during which, unlike in Hinduism, the family is not considered impure. From the time of death until cremation, the Siri Guru Granth Sahib should be recited in full, and if this is not possible, the recitation continues afterwards until it is complete.

In some cultures, after a thirteen-day mourning period, a large feast will be held for relatives and community members, during which there will be a turban ceremony, in which a new turban is presented to the eldest son to signify the transfer of paternal authority. As his father before him, he now becomes the head of the household.

A widow is permitted to discard her long white *chunni* (scarf) of widowhood after the thirteen days' mourning, and having been ritually bathed by female relatives is able to return to bright clothing, if she chooses.

The anniversary of a death is remembered and mentioned during the regular Sunday service.

SOME USEFUL WORDS AND PHRASES

Adi Granth the first version of the Siri Guru Granth Sahib

Agni sacred fire

Amrit water of immortality, a mixture of water and sugar stirred with a double-edged sword

Amrit Sanskar ceremony that initates a person into the Khalsa brotherhood

Anand Karaj ('happy event'), wedding ceremony

Ardas prayer of supplication, pleading for blessings and support

Awagaun cycle of life, death and rebirth

Dharmsal righteousness

Diwan Hall the main hall and worship area of a *gurdwara*

Giani a Sikh religious scholar who leads the service in the *gurdwara*

Granthi the official in charge of managing the *gurdwara*. He is not an ordained priest and has no special rights or status

Gurbani sacred text; short extracts from the writings of the Gurus

Gurdwara Sikh temple

Gurpurb Gurus' remembrance days

Guru spiritual teacher or leader

Haumai ego

Hukam divine will, or command

Hukamnama hymn randomly selected and taken as God's will or command for the day

Karah prashad blessed food

Karma the belief that what you do in this life affects your subsequent lives. It is possible to modify your *karma* with the grace of the Guru or God

Kirpan sword

Kurmai engagement ceremony

Langar community kitchen, meal

Manmukh self-centred

Matha taykna kneeling and touching the forehead to the floor, honouring the wisdom in the holy book

Mehendi the tradition of decorating the skin, especially the hands ,with intricate patterns using henna paste

Mela fair

Milni ritual meeting of heads of the two families before a marriage

Mukti liberation from the cycle of llife, death and rebirth

Nishan sahib Sikh flag

Nitnem prayers, said three times a day

Panj kakaar the five emblems (the Five Ks: kesh, kara, kanga, kacha, kirpan) worn by Sikhs

Panj piyare five beloved ones, the first Sikh initiates

Prakash ritual in the *gurdwara* of opening the holy book for the day

Ragi musician who plays and/or sings devotional songs

Rehat Maryada Sikhs' strict code of conduct

Sangat congregation

Satsang gathering of devotees for inspirational worship and meditation

Shabad devotional song, hymn

Sikh student or disciple

Siri Guru Granth Sahib the Sikhs' holy book

Sukhasan ritual in the *gurdwara* of closing the holy book for the day

GREETINGS

'Sat Sri Akal' 'God is true and timeless'. The Sikh greeting, accompanied by the *namaste* gesture (palms and fingertips touching, and a bow of the head)

Chapter 7

BUDDHIST
CEREMONIES

WHAT BUDDHISTS BELIEVE

Buddhism is more of a philosophy and a way of life than a faith, as Buddhists do not believe in a creator God. Individuals take responsibility for their thoughts, words and actions so as to be more content with their own lives, to help others and generally to live more effectively. The goal of the Buddhist is the attainment of *nibbana*, or *nirvana*, a state beyond all confusion and suffering. Buddhist practice is said to create joy, happiness, spontaneity, loving-kindness (*metta*), generosity, compassion and wisdom.

Much emphasis is placed on various forms of meditation, the most basic of which use the breath to help focus the mind, with the belief that regular practice, combined with study of the Buddha's teachings, leads to the cessation of suffering and, ultimately, enlightenment.

Prince Siddhartha Gautama, who later became the Buddha, was born in around 563 CE into a wealthy royal family of the Shakya clan in north-eastern India. Growing up, he lived a privileged, sheltered existence, protected from the harsh realities of life. In part this was the result of a deliberate decision by his father, the king. Soon after Siddhartha's birth a holy man saw the infant and prophesied that he would either become a great *chakravartin* ('wheel-turning king') or a great spiritual leader; being of the warrior caste, his father wanted him to

ABOVE Monumental seated Buddha from the thirteenth century at Kamakura, Japan.
PREVIOUS PAGE Buddhist monks meditating on Vulture Peak, Rajgir, India.

WHAT BUDDHISTS BELIEVE

be the former. To prevent his son from discovering suffering and the impermanence of life (*anicca*), the king arranged for him always to be cloistered in palaces, surrounded only by pleasure and beauty. However, having an enquiring mind and natural curiosity, Siddhartha felt imprisoned. With the help of a trusted servant he made four secret trips to the outside world, and for the first time encountered old age, sickness and death, which, his servant assured him, happened to everyone. He also encountered a poor but radiantly peaceful *sadhu*, or wandering holy man.

Shaken by his experiences, he left his wife and child and at the age of twenty-nine embarked upon a spiritual quest for the solution to the problem of suffering and mortality. He spent the next six years learning the ways of the holy men, fasting and living a life of such extreme asceticism that it took him to the brink of death. Only at that moment did he realise that this path would not give him the answers he sought, and he discovered the 'Middle Way', between the extremes of self-mortification and self-indulgence. Abandoning his

THE FOUR NOBLE TRUTHS

Dukkha (the suffering nature of experience)

The truth that birth, ageing, illness, despair, desire, anger, worry, failure, the impermanence of pleasure and fear of death cause suffering.

Samudaya (the origin of suffering)

The truth that suffering is caused by the constant *tanha* (craving) for life to be different in some way, for sensual pleasures and the wish to avoid unpleasant things.

Nirodha (the cessation of suffering)

The truth that freedom from suffering is possible through the removal of desire, hatred and ignorance.

Marga (the path to release)

The truth of the way to achieve freedom from suffering, known as the Noble Eightfold Path.

THE EIGHTFOLD PATH

This teaching lays out eight precepts to follow on the path to enlightenment. They fall under three headings.

Panna (discernment or wisdom)
Samma ditthi: right seeing and understanding
Understanding of the Four Noble Truths, which includes the belief of 'do good, get good' (*kamma*, or *karma*).
Samma sankappa: right thinking, or right intent
Thinking skilfully and intending not to harm any other living creature.

Sila (virtue and morality)
Samma vaca: right speech
The intention to be kind and truthful in what we say, both to ourselves and to others.
Samma kammanta: right conduct
This follows the Five Precepts – to train not to kill or harm; not to steal; not to misuse sex (for example, not to commit adultery); not to lie; and to avoid intoxicants (drugs, alcohol) that cloud the mind.
Samma ajiva: right livelihood
Having a job or occupation that does not cause harm to others, and may be of service to them in some way.

Samadhi (concentration/meditation)
Samma vayama: right effort
Pursuing a path that will lead us away from wrong thinking and action.
Samma sati: right mindfulness
Working towards clear understanding of our physical and emotional feelings, as well as our thoughts.
Samma samadhi: right concentration
Using meditation to develop the mind towards insight and understanding.

austere life-style, he devoted himself to meditation. It is said that while immersed in contemplation under a fig tree – which came to be called the *bodhi* tree, or 'tree of enlightenment' – he attained the highest state of knowledge and became the Buddha ('one who has awakened to the truth').

The Buddha later gave his first discourse, the *Dhamma-cakkappavattana-sutta* ('Setting the wheel of *dhamma* [truth] in motion'), to his first five followers. This discourse expounded the Middle Way and contained the essence of the core beliefs of Buddhism now framed within the Four Noble Truths.

To be or to become a Buddhist is to 'take refuge' in the Three Treasures, or Three Jewels, and to repeat this vow in front of a monk in a formal setting: 'I take refuge in the Buddha', 'I take refuge in the *dharma* (truth)' and 'I take refuge in the *sangha* (spiritual community)'. At this time, a new name is often given to the person making the vow. This might be a Sanskrit name or, in the West, a translation. It is up to the individual whether they choose to use the name or not.

Karma, Kamma

Fundamental to Buddhism is the belief in reincarnation, and to understand this it is necessary first to know that *samsara*, our world of confusion, driven by greed, hatred and delusion, is endless, with all beings passing from one state to another. However, Buddhists believe that how life is lived has a powerful impact in creating good or bad outcomes for now and the future, and is determined by our *karma* (intentional actions). This effectively means that the more one follows the teachings of the Buddha, the further one will go on the path to awakening and freedom from suffering.

SACRED WRITINGS

In Buddhism there is no one holy book. The collection of Buddhist texts known as the Pali canon is sometimes called the *Tripitaka*, or the 'Three Baskets', reflecting three groups of teachings. The *Vinaya Pitaka* lays down the training and discipline for monastic life; the *Sutta Pitaka* is divided into five parts (the five *Nikaya*, which contain the Buddha's teachings and discourses); and the *Abhidhamma Pitaka*, which was written after the Buddha's death and is an extensive philosophical and psychological analysis of his teachings.

There are many other important Buddhist writings in Pali, Sanskrit, Chinese and other Asian languages. There is also a strong tradition of teaching through the use of stories, and many of these are contained in the Jataka tales, which recall the previous incarnations of the Buddha.

Pali was one of the languages that evolved from Sanskrit, the classic literary language of India. It is the scriptural language of Theravada Buddhisim, while Sanskrit is that of Mahayana Buddhism. Spellings differ according to the language of the text; for example, the Buddha's original name is Gotama in Pali, Gautama in Sanskrit. *Dhamma* in Pali is *dharma* in Sanskrit; *kamma* in Pali is *karma* in Sanskrit.

BRANCHES OF BUDDHISM

Buddhism is not a highly organized religion. Following the death of the Buddha there was a difference of opinion about the correct interpretation of certain aspects of his teachings. This gave rise to two main schools of thought.

Theravada

The school found today in South-East Asia (Sri Lanka, Myanmar, Thailand and Cambodia) is Theravada, the 'Teaching of the Elders', also called Hinayana, the 'Small Vehicle', by its opponents. The focus here is on the individual's attainment of enlightenment through his or her own efforts, by leading a very simple and strictly disciplined life. For this reason the monastic life is generally recommended (monks and nuns learn the *Vinaya*, with its 227 monastic rules, by heart), but Theravada is also widely followed by lay practitioners, both male and female, with varying levels of discipline. The main meditation practices taught in Theravada are *samatha* (calm abiding) and *vipassana* (insight), but these are used in all branches of Buddhism.

Mahayana

The distinctive teaching of Mahayana Buddhism, the 'Great Vehicle' (found in Tibet, Mongolia, China, Japan, Korea and Vietnam), is that of compassion for all sentient beings. At its centre is the *bodhisattva*, a person on the path to enlightenment who out of compassion takes a vow not to enter nirvana until all sentient beings are liberated.

The Buddhism of Tibet is essentially Mahayana, but with the addition of Vajrayana (the 'Diamond Vehicle'), which uses specific practices to attain enlightenment in a single lifetime. Many Tibetans regard the Dalai Lama as their spiritual leader and he is generally regarded as the living embodiment of Avalokitesvara, the Bodhisattva of Compassion.

Zen

Part of the Mahayana tradition, Zen Buddhism came to Japan and Korea from China, where it was known as Ch'an. It is said to have originated when the Buddha held up a single flower to a student who smiled because he understood the meaning of the Buddha's teaching through this wordless transmission. Zen emphasises an intense teacher-to-student relationship, and requires great meditative discipline. *Koans* – short, stylised spiritual riddles – are often given to students to help them go beyond the conceptual mind and lead them closer to awakening.

Devotional Buddhism

Also very popular in China and Japan are various forms of devotional Buddhism, where the focus is either on wishing for rebirth in a transcendent realm or 'pure land', where negative karmic accumulations would evaporate and *nirvana* would be attained in the next lifetime, or on devotion to a particular Mahayana *sutra* (scriptural text) as embodying the truth. One example of this is Nichiren Shu, which was founded in Japan and which focuses on the *Lotus Sutra* as the essential teaching. The main practice involves chanting the title and one or two other portions of the text.

All the major traditions of Buddhism are practised in the Western world. Interestingly, Buddhism has all but vanished in the country of its origin, India, and is practised there only by a very small minority.

ABOVE 'Riding the ox home', by the fifteenth-century Zen painter Shubun. In the parable of the Ox-Herding pictures the ox represents Buddha nature, or one's true self.

PLACE OF WORSHIP

A place of gathering for the Buddhist *sangha* (community) is generally known as a temple or a centre in the West. In the East, names include *vihara*, *wat* and *gompa*, according to the country and the form of Buddhism. Worship in Buddhism is not the same as in many other religions, because, as we have seen, it is predominantly about following the teachings of the Buddha, through both study and meditation. However, in most Buddhist traditions there are ceremonies where devotional texts are chanted, though not on set days of the week.

The key people connected with temples and monasteries are known by different titles, depending on the tradition. For example, in the Theravada tradition, a senior leader or teacher might be known as an abbot or an Ajahn, with the female equivalent being a sister, while

ABOVE The temple building at Kagyu Samyé Ling, a Tibetan Buddhist monastery in Eskdalemuir, south-west Scotland.

in Tibetan Buddhism you might encounter the titles of Lama (spiritual leader), Rinpoche ('precious teacher') or Khenpo. The term 'Venerable' is usually applied as a mark of respect to an ordained *bhikkhu* (monk). Ordained nuns in the Theravada tradition wear white, while monks wear ochre/orange robes. Mahayana robes are maroon and Zen robes black or grey. Monks and nuns have shaven heads, and lead strict lives dedicated to living and sharing the teachings of the Buddha. They have no personal possessions, and what they eat and wear is usually donated by the lay (non-monastic) community who support the temple or centre.

In most traditions, Buddhist monks and nuns may leave the monastic life at any time, although this would be frowned upon in certain cultures. In some instances, a lay person can become a monk or nun for a short period of time, perhaps three months or more, before returning to non-monastic life. Again, this depends very much on culture and tradition.

There are many sacred items associated with Buddhism, and in the Tibetan tradition you are likely to see prayer wheels. Sometimes called *mani* wheels, these contain thousands of prayers, and it is said that by rotating the wheel you distribute loving-kindness and compassion to yourself and others. They vary greatly, from hand size to enormous. Within the

ABOVE Prayer wheels at Kagyu Samyé Ling Monastery.

Vajrayana tradition, the *ghanta* (Tibetan bell) and *dorje* (accompanying striker) are profound representations of wisdom and compassion.

Prayer flags, or *lung-ta*, meaning 'wind horse', are a series of separate pieces of cloth in recurring colours (each colour representing the elements) that are sewn on to long cords. Traditionally these have Buddhist prayers printed on them, which are thought to spread throughout the surrounding landscape as the flags are moved by the wind, and it is said that the more frayed the flags, the more prayers have been answered. You are particularly likely to see these around the outside of a Buddhist temple or a stupa (a holy monument or shrine containing sacred images and holy relics, and a symbol of enlightenment). At city temples or centres, they are usually hung only on special festival days.

Other items now popular in Western mainstream culture, but actually not related to Buddhism, are Tibetan 'singing bowls', hand-made from seven different metals, in which the sound is created by rotating a

ABOVE Stupa at Samyé Ling. The form and contents of the stupa express the balance and purification of earth, water, fire, air and space.

wooden striker carefully around the outside of the bowl's rim, and *tingshas* – two circular metal cymbals attached one each end of a leather cord. Various uses are to do with personal preference rather than religiously connected.

INSIDE A TEMPLE

When visiting a Buddhist temple or centre, one of the first things you will notice is the smell of the incense that is regularly burned. The atmosphere is devotional, with an air of stillness. There is likely to be an outer lobby and, in some centres, a refreshment room.

The lobby leads into the Shrine Room, which is peaceful and colourful, with cushions on the floor and probably some chairs towards the back. There might be *thangkas* (elaborate wall hangings). The central focus at the front of the room on a raised platform will be a *rupa* (statue of the Buddha), which is likely to be surrounded by candles, flowers and sometimes seven small brass bowls offering different items of water (symbolic of drinking and purification), flowers, incense, candle,

fragrance and food (usually rice). As the first images of the Buddha were made some three hundred years or so after his death, no one knows what he looked like, but the common features usually depicted, with varying cultural differences, are robes (the sign of monkhood); the hair topknot (varying stories

ABOVE Dharma Hall at Providence Zen Center, Rhode Island, USA. The Dharma Hall is the main assembly and lecture hall in a Zen monastery.

abound of what it symbolises, from previous royal status to connection with the heavens); long ear lobes (listening and a wealth of wisdom) and a range of *mudras* (symbolic hand gestures, each with a different meaning, such as compassion, awakening, and so on). Some statues might also be surrounded by a halo to symbolise the sacred nature of the Buddha. It is important to remember that a statue of the Buddha is a symbol of enlightenment, which is revered rather than worshipped.

SERVICES

Although there are no set days for this, Buddhists do gather together to meditate and perform *puja* (act of devotion, or offering) ceremonies, especially on full moon days, certain festivals and holy days, when monks will also offer teachings. However, practising Buddhists spend some time in daily home-based meditation, and may also perform *puja* before a shrine, which might be a simple shelf holding a statue of the Buddha as a focus for devotion, with some flowers, incense and candles as offerings, or might be something more elaborate in a room reserved purely for that purpose. Alternatively, they might visit the Shrine Room of a Buddhist temple or centre for reflection, meditation and reading

the Buddha's teachings. There is also a tradition of taking periods of time on retreat to study Buddhist teachings in greater depth, and to deepen meditation practice.

ABOVE Offering incense at the temple of Wat Phra Kaeo in the Grand Palace compound in Bangkok, Thailand.

WHAT IS HAPPENING?

◆ If you are attending a class for meditation or teaching, you may find that monks or nuns are present, and it is customary for practising Buddhists to bow slightly to them with hands cupped (only fingertips and palms touching to emulate the shape of the lotus bud) as a mark of respect for their dedication to a life of devotion for the good of all, and for their knowledge. You might see

Buddhists kneel and prostrate themselves (touching the forehead, nose, hands, knees and toes to the ground) in front of a statue of the Buddha, or perform a full-length body prostration. These acts of devotion are not idolatrous but marks of respect for their symbolism, that is, the teachings that lead to liberation from suffering. As a visitor you would not be expected to do any of these.

◆ A meditation or teaching session always starts and ends with a bell or gong, and might include chanting and prayer, depending on the focus for that occasion.

ABOVE Chanting at 5:00 a.m. in the Sutra Hall at Bodhi Manda Zen Center, Jemez Springs, New Mexico, USA.

Some monks and lay people use *mala* beads (prayer beads) to count *mantras* (repetitive Sanskrit prayers), which are repeated in sets of twenty-seven, fifty-six or 108. A large *meru* ('mountain' bead) provides a starting and ending point. Originally the beads were seeds from a *bodhi* tree, but nowadays many  different materials are used, from wood to gemstones. Catholics, Muslims, Hindus, Sikhs, Orthodox Christians and Baha'i also use prayer beads. In a non-religious context these are often called 'worry beads' – something to focus on and take your mind off your worries!

The most commonly chanted *mantra* of Tibetan Buddhism is '*Om Mani Padme Hum*' ('Praise to the Jewel in the Lotus'), which through repetition and attention on Chenrezig (the Buddha of Compassion) is said to awaken or enhance that quality within a devotee.

Frequently classes of Buddhist teachings and meditation are offered on a donation (*dana*, practice of generosity) basis, in which students give what they can afford, which might even be nothing. This is part of the Buddhist philosophy of making the teachings of the Buddha available to everyone. A donation could be of flowers, candles or incense for the temple, food for the *sangha*, or in Western cultures it is most likely to be money. The key to giving is that it is done freely and wisely. A small amount of anything given from the heart is worth more than a large amount given by a rich man without much thought. This is why, in Buddhist countries, monasteries are supported by the local communities, and people often feed monks before they feed themselves.

WHAT DO I DO?

❖ Before entering the Shrine Room leave your shoes in the appointed area (for warmth, you might want to keep socks on). Clothing needs to be modest, with legs, arms and chest covered, but not your head. It should also be comfortable, as you will usually be sitting cross-legged on a cushion, although in the West chairs are often provided as well.

❖ As a mark of respect, remember never to point your feet towards the main statue of the Buddha. If you are uncomfortable it is not appropriate to stretch your legs out in front of you; it is better to stand up very quietly and leave the room, or find a chair.

❖ Meditation is generally done sitting cross-legged on floor cushions, although in many Buddhist traditions it is equally acceptable to sit in a chair. Sometimes students are encouraged to work with discomfort as part of the learning process, and on certain ten-day retreats employing the *vipassana* technique, for example, chairs are discouraged. Hands rest gently in your lap so that they overlap with palms upwards, or so that the index finger and thumb are touching.

❖ A plate, box or bowl will be provided for your donation, and sometimes this is a bowl of fruit on the shrine into which you place some money. After the session, light refreshments will be available.

FESTIVALS AND HOLY DAYS

THE BUDDHIST CALENDAR

The Buddhist calendar is lunar based, and therefore the months when festivals and holy days occur will vary from country to country and according to local traditions, so accurate dates and times in any year are best obtained from Buddhist internet sites of the relevant traditions. The only festival that is celebrated worldwide by Buddhists is Wesak.

THE MONTHS OF THE YEAR IN PALI/SANSKRIT		
Pali	**Sanskrit**	
Citta	Caitra	(February–April)
Vesakha	Vaisakha	(March–April)
Jettha	Jyaistha	(April–June)
Asalha	Asadha	(May–July)
Savana	Sravana	(June–August)
Pottapada	Bhadrapada	(July–September)
Assayuja	Asvina	(August–October)
Kattika	Karttika	(September–November)
Maggasira	Margasirsa	(October–December)
Phussa	Pausa	(November–January)
Magha	Magha	(December–February)
Phagguna	Phalguna	(January–March)

LOSAR (TIBETAN BUDDHIST NEW YEAR)

This is a three-day festival during which friends and family visit each other and exchange gifts. Traditionally it is a fifteen-day celebration, but the major focus is on the first three days. As a new year, it is considered a new beginning, and Buddhists attend ceremonies at beautifully decorated monasteries where various rituals are performed with incense to drive away evil spirits, and there is plentiful food and dancing, which mirrors the celebrations of Tibet's earlier indigenous Bon religion. At the Namgyal Monastery of Dharamsala in India, the home of the exiled Dalai Lama, his Holiness leads a long procession of monastic and lay dignitaries to the top of the mountain to offer a 'sacrificial cake' to the great protector goddess Palden Lhamo.

In Western cultures this is likely to be only a one-day celebration, and your Buddhist friends might spontaneously invite you to a special *puja a*t the temple, followed by a feast.

PARINIBBANA (NIRVANA DAY) (February)

The word *parinibbana* means 'passing away', and is a Mahayana Buddhist festival that marks the Buddha's death at the age of eighty after the forty-five years of

ABOVE Reclining Buddha in Polonnaruwa, Sri Lanka. When he left this life at the age of eighty, Buddha attained the ultimate *nirvana*.

teaching that followed his enlightenment. Buddhists celebrate by visiting temples, monasteries or centres to spend time in meditation and reflection on the Buddha's teachings about the impermanence of life. It is seen as a time to consider personal mortality, and remember the recently deceased.

MAGHA PUJA

This is the second most important Buddhist festival, and commemorates the day that Buddha predicted his death, and recited a summary of his teachings together with a code of discipline to a very large gathering of monks previously ordained by him. More of a monastic celebration, it is a chance for monks and nuns to come together in *sangha* to share knowledge and experience, and to discuss the teachings of Buddha. In the West, this day is known as Sangha Day, and is celebrated towards the end of the year.

THE NEW YEAR (April)

The new year in both Mahayana and Theravada traditions starts on the first full moon in April, although in the West, if this is a weekday it will usually be moved to the nearest Sunday. Buddhists will celebrate by visiting a temple or centre, offering food to the monks and receiving blessings in return, listening to teachings, chanting and meditating. In the Theravada tradition, if there is a temple, or an outside area that can be prepared appropriately, there will be a candlelit evening procession, with incense, flowers and chanting, that circles the sacred area three times as a reminder of the virtues of the Buddha. For Theravada Buddhists in Thailand this celebration, on 13 April, is called Songkran.

WESAK, VESAK, VESAKHA (BUDDHA DAY)

This day celebrates the first of the Three Jewels, 'I take refuge in the Buddha', and is considered particularly important because it commemorates the Buddha's birth, enlightenment, and attainment of *nirvana* (when he died and transcended the cycle of reincarnation). It is a colourful festival, for which homes are decorated with flowers and incense is burned. Buddhists visit their local temple for services and teachings, and to give offerings to the monks.

In Western cultures Wesak cards, depicting the Buddha or a lotus flower (symbol of purity and truth) are often sent, and there might be a celebratory meal.

In the Theravada and Mahayana traditions, Buddha Day is usually around May or June, and in Zen Buddhism it is celebrated on 8 December as Bodhi Day.

ABOVE Buddhist monks parading through downtown Seoul during the three-day Lotus Lantern Festival celebrating Buddha's birthday.

WHAT DO I DO?

❖ Because of their belief that it is wrong to take life, many Buddhists are vegetarian. Some might eat fish, eggs, or dairy products, while others are vegan, and eat no animal products of any kind, including for example milk, eggs and honey. Others might also choose not to eat onions or garlic. If you are invited for a meal, you are likely to eat fresh salads, rice, vegetables and fruit.

❖ Generally alcohol is not drunk but there are many different feelings about this, so it is best to check before you go. Equally, if you are inviting Buddhist guests, find out what is acceptable and what is not. When inviting any guest you might not know well, it is advisable to ask their preferences in advance.

ABOVE Dragon lantern. The Lotus Lantern Festival includes street performances and a massive lantern parade near the Jogye Temple in Seoul.

HANAMATSURI (FLOWER FESTIVAL)

This festival is predominantly celebrated by Japanese Buddhists and honours the birth of Buddha.

WHAT HAPPENS?

◆ If you are invited to attend a temple for the Flower Festival, during the service you will see a shrine of flowers, representing the garden in Lumbini (in modern-day Nepal), where the Buddha was born, created in front of the main temple shrine. A small statue of the infant Buddha is placed in the shrine, and after offering flowers, the community gently pours sweet tea over the image to represent the gentle rain that was said to fall at his birth.

ASALHA PUJA, OR DHAMMACAKKA (DHARMA DAY)

Theravada and Western Buddhists celebrate this day in the month of Asalha, on the anniversary of the Buddha's first discourse. It is the second of the 'Three Jewels', and is marked with readings from the teachings and gratitude for the Buddha's life. The evening's full-moon vigil is likely to include a discourse chanted in its original Pali language.

VASSA (THE 'RAINS RETREAT')

On the day after Dharma Day in the Theravada calendar, in the countries of South-East Asia, monks traditionally gave up their nomadic living and prepared to stay in one place for the three-month rainy season. For all Buddhist monks this is a period of retreat and a time of penitence, self-examination and forgiveness.

PADMASAMBHAVA DAY (September)

On this day Tibetan Buddhists honour this great saint, also known as Guru Rinpoche, who was the first Indian monk to take Buddhism to Tibet in the eighth century. Celebrations might include dressing colourfully, chanting, reading stories from his life and sharing a communal meal.

PAVARANA ('ADMONISHMENT') (Usually in October)

This ends the 'Rains Retreat' on the full moon of the eleventh lunar month. In monasteries, because of the containment over such a long period of time, the Buddha devised a number of ceremonies including one where monks would be encouraged to give gentle feedback to each other about any behaviour that could be reflected on.

KATHINA DAY

The date of Kathina Day will vary depending on when the rainy season starts and ends. A Theravada festival that takes place at the end of the 'Rains Retreat', in South-East Asia, it involves the formal giving by the lay community to the monastic community of a quantity of cloth that is then made into a robe and given to a nominated monk or monks. It is a form of ceremonial almsgiving, and is accompanied by a celebratory meal for the lay community. Monks are not present at this. Traditionally, and still in some countries, the cloth would have been white, so as well as sewing the robes within a certain time limit, the monks also had to dye them. *Kathina*, after which the day is named, means the wooden frame that was originally used in making the robes.

SANGHA DAY (FULL MOON DAY) (November)

Celebrated by Western Buddhists in November (see Magha Puja), this is the third of the 'Three Jewels' ('I take refuge in the *sangha*'), and is a joyous celebration of friendship, when Buddhists, both monastic and lay, gather to celebrate their worldwide community and exchange gifts.

ABOVE Monks working on a sand mandala in New Hampshire, USA. In this Tibetan Buddhist tradition, mandalas are created from coloured sand and then destroyed, to symbolise the transitory nature of material life.

RITUALS AND CEREMONIES

BIRTH

Within the Buddhist belief in reincarnation, it is said that to be born human is rare, so birth is a time for celebration. While there are no specific religious ceremonies, babies are generally taken to a Buddhist temple to be blessed.

WHAT HAPPENS?

◆ The blessing will probably open with the lighting of candles and incense, the ringing of a sacred bell, and chanting either by monks or by everyone present, in which case chant sheets will be given. These might be in Sanskrit or Pali, and in the West would probably have an English translation, so that you can follow the meaning.

◆ Everyone will say a prayer for the baby's wisdom, health and prosperity, and a monk or the abbot of the temple, depending on the tradition, will give a blessing and perhaps a *Dharma* talk.

◆ In some temples, the grandparents, parents and spiritual guardians of the baby may give a reading of some kind, but this depends on the temple or centre and their personal approach.

◆ There will be more chanting, and when the blessing is concluded the candles will be extinguished. A bell will be rung to signify the end.

◆ There will then be food, tea and socialising.

WHAT DO I DO?
❖ Presents are very welcome, as is a congratulatory 'new baby' card.

COMING OF AGE

There are no Buddhist coming-of-age ceremonies, but Western families may choose to mark the occasion with

ABOVE Young novice monks at the Kothduwa temple in the Maduganga estuary in southern Sri Lanka.

a celebration of some kind. In South-East Asia, some families encourage their adolescent sons to become monks for about three months as a rite of passage.

MARRIAGE

In the West a few temples are licensed to perform weddings, but as marriage is not a sacred ceremony in Buddhism, most weddings will be civil ceremonies that might be followed by a blessing at a temple or centre. What is required of a Buddhist couple is that they respect each other, and work to live harmoniously.

ABOVE Boy monks at the temple of Angkor Wat in Cambodia.
OPPOSITE Marriage ceremony in Thailand.

WHAT HAPPENS?

◆ For their blessing, the bride and groom are likely to wear what they wore for their civil ceremony, or clothing according to their own tradition, such as Thai, Japanese or Korean. As always, because the Shrine Room is a devotional area, there will be candles, incense and flowers,

◆ The blessing will probably last about thirty minutes and a bell or gong will be rung to signal the start and end. The person leading the blessing might be seated on a raised platform, and people stand up, as a mark of respect, as they enter and leave.

◆ The blessing may include chanting by monks, or monks and nuns, from the sacred texts. Generally, there is no particular involvement by the couple or guests other than to sit and listen, although wedding rings may be exchanged. For the most part, everyone remains seated throughout the blessing.

◆ In the Thai tradition, the monk will sprinkle the couple with blessed water.

◆ There is no regular form for a post-blessing celebration, and it will be whatever the couple and their families decide.

WHAT DO I DO?

❖ If you are invited to a blessing, the same guidelines apply as those for services in general: wear comfortable, modest clothing to cover your arms, legs and chest.

❖ Shoes are taken off before entering the Shrine Room.

❖ Remember to turn off your cell phone.

❖ Remember that feet should never point towards the Buddha.

❖ It is usually acceptable to take photos or video the blessing, but make sure to check this first.

❖ A Buddhist couple will welcome congratulatory cards and gifts, especially those relating to Buddhism – perhaps candles, a beautiful incense holder or vase, or a statue of the Buddha. They may, of course, have a traditional wedding gift list.

DEATH

In Buddhism, death is a merely a transition from one state of being to another, continuing an onward journey that will include rebirth. So while the body of a deceased person will be treated with respect, and probably not moved for a short period to allow the transition to be completed, it is considered an uninhabited shell. Therefore Buddhists often donate their organs for medical use as an act of *dana*, which continues their lifelong intention to be of service to all sentient beings.

Naturally, Buddhists experience grief and bereavement at the loss of a loved one, but because of their belief in reincarnation and the law of *karma*, there can also be joy in the sense that the deceased will now be on the path to awakening in their future lives.

WHAT HAPPENS?

♦ As part of returning to the elements, Buddhists are cremated, and coffins are likely to be as eco-friendly as possible. The coffin might be open, as a reminder of the impermanence of life. The emphasis of the funeral service is usually on performing rituals and reciting texts for the benefit of the deceased.

♦ At a temple, the service might last up to an hour, and the format may vary. Generally it will start with the ringing of a bell. Incense and candles will be burning at the shrine and there will be meditation, chanting, prayers, and in some cases poems, readings from the Buddha's teachings and perhaps songs.

♦ At a crematorium chapel, what is included will be dictated by the time available, which will usually be a maximum of thirty minutes. However, it is very unlikely that incense will be burned, and candles might not be allowed.

♦ More elaborate funeral services are likely in the countries of origin.

WHAT DO I DO?

❖ If you are invited, flowers are very welcome, as are condolence cards.

❖ Most people choose to wear smart, dark clothing.

❖ As the coffin enters everyone stands, after which people generally remain seated until the service ends, but you can, of course, take your lead from your neighbours in case of variations.

❖ There may or may not be a post-funeral gathering, but you will know this in advance.

SOME USEFUL WORDS AND PHRASES

Anicca the impermanence of life

Bhikkhu monk

Bodhisattva a person on the path to enlightenment

Dana the practice of generosity; 'giving and letting go'

Dharma truth

Eightfold Path eight precepts to follow on the path to Enlightenment

Enlightenment complete freedom from *samsara*; the reaching of *nirvana*

Gompa Buddist monastery or centre of learning in some north-eastern Asian countries

Karma the law of cause and effect; the belief that what you do in this life affects your subsequent lives

Khenpo title given to a respected senior monk; also a level of advanced learning

Koan riddle, used to help concentrate the mind in meditation

Lama spiritual leader, teacher

Lotus flower symbol of purity and truth

Mahayana sutras scriptural texts

Mantra repetitive prayers

Middle Way the practice of moderation, non-extremism

Mudra symbolic spiritual hand gesture

Nibbana, nirvana the state beyond all confusion and suffering

Puja act of devotion, or offering

Rinpoche 'precious one', an honorific title given within Buddhism to, for example, a great teacher

Sadhu holy man

Samatha meditation practice of 'calm abiding'

Samsara endless cycle of birth, death and rebirth in our world driven by greed, hatred and delusion; the opposite of enlightenment

Sangha spiritual community

Stupa holy monument or shrine containing sacred images and holy relics, symbol of Enlightenment

Thangka painted or embroidered wall hanging or banner

Tripitaka ('three baskets') early Buddhist writings

Vihara Sanskrit/Pali term for a monastery

Vipassana meditation practice of 'insight', or seeing things as they really are

Wat in Far Eastern countries, such as Cambodia, Laos and Thailand, a monastic temple and its precincts

FURTHER READING

There are, of course, libraries full of books on religion. As a starting point, the following may be useful.

Bowker, John (ed.). *The Oxford Dictionary of World Religions*, Oxford/New York, Oxford University Press, 1997.

Buddhist Society. *1001 Pearls of Buddhist Wisdom*, London, Duncan Baird Publishers, 2006.

Cook, Michael. *The Koran, a very short introduction*. Oxford, Oxford University Press, 2000.

Cross, F. L. (ed.). *The Oxford Dictionary of the Christian Church*, London/New York/Toronto, 1958 (reprinted 1966).

HH Dalai Lama and Howard C. Cutler. *The Art of Happiness*. London, Hodder and Stoughton, 1999.

Durden-Smith, Jo. *The Essence of Buddhism*, Royston, Eagle Editions Ltd, 2004.

Duggal, K. S. *Sikh Gurus, Their Lives and Teachings*, New Delhi, UBS Publishers' Distributors Ltd, 2001.

Frager, Robert. *The Wisdom of Islam*, Hampshire, Godsfield Press, 2002.

Frawley, Dr David. *Hinduism: the Eternal Tradition (Sanatana Dharma)*, New Delhi, Voice of India, 2008.

Parrinder, Geoffrey. *Mysticism in the World's Religions*, Oxford/Rockford USA, Oneworld Publications, 1995.

Snelling, John. *The Buddhist Handbook: A Complete Guide to Buddhist Teaching and Practice*, London, Century Hutchinson, 1987.

Unterman, Alan. *Dictionary of Jewish Lore and Legend*, London, Thames and Hudson, 1991.

Ware, Timothy (Bishop Kallistos Ware). *The Orthodox Church*, London, Penguin Books, 1997.

The 'Simple Guides: Religion' series, published by Kuperard/Bravo, London:

Clark, Katherine. *The Orthodox Church*, 2009.

Hartley, Edmund. *The Roman Catholic Church*, 2009.

Kalsi, Sewa Singh. *Sikhism*, 2007.

Kingsland, Venika Mehra. *Hinduism*, 2008.

Rhymer, David. *The Protestant Tradition*, 2008.

Robinson, Danielle. *Islam*, 2007.

St Ruth, Diana and Richard. *Theravada Buddhism*, 2007.

St Ruth, Diana and Richard. *Zen Buddhism*, 2008.

Starr-Glass, David. *Judaism*, 2008.

Useful Websites

The author recommends the following sites for those interested in interfaith studies:

http://www.interfaithfoundation.org
The Interfaith Foundation in the United Kingdom

http://www.onespiritinterfaith.org/index.html
The Interfaith Foundation in the United States

http://www.newseminary.org/
The New Seminary, a non-profit organisation in New York that offers spiritually based education programmes

Akasha Lonsdale's own website is:
http://www.simplydivineceremonies.com

INDEX

PHOTOGRAPHIC ACKNOWLEDGEMENTS

Cover images

Front: Jewish wedding, rosary, christening scene, Hindu *arati* ritual, Muslim man at prayer © *Fotolia.com*; reading from the Torah scrolls © *Dreamstime.com*

Front and spine: religious symbols motif © *iStockphoto.com*

Back flap: © Akasha Lonsdale

Text pages

The photograph on page 62 is reproduced by permission of Maria Esther Birchall.

The icon of the Holy Virgin on page 87, painted by Panayiotis Koumoundouros, is reproduced by permission of Katherine Clark.

The photograph on page 167 is reproduced by permission of Hilah and Eitan Rubin-Razinsky.

Images on pages 16, 145, 154, 162 © *iStockphoto.com*; 58, 65, 66, 117, 151 © *Dreamstime.com*

Images on the following pages are reproduced under Creative Commons Attribution ShareAlike Licenses 1.0, 2.0, 2.5 and 3.0.

Chapter 1

Pages 12 © J D Treat; 18 © Rvin88; 19 © Ej.culley; 20 © Rowan of Ravara; 21 © Fingalo Christian Bickel; 25© Marian Lambert; 37 © Micha L. Rieser; 45 © Wolfgang Sauber; 46 © Peter Mackriell; and 56 © Holger.Ellgaard.

Chapter 2

Pages 82 © Schekinov Alexey Victorovich; 86 © Lemur12; 88 © Taamu; 90 © Frettie; 91 © Viktor Andreev; 93 © Adriatikus; 94 © Aleksandr Kurilov; 100 © Yerey Maksim Massalitin; 103 © 'me'; and 107 © Maggas.

Chapter 3

Pages 122 © Adiel Io; 125 © Horsch, Willy; 127 © Daniel Ullrich, Threedots; 129 © Juda S. Engelmayer; 130 © David Berkowitz; 142 © Olve Utne; 148 (top) © stu_spivack; 148 (bottom) © Ja'akov; 155 © user:shako; and 156 © Aviv Hod.

Chapter 4

Pages 174 © Ali Mansuri; 179 © shioshvili; 180 © Baldiri; 182 © Agencia Brasil; 187 and 188 © Ahmed Rabea; 191 © Arisdp; 192 © Trueblue74; 193 © Hamed Saber; 195 © Muhammad Mahdi Karim; 201 and 202 © Lee Jordan; and 203 © Monjurul Hoque.

Chapter 5

Pages 210 © Claude Renault; 213 © Steve Jurvetson; 217 © Deepak Gupta (CC 2.0 Germany); 225 © Kawanet; 231 © Vijay Bandari; 233 © Dhondusaxena; 245 © Tejal Patel; 247 © Jaisingh Rathore; 249 © Jovika; 251 © Appaiah; and 252 © m-bot.

Chapter 6

Pages 260, 267 and 279 © J Singh; 266 © Hari Singh; 270 © Ken Wieland; 272 © Gophi; 273 © Ddalbiez; 275 and 284 © Jasleen Kaur; 282 © Sixtybotts; 287 © Sunny Gill265; and 291 © Ashish 100.

Chapter 7

Pages 298 © 'myself'; 300 © Eckhard Pecher; 306 and 308 © Robert Matthews; 309 © Arunas Kulikauskas; 310 © Laughlin Elkind; 311 © Peter Burr; 312 © Chris 73; 315 © Lankapic; 318 © Benjamin Krause; 321 © Mozart Diensthuber; 323 © Maedin Tureaud; and 324 © sam garza.